Governance in World Affairs

Governance in World Affairs

ORAN R. YOUNG

CORNELL UNIVERSITY PRESS

Ithaca and London

First published 1999 by Cornell University Press
First printing, Cornell Paperbacks, 1999

Printed in the United States of America

LIBRARY OF CONGRESS CATALOGING-IN-PUBLICATION DATA
Young, Oran R.
    Governance in world affairs / Oran R. Young.
        p.   cm.
    Includes index.
    ISBN 0-8014-3656-7 (cloth). — ISBN 0-8014-8623-8 (paper)
        1. International relations.   2. World politics.   3. International
    cooperation.   I. Title.
    JZ1318.Y68   1999
    327.1'7—dc21   99-23804

Cornell University Press strives to use environmentally responsible suppliers and materials to the fullest extent possible in the publishing of its books. Such materials include vegetable-based, low-VOC inks and acid-free papers that are recycled, totally chlorine-free, or partly composed of nonwood fibers. Books that bear the logo of the FSC (Forest Stewardship Council) use paper taken from forests that have been inspected and certified as meeting the highest standards for environmental and social responsibility. For further information, visit our website at www.cornellpress.cornell.edu.

Cloth printing   10 9 8 7 6 5 4 3 2 1
Paperback printing   10 9 8 7 6 5 4 3 2 1

To

Elise Boulding
Jean Hennessey
Jim Hornig
Gene Lyons
Leonard Rieser

whose support at Dartmouth has made all the difference

Contents

Preface

The approach to governance in world affairs which I present in this book is the culmination of a long-term research program whose earlier findings are reported in *International Cooperation* (Cornell 1989) and *International Governance* (Cornell 1994). This new book is self-contained and intended to be read as a comprehensive account of the regime-theoretic approach to global governance. It builds on ideas I have developed in detail in earlier publications.[1] But at the same time, the book reflects an ongoing effort to refine our grasp of the essential character of regimes as governance systems, to fill gaps left by prior work in the field, and to present an integrated account of regime theory as a way of thinking about governance in world affairs.

The scope of this work is broader than that of its predecessors. As before, environmental and resource regimes constitute the empirical testbed for the development of my thinking about international institutions. But here, I turn repeatedly to questions of generalizability *across* issue areas, and I seek to pinpoint the place of issue-specific regimes in the broader settings of international society and global civil society. Two key threads run through the chapters of this book, weaving the arguments presented into an integrated whole. One centers on the idea that regimes are dynamic systems. As a result, an understanding of regime formation is simply a springboard for inquiries into the effectiveness of these arrangements once they become operational as well as the processes through

1. In addition to *International Cooperation* and *International Governance*, see Oran R. Young and Gail Osherenko, eds., *Polar Politics: Creating International Environmental Regimes* (Ithaca: Cornell University Press, 1993), and Oran R. Young, *Creating Regimes: Arctic Accords and International Governance* (Ithaca: Cornell University Press, 1998).

which they change over the course of time. The other unifying thread concerns the importance of initiating a dialogue between two distinct ways of thinking about international institutions—the collective-action perspective arising from the fields of economics and public choice, and the social-practice perspective flowing from the fields of sociology and anthropology. Within the framework established by these overarching theoretical concerns, four substantive themes give this book its distinctive flavor: regime tasks, the effectiveness of institutions, regime change, and institutional linkages. Taken together, these theoretical and substantive concerns define what I see as the cutting edge of regime theory.

The study of international regimes is progressing simultaneously on two levels. The analytic tools needed to think systematically about individual regimes are developing rapidly, as exemplified by the growth of interest in institutional effectiveness and change. Equally important, however, the study of regimes is becoming embedded in the larger intellectual movement associated with the idea of "governance without government" at the international level.[2] To the extent that the emergence of issue-specific regimes meets the rising demand for governance in international society, the sharpening of these analytic tools will take on meaning that extends well beyond the production of knowledge about regimes per se. The challenge before us, then, is not only to broaden and deepen our understanding of an empirical phenomenon of growing significance but also critically to assess a new way of thinking about the provision of governance in international society. Because rising doubts question the effectiveness of governments in solving problems of governance at the domestic level, efforts to understand decentralized governance systems at the international level may find a sizable audience among those whose interests center on other levels of social organization as well.

As ALWAYS, it is a pleasure to record the debts I have incurred in carrying out the research reported in this book. The spread of regime analysis to Europe during the 1990s is a striking development; it has allowed me to engage in a productive dialogue with such scholars as Thomas Bernauer, Helmut Breitmeier, Andreas Obser, Volker Rittberger, Peter Sand, Olav Schram Stokke, Arild Underdal, Jørgen Wettestad, and Michael Zürn. The regimes research agenda is now being picked up by scholars in Japan and elsewhere in Asia. In fact, the final chapter of this book responds, in part, to a Japanese request for a paper reflecting the evolution of regime theory from its American origins. I view this as a promising development, and I

2. James N. Rosenau and Ernst-Otto Czempiel, eds., *Governance without Government: Order and Change in World Politics* (Cambridge: Cambridge University Press, 1992).

welcome the opportunity to refine the core ideas of regime theory through interactions with scholars working in other countries and approaching the common agenda from varying perspectives.

Roger Haydon, my editor at Cornell University Press, has played a key role in the development and publication of all the books I have published with the press. He prodded me in the 1980s to produce *International Cooperation*, and he has consistently expressed the view that the fruits of my research program deserve a wide audience. Konrad von Moltke, my colleague at Dartmouth and collaborator in matters pertaining to global governance, has provided an invaluable sounding board for my ideas on international regimes. I hope I have succeeded in playing the same role for him. Gene Lyons and Michael Mastanduno, past and present directors of the John Sloan Dickey Center for International Understanding at Dartmouth, have provided much-appreciated backing for my ongoing work on issues of governance in international society. Nicki Maynard, my assistant for many years, and the student assistants who work under her direction have helped in many ways to render my work environment productive. To them, I owe a debt of gratitude that is hard to capture.

I am grateful for permission to include in this book materials that originally appeared elsewhere. Chapter 1 is a revised version of the concluding essay in Oran R. Young, ed., *Global Governance: Drawing Insights from the Environmental Experience* (Cambridge: MIT Press, 1997). An earlier version of Chapter 5—prepared initially for presentation at the 1998 annual meeting of the American Association for the Advancement of Science— appeared as "The Effectiveness of International Environmental Regimes: A Midterm Report" in *International Environmental Affairs* 10 (Fall 1998), 267–89. Chapter 7 is based on my "Institutional Linkages in International Society," *Global Governance* 2 (January–April 1996), 1–24.

Finally, material support for the work reported in this book has come from a variety of sources over the years, including the Ford Foundation, the International Institute for Applied Systems Analysis, the MacArthur Foundation, and the National Science Foundation as well as the Dickey Center at Dartmouth. Without the generosity of these funders, my research program would remain extremely limited.

ORAN R. YOUNG

Wolcott, Vermont

Acronyms and Abbreviations

AEPS	Arctic Environmental Protection Strategy
AGBM	Ad Hoc Group on the Berlin Mandate
AHLs	Allowable harvest levels
AMAP	Arctic Monitoring and Assessment Programme
ATCMs	Antarctic Treaty Consultative Meetings
ATS	Antarctic Treaty System
BEAR	Barents Euro-Arctic Region
CAFF	Conservation of Arctic Flora and Fauna
CCAMLR	Convention on the Conservation of Antarctic Marine Living Resources
CFCs	Chlorofluorocarbons
CITES	Convention on International Trade in Endangered Species of Wild Fauna and Flora
COP	Conference of the parties
CPRs	Common pool resources
CRAMRA	Convention on the Regulation of Antarctic Mineral Resource Activities
CSD	Commission on Sustainable Development
DSPs	Dispute settlement procedures
ECOSOC	Economic and Social Council
EEZs	Exclusive economic zones
EMEP	Environmental Monitoring and Evaluation Programme
EPA	Environmental Protection Agency
EU	European Union
FAO	Food and Agriculture Organization
FCCC	Framework Convention on Climate Change

G-8	Group of 8
GATT	General Agreement on Tariffs and Trade
GEF	Global Environment Facility
GNP	Gross national product
IASC	International Arctic Science Committee
ICSU	International Council of Scientific Unions
IIASA	International Institute for Applied Systems Analysis
IMF	International Monetary Fund
IPCC	Intergovernmental Panel on Climate Change
IRD	International Regimes Database
IWC	International Whaling Commission
LMEs	Large marine ecosystems
LRTAP	Long-Range Transboundary Air Pollution
MOP	Meeting of the parties
MARPOL	International Convention for the Prevention of Pollution from Ships
MSY	Maximum sustainable yield
NAFTA	North American Free Trade Agreement
NAMMCO	North Atlantic Marine Mammals Commission
NCPs	Noncompliance procedures
NGOs	Nongovernmental organizations
NIEO	New International Economic Order
NMP	New Management Procedure
NOx	Nitrogen oxides
NPT	Nonproliferation Treaty
NSF	National Science Foundation
OECD	Organization for Economic Cooperation and Development
POPs	Persistent organic pollutants
RMP	Revised Management Procedure
SCAR	Scientific Committee on Antarctic Research
SIRs	Systems for implementation review
SO_2	Sulfur dioxide
SSTs	Supersonic transports
TACs	Total allowable catches
TNCs	Transnational corporations
UN	United Nations
UNCED	United National Conference on Environment and Development
UNCLOS	United National Convention on the Law of the Sea
UNDP	United Nations Development Programme
UNEP	United Nations Environment Programme

UNESCO	United Nations Educational, Scientific, and Cultural Organization
VOCs	Volatile organic compounds
WHO	World Health Organization
WTO	World Trade Organization
WWF	Worldwide Fund for Nature

CHAPTER ONE

Governance without Government

The demand for governance in world affairs has never been greater. Broadly speaking, this development is a product of rising interdependencies among the members of international society and—to anticipate a phenomenon discussed later in this chapter—global civil society, which make it increasingly difficult for states or other autonomous actors to isolate themselves from events occurring in other parts of the world, however much they might wish to do so. The repercussions of upheavals such as the disintegration of the former Soviet Union and the bloody civil war in the former Yugoslavia are inescapable, even for those located at opposite ends of the Earth. The economic consequences of financial crises in East and Southeast Asia reverberate throughout the global economy. Greenhouse gases emitted anywhere in the world affect the global climate system. And these examples are merely illustrative of a broad range of developments that make it impossible for any state or other actor to isolate itself from the impacts of outside events in today's world.

The end of the cold war triggered a moment of euphoria during which it seemed that the emergence of a new world order was at hand and that the promise of the United Nations as an intergovernmental mechanism for solving problems of international governance would finally be realized. This bubble soon burst, however, giving way to mounting skepticism about the capacity of the United Nations to cope with an array of pressing problems. The failure of United Nations peacekeeping missions in Bosnia, Rwanda, and Somalia has raised profound questions about the ability of the organization to deal effectively with current threats to international peace and security. The pronounced tendency of the members of the group of seven leading industrial countries plus Russia (the G-8), the

Organization for Economic Cooperation and Development (OECD), the European Union (EU), and the North American Free Trade Agreement (NAFTA) to avoid the United Nations (UN) has marginalized the world organization with regard to large-scale economic issues.[1] The obvious shortcomings of such arrangements as the Commission on Sustainable Development, established as a legacy of the 1992 United Nations Conference on Environment and Development, highlight the limited capacity of the UN to solve problems involving human/environment relations.

What is to be done in the face of this apparent gap between the demand for governance and the supply of governance at the international level? Some observers react to this question with a deep sense of frustration and growing pessimism regarding humankind's ability to cope with the world's troubles. Anticipating a "coming anarchy," they offer no clear recipe for contending with the crisis of governance they foresee.[2] A second response to the growing demand for governance emphasizes efforts to reform the UN as a preferred mechanism for the supply of global governance. Those who espouse this approach have devoted much time and energy to drawing up elaborate blueprints for restructuring the organization to increase its capacity to deal with a wide range of governance problems. A particularly notable contribution in a long line of such prescriptive programs is articulated in the report of the Commission on Global Governance titled *Our Global Neighborhood*.[3]

Yet a third response emphasizes the distinction between governance and government and directs attention to a variety of innovative social practices that have come into existence during the postwar era to solve discrete or distinct problems by creating regimes or sets of roles, rules, and relationships that focus on specific problems and do not require centralized political organizations to administer them.[4] Whereas the second option looks to the United Nations System and calls for a comprehensive, legally bind-

---

1. For an account that explores the growth of this tendency to develop economic arrangements outside the ambit of the United Nations, see Gene M. Lyons, "International Organizations and National Interests," *International Social Science Journal* 47 (1995), 261–76.

2. The phrase "coming anarchy" is from Robert D. Kaplan, "The Coming Anarchy," *Atlantic Monthly*, February 1994, 44–46, 48–49, 52, 56, 58–60, 62–63, 66, 68–70, 72–76. For a thoughtful discussion of the "new pessimism," see Charles William Maynes, "The New Pessimism," *Foreign Policy*, no. 100 (Fall 1995), 33–49.

3. Commission on Global Governance, *Our Global Neighborhood: The Report of the Commission on Global Governance* (Oxford: Oxford University Press, 1995). For a succinct account of the recommendations of the commission, which was chaired by Ingvar Carlsson and Shridath Ramphal, see Ingvar Carlsson, "The U.N. at 50: A Time to Reform," *Foreign Policy*, no. 100 (Fall 1995), 3–18.

4. For a survey of the state of regime analysis, see Marc A. Levy, Oran R. Young, and Michael Zürn, "The Study of International Regimes," *European Journal of International Relations* 1 (September 1995), 267–330.

ing, and state-centered approach to international governance, the third response looks to piecemeal or issue-specific arrangements that may or may not be legally binding, may or may not assign some role to the UN or its specialized agencies, and often accord important roles to nonstate actors. Creative efforts of this sort are particularly notable in—but by no means confined to—the realm of environmental issues.[5]

Without passing judgment on other responses, I present a critical assessment of the potential of this third response to the challenge of governance in world affairs. There is no denying the appeal of this approach, given its pragmatic focus on well-defined problems, its promise of crafting regimes that do not require expensive and corruptible bureaucratic organizations, and its sense of optimism about the prospects for solving problems without radically transforming the character of international society. But such appeal should not deter a critical assessment of this way of thinking. On the contrary, it highlights the importance of taking a hard look at the real potential of issue-specific regimes.

Proceeding in this spirit, I pose and seek to answer the following questions in this book:

- What exactly are regimes, and how do they differ from organizations such as the United Nations that loomed large in earlier efforts to meet the demand for governance in international society?
- Are we witnessing the emergence of a global civil society alongside international society, and what are the implications of this development for governance in world affairs?
- Are some sorts of problems well suited to treatment through the formation of international or transnational regimes, whereas others cannot be solved in this way?
- Under what conditions are issue-specific regimes likely to prove successful or effective in solving the problems that motivate their creation?
- What broader—sometimes unintended—consequences for international society and global civil society are likely to flow from the formation and operation of a growing collection of regimes?

REGIMES AS SOURCES OF GOVERNANCE

The blossoming of interest in international regimes as mechanisms for solving problems of governance has brought with it new concepts as well

---

5. Oran R. Young, *International Governance: Protecting the Environment in a Stateless Society* (Ithaca: Cornell University Press, 1994).

as revised definitions of familiar concepts. Thus, we now talk about "social institutions," "social practices," "governance systems," "mechanisms of social control," and "organizations" in addition to "regimes" as such. This poses two problems.[6] First, there is a lack of agreement on the use of some terms, which complicates efforts to compare and contrast different arguments about fundamental questions regarding the formation and effectiveness of regimes. Additional difficulties arise when we seek to move on to operationalize these concepts for purposes of empirical analysis. As a result, it is often hard to subject divergent hypotheses to empirical evaluation in order to single out those propositions which stand up well to testing and discard those which do not.

Even more fundamental is the split between those who adopt a *contractarian* perspective and those who think in *constitutive* terms in seeking to identify and understand international regimes. Contractarians assume the prior existence of actors with a clear sense of their own identities and the interests flowing from these identities. Such actors will be motivated to create institutional arrangements when they find that proceeding individualistically leads to joint losses or to an inability to reap joint gains. On this account, regimes are devices created by self-interested actors to solve or at least ameliorate collective-action problems (for example, security dilemmas, trade wars, and tragedies of the commons).[7] The constitutive perspective, by contrast, assumes that institutions play a major role in defining the interests of participants and even in shaping their identities. States seeking membership in the European Union, for example, must adjust their domestic systems to conform to the requirements of the union. Thus institutions have formative effects on their members rather than the other way around.[8]

In one sense, there is no need to choose between these analytic perspectives. They offer different starting points that produce distinct lines of inquiry, each of which may broaden and deepen our knowledge of governance in international society. Moreover, it is perfectly possible to adopt the view that actors and institutions are mutually constitutive. Thus, participation in social institutions can affect how members frame their inter-

6. For an overview of the new institutionalism in international relations, see Young, introduction to ibid.

7. For a sophisticated introduction to this approach, see Russell Hardin, *Collective Action* (Baltimore: Johns Hopkins University Press, 1982).

8. Alexander Wendt, "The Agent-Structure Problem in International Relations Theory," *International Organization* 41 (1987), 335–70, and Alexander Wendt, "Anarchy Is What States Make of It—the Social Construction of Power-Politics," *International Organization* 46 (1992), 391–425.

ests and understand their identities, even when they have distinct identities established prior to participation.[9] Yet clashes between advocates of these two perspectives, who often disagree about epistemological as well as conceptual or analytic matters,[10] have heightened the problem faced by those devising a practical means of identifying the universe of international regimes and assessing the potential of this approach to meet the rising demand for governance in international society.

How should we proceed in the face of these conceptual complications? The answer I propose and seek to defend in this book is a highly pragmatic one. Despite conceptual problems, most observers recognize international regimes in operation and largely agree when it comes to identifying specific regimes. In environmental matters, for example, regimes govern an array of distinct functional problems (for example, the dumping of wastes at sea, intentional discharges of oil, international trade in endangered species of fauna and flora, transboundary fluxes of airborne pollutants, transboundary movements of hazardous wastes, ozone depletion, the loss of biological diversity, and climate change) as well as a variety of geographically delimited areas (such as the Great Lakes, the Rhine River, the Svalbard Archipelago, Antarctica, and various regional seas). Some regimes reflect functional and geographic concerns at the same time, as in the case of the regime designed to protect the North Sea from the disposal at sea of harmful substances and from land-based runoffs. There remain disagreements about the existence of regimes in some cases, often when a regime is embryonic or in its earliest stages of development (for instance, the arrangements spelled out in the 1992 Framework Convention on Climate Change). But what is most striking is that such disagreements generally occur at the margins of this universe of cases and that a high degree of consensus exists regarding the core set of regimes.

What do these specific regimes have in common that can help define attributes of regimes in general? Regimes are sets of rules, decision-making procedures, and/or programs that give rise to social practices, assign roles to the participants in these practices, and govern their interactions. Regimes can and certainly do vary along a number of dimensions, most obviously in their functional scope, geographic domain, and membership. In this connection consider the spread between the Great Lakes water qual-

9. Alexander Wendt, "Collective Identity Formation and the International State," *American Political Science Review* 88 (June 1994), 384–96.

10. For a particularly articulate expression of nonpositivist views on the nature of regimes and how to study them, see Friedrich Kratochwil and John Gerard Ruggie, "International Organization: A State of the Art on an Art of the State," *International Organization* 40 (Autumn 1986), 753–75.

ity regime, which has two members and focuses on water quality in a limited area, and the climate regime, which is global in scope and likely to draw in almost all members of international society as it develops. There is also considerable variation in decision-making procedures, compliance mechanisms, revenue sources, and dispute resolution processes. The degree of formalization is another significant dimension, with some regimes resting on legally binding conventions or treaties and others founded on "soft" law agreements (such as ministerial declarations, executive agreements, or even more informal understandings).

Beyond this, a number of more analytic distinctions have emerged in the literature on international regimes.[11] Although complex mixes are common, individual regimes may be (1) largely regulatory in that they emphasize the formulation of rules or behavioral prescriptions; (2) predominantly procedural, focusing on mechanisms for arriving at collective choices; (3) primarily programmatic in that they lead to joint or collaborative projects; or (4) essentially generative, highlighting new ways of thinking about problems. Regimes also vary in strength or depth as measured by the density, specificity, and range of their operative provisions. Many regimes (for example, the Antarctic Treaty System and the European transboundary air pollution regime) become stronger as they develop over time. Additionally, individual regimes may be nested into overarching institutional arrangements or integrated into larger structures pertaining to broader issue areas (as with the regime for straddling stocks of fish in relation to the encompassing law of the sea or the regimes dealing with specific commodities such as sugar, coffee, or tin in relation to the overarching regime dealing with international trade in goods and services).

Like other social institutions, international regimes come in many sizes and shapes. Yet they share a number of features that allow us to place them in the same universe of cases and separate them from the entities (such as the various components of the United Nations System) emphasized in other approaches to governance in international society. As the regimes designed to protect stratospheric ozone and to regulate trade in endangered species of fauna and flora suggest, international regimes are almost invariably responses to specific problems; they do not seek to provide comprehensive systems of public order for geographically or socially defined areas. Although states loom large in such arrangements, a variety of non-state actors have also become important players in these institutional arrangements. Taken together, regimes form a horizontal rather than a vertical or hierarchical system of public order. The result is a complex pattern

---

11. For a fuller account, see Levy, Young, and Zürn, "Study of International Regimes."

of decentralized authority. One of the strengths of this horizontal structure of governance is the capacity of individual regimes to survive serious failures in other components of this system of international order. The opposite side of the coin, however, is an underdeveloped capacity to sort out overlaps and intersections. Individual regimes are created for different purposes by different actors who usually make little or no attempt to coordinate their efforts or to identify the links between regimes.

Relatively speaking, regimes are lightly administered. If we draw a distinction between regimes as institutions and organizations as material entities possessing offices, budgets, personnel, and legal personalities, it is possible to say that this approach to governance highlights the idea of "governance without government" and may fulfill the function of governance while minimizing the establishment of new bureaucracies or administrative entities.[12] Of course, much of the work of implementing the provisions of international regimes is left to individual members that are typically highly organized, whether they are states or various types of non-state actors. Moreover, regimes vary in the extent to which their day-to-day operation requires the presence of organizational capacity at the international or transnational level. Whereas the 1959 Antarctic Treaty—the core element of the Antarctic Treaty System—operates without any standing administrative apparatus, the organizational arrangements initially envisioned in connection with deep seabed mining—the International Seabed Authority and the Enterprise—would have brought into existence an unprecedentedly elaborate set of organizations. No doubt, the ambitious character of this arrangement is one reason why the administrative provisions pertaining to deep seabed mining set forth in part 11 of the 1982 Law of the Sea Convention fell by the wayside, even though the convention as a whole finally entered into force in 1994, almost twelve years after being opened for signature.

What is more, regimes often acquire increased organizational capacity as they evolve through time. With respect to the Antarctic Treaty System, the addition of elements dealing with living resources and environmental protection has added an increasingly complex administrative apparatus, including a commission responsible for issues relating to the use of living resources and a committee responsible for implementing provisions relating to environmental protection. Yet secretariats associated with environmental regimes are more likely to have from five to twenty staff members

12. The phrase "governance without government" is from James N. Rosenau and Ernst-Otto Czempiel, eds., *Governance without Government: Order and Change in World Politics* (Cambridge: Cambridge University Press, 1992).

in contrast to the hundreds employed by organizations within the United Nations System.[13]

REGIMES AND SOCIETIES

International regimes do not operate in a social vacuum. Just as students of domestic systems draw a distinction between the state and civil society, those concerned with international affairs look on the states system as a society of states. Reasonably well-defined principles deal with membership in international society, and rules govern interactions among the members of this society (such as the rule prescribing nonintervention in the domestic affairs of individual members).[14] Although there is no state as such in international society, we can still pose questions about the relationship between regimes and the society of states within which they operate that parallel the questions which students of domestic systems ask about state/society relations.

Both the constitutive principles of international society and the more specific rules that have emerged to put them into practice are violated from time to time. These arrangements also evolve steadily over time. There has, for example, been much discussion of de facto shifts in the idea of sovereignty as a constitutive principle of international society.[15] Even so, many—perhaps most—students of international regimes have focused on international society, assuming that the members of regimes are states and proceeding to analyze the effectiveness of regimes within an analytic framework tied to the states system.[16]

Understandable as it may seem as a basis for analysis, this state-centric approach runs the risk of introducing a conservative bias into regime the-

13. The literature on international secretariats is sparse. But see "International Secretariats," a background paper prepared for the workshop on international secretariats at the Rockefeller Brothers Conference Center, Pocantico, New York, 15–18 June 1995 (available from the Institute on International Environmental Governance at Dartmouth College).

14. The elaboration of this idea is the defining feature of the British school of thought on international affairs. Perhaps the best-known expression occurs in Hedley Bull, *The Anarchical Society: A Study of Order in World Politics* (New York: Columbia University Press, 1977). See also Oran R. Young, "System and Society in World Affairs: Implications for International Organizations," *International Social Science Journal* 47 (1995), 197–212.

15. Gene M. Lyons and Michael Mastanduno, eds., *Beyond Westphalia: State Sovereignty and International Intervention* (Baltimore: Johns Hopkins University Press, 1995), and Thomas J. Biersteker and Cynthia Weber, eds., *State Sovereignty as Social Construct* (Cambridge: Cambridge University Press, 1996).

16. See, for example, Stephen D. Krasner, ed., *International Regimes* (Ithaca: Cornell University Press, 1983), and Volker Rittberger, ed., *Regime Theory and International Relations* (Oxford: Clarendon, 1993).

ory and fails to confront many interesting developments currently under way in international and transnational affairs. There is no reason to believe that states are on their way out as centers of power and authority. Yet evidence shows that a second social system is growing up around the society of states, a system that is coming to form a part of the social environment within which regimes operate. Increasingly described as *global civil society*, this system is made up of a variety of nonstate actors, including interest groups, professional associations, and corporations, that operate above the level of the individual but below or apart from the level of any structure of governance.[17]

Many ambiguities surround the concept of global civil society at this stage. Does global civil society qualify as a society in the sense that it has widely accepted constitutive principles covering such matters as membership and interactions among its members? Is global civil society a single phenomenon to be considered on a par with international society? Does it make sense, for instance, to include the world economy or the worldwide system of modes of production as part of global civil society, or are we better off reserving the idea of civil society for actors and interactions that are essentially noneconomic and nonpolitical in character?[18] Does global civil society have a life of its own, or is it more appropriately treated as a set of developments modifying the character of international society?[19] In the end, can we define the concept of global civil society with sufficient precision to make it possible to distinguish it from international society and to permit confident judgments concerning its strength as well as how much this strength is increasing or decreasing?

These are formidable questions. Even so, the concept of global civil society clearly has something to offer to students of international or transnational governance. To begin with, it highlights the risk of regime theory becoming overly state centric in the sense of assuming that membership in international regimes is—or should be?—confined to states. We are experiencing the emergence of a variety of recognized and significant roles for nonstate actors in the development and operation of international re-

17. Paul Wapner, "Governance in Global Civil Society," in Oran R. Young, ed., *Global Governance: Drawing Insights from the Environmental Experience* (Cambridge: MIT Press, 1997), 65–84, and Ronnie D. Lipschutz, *Global Civil Society and Global Environmental Governance* (Albany: State University of New York Press, 1996).

18. For a range of perspectives on this issue, see William R. Thompson, ed., *Contending Approaches to World System Analysis* (Beverly Hills: Sage, 1983).

19. For an account suggesting that global civil society is presently a source of criticism of international society rather than an alternative source of world order, see Richard A. Falk, "The World Order between Inter-State Law and the Law of Humanity: The Role of Civil Society Institutions," in Danielle Archibugi and David Held, eds., *Cosmopolitan Democracy: An Agenda for a New World Order* (Cambridge: Polity, 1995), 163–79.

gimes.[20] Some of these actors (for example, multinational corporations) have proven remarkably adept at finding ways to achieve their goals within institutional frameworks established by international regimes. Beyond this lies the realm of relations between nonstate actors and global civil society. Just as international regimes have proliferated to deal with a variety of problems arising in international society, we may speak of transnational regimes as mechanisms for solving problems arising in global civil society. Consider, for instance, the global insurance regime that has evolved in conjunction with the dramatic growth in world trade during the postwar era. It is fair to say as well that membership in global civil society is significant in constitutive terms for many nonstate actors—such as the Worldwide Fund for Nature and Greenpeace—in the same way that membership in international society has constitutive implications for states.[21] It makes no more sense to try to grasp the identity of many nonstate actors without understanding their involvement in global civil society than it does to think of states without paying attention to their connection to international society.

A question arises at this point about the extent to which global civil society should be regarded as a mechanism for the performance of the function of governance. In fact, this idea risks confusing the issue. Regimes are sets of roles, rules, and relationships that arise to deal with issue-specific problems, whether these problems are associated primarily with the society of states or with global civil society. What is needed to make progress analytically is a clear separation between regimes, on the one hand, and both international society and global civil society, on the other.[22] The point of drawing such a distinction, which parallels the state/society distinction with regard to domestic systems, is not to argue that regimes and society are unrelated to each other. On the contrary, the distinction opens up a new research agenda that focuses precisely on the links between regimes and societies. Are regimes easier to create and operate successfully in some societal settings than in others? Can we draw useful distinctions be-

---

20. Thomas E. Princen and Matthias Finger, *Environmental NGOs in World Politics: Linking the Local and the Global* (London: Routledge, 1994), and Paul Wapner, *Environmental Activism and World Civic Politics* (Albany: State University of New York Press, 1996).

21. For some interesting observations on the case of Greenpeace, see Paul Wapner, "In Defense of Banner Hangers: The Dark Green Politics of Greenpeace," in Bron Raymond Taylor, ed., *Resistance Movements: The Global Emergence of Radical and Popular Environmentalism* (Albany: State University of New York Press, 1995), 300–314.

22. Whereas regimes are issue-specific institutions focused on the supply governance, societies are socially defined groups that share general principles or rules regarding membership and prescriptive standards pertaining to interactions with one another. Thus, international society is a society of states; regimes like those dealing with Great Lakes water quality, Antarctica, or stratospheric ozone operate within this society. For relevant background, see Jean L. Cohen and Andrew Arato, *Civil Society and Political Theory* (Cambridge: MIT Press, 1992).

tween international regimes whose members are states and transnational regimes whose members are various types of nonstate actors? Are some types of regimes better suited to operation in conjunction with international society in contrast to global civil society, and vice versa? What about the prospects for regimes whose membership includes a mix of states and nonstate actors? These and other similar concerns are important issues that come into focus once we make a clear separation between regimes and society; they cannot be posed, let alone answered, in the absence of such a distinction.

Thus we can distinguish initially between two pure types of regimes that are relevant to the supply of governance in world affairs. International regimes, the central concern of most contributors to the new institutionalism in international relations, are institutional arrangements whose members are states and whose operations center on issues arising in international society. Arms control regimes, such as the arrangement governing nuclear nonproliferation, exemplify this category of institutions. Transnational regimes, by contrast, are institutional arrangements whose members are nonstate actors and whose operations are pertinent to issues that arise in global civil society. The rapidly emerging social practice connecting users of the World Wide Web is an example.

Although these pure types are interesting for analytic purposes, real-world regimes are often—perhaps normally—a mix of international regimes in which nonstate actors play significant roles and transnational regimes in which states have important roles to play.[23] What is more, societal influences can and often do cut across the pure types of regimes. The forces at work in global civil society can exert considerable pressure on the operation of international regimes. Much the same can be said of the pressure international society exerts on the operation of transnational regimes. It follows that we must pay greater attention to arrangements in which states and nonstate actors interact with one another in complex ways, rather than clinging to the familiar assumptions of a state-centric world. To facilitate discussion, I use the phrase *global governance* in this book to refer to the combined efforts of international and transnational regimes.

THE EFFECTIVENESS OF REGIMES

It would be a mistake to expect international and transnational regimes to meet every demand for governance in world affairs. Although the num-

23. Debora L. Spar, *The Cooperative Edge: The Internal Politics of International Cartels* (Ithaca: Cornell University Press, 1994), and Virginia Haufler, *Dangerous Commerce: Insurance and the Management of International Risk* (Ithaca: Cornell University Press, 1997).

ber of such arrangements has increased rapidly in recent decades, especially in the realm of environmental affairs, regimes do not arise to deal with every problem on the global political agenda. In fact, the effort to explain why regimes emerge in response to some problems but not others is a major preoccupation of students of global governance. The striking contrast between international efforts to regulate transboundary movements of sulfur dioxide and nitrogen oxides and a variety of other toxic substances, for example, is a phenomenon that calls for sustained analysis. Even when regimes do come into being, the absence of any hierarchical structure capable of welding these issue-specific arrangements into an integrated world order means that gaps and overlaps among discrete regimes will be common. Some institutional linkages are beneficial in the sense that separate regimes serve to reinforce each other, thereby contributing to the fulfillment of their respective goals. But the occurrence of mutual interference is also inevitable from time to time.[24] Under the circumstances, there is no basis for expecting regimes to offer a simple and comprehensive solution to the problem of governance in world affairs.

Turning to specific regimes, however, it is natural to inquire into their effectiveness or success in solving the problems that motivate their establishment. Any comprehensive consideration of this subject would entail use of a number of criteria to assess the performance of regimes, over and above considerations relating to the substantive features of particular problems. An *economic criterion* stresses efficiency and asks whether the same results could have been achieved at a lower cost or, alternatively, better results achieved at the same cost. A *political criterion* directs attention to equity and raises questions about the fairness both of the results of institutional arrangements and of their procedures or processes. Although *equity* is notoriously difficult to define and operationalize, the issue of fairness cannot be set aside as a major concern. When it comes to environmental regimes, there is also an *ecological criterion* that emphasizes the degree to which the results flowing from institutional arrangements are sustainable in that they do not disrupt key biotic or abiotic systems. A well-known example of this concern is the vigorous debate in more recent years about an analytic construct known as the "tragedy of the commons," which centers on issues relating to the consequences of alternative structures of property rights.[25]

An alternative perspective on the performance of regimes involves the

24. Oran R. Young, "Institutional Linkages in International Society: Polar Perspectives," *Global Governance* 2 (January–April 1996), 1–24.

25. For a good sample, see Bonnie McCay and James Acheson, eds., *The Question of the Commons: The Culture and Ecology of Communal Resources* (Tucson: University of Arizona Press, 1987).

idea of process management in contrast to—or as a supplement to—problem solving when it comes to the results that social institutions produce.[26] On this account, we need to recognize that some problems are extremely difficult or even impossible to solve within any reasonable time frame. Many cases of ethnic conflict come to mind immediately in this connection. But intractable environmental problems, such as those associated with the treatment of toxic wastes or anthropogenic interference in the global carbon cycle, are easy to identify as well. In such cases, regimes may be more effective in managing or containing problems than in solving them. The idea of process management also helps us to grasp the role that regimes can play in deepening or even transforming our understanding of the problems that lead to their creation. In such cases as climate change, where the physical and biological systems involved are poorly understood, this form of process management can become a central feature of the performance of institutional arrangements. Although there is a natural tendency to think in terms of problem solving in evaluating the performance of regimes, the idea of process management deserves greater attention in future analyses of institutional effectiveness.

Even so, this line of thought is not free from controversy. Consider a point that parallels the central issue in a well-known debate among students of conflict. This debate pits those who focus on conflict resolution and see management as a process that is likely to reduce pressures on the parties to resolve their differences against those who emphasize conflict management and see resolution as an ideal whose pursuit may prove detrimental to the effort to control or contain conflicts. Success in the development of regimes that emphasize process management may sometimes reduce pressures to solve problems. But the single-minded pursuit of regimes capable of solving problems can lead to outright failure. There is no simple way to resolve this debate; the arguments on both sides have merit, at least under some circumstances. Yet the idea of process management is a welcome addition to the growing stream of work that hitherto has looked at institutional effectiveness primarily in terms of problem solving.

However we approach the effectiveness of international and transnational regimes, virtually everyone agrees that actual regimes vary dramatically in these terms and that many individual regimes undergo substantial changes over time with regard to effectiveness. The prevailing view is that the regime created to deal with Great Lakes water quality has been relatively successful, for example, but that many other arrangements dealing

26. I am indebted to Angela Cropper of the United Nations Development Programme for drawing this distinction to my attention.

with lakes or river basins have performed poorly.[27] The regime governing problems of pollution in the North Sea has grown stronger with the passage of time, whereas many international fisheries regimes have proven increasingly disappointing. There is general agreement that the regime dealing with intentional discharges of oil at sea became markedly more effective following a switch during the 1970s from a system of discharge standards to a system based on equipment standards. For its part, the regime for whales and whaling appears to have become increasingly effective during the 1970s and early 1980s, before undergoing a de facto transformation of constitutive principles from conservationism to preservationism which raises questions about whether it is meaningful to compare the regime's effectiveness today with its earlier performance. Overall, the dominant impression regarding the effectiveness of international and transnational regimes is one of variance, an observation that leads us to inquire about factors that determine success or failure. This is true whether the assessment focuses only on problem solving or opens out into consider ations of efficiency and equity or of process management in contrast to problem solving.

This conclusion suggests the need for an extensive program of research related to governance in world affairs. Not only is it important in analytic terms to focus attention on the determinants of institutional effectiveness, but it is also essential to make progress in this area if the study of regimes is to yield results of interest to practitioners. Students of regimes have devoted increasing attention to various aspects of effectiveness.[28] It is premature to offer any definitive judgment regarding the results of these studies; more research is needed. Still, it is not unreasonable to ask for a midterm report regarding efforts to understand the forces that explain observed variance in the performance of international and transnational regimes.

The bottom line of such a report is by no means clear-cut (see Chapter 5). Recent research has produced a long and rapidly growing list of fac-

---

27. Some close observers believe that the Great Lakes water quality regime is facing growing threats to its effectiveness. See Lee Botts and Paul Muldoon, *The Great Lakes Water Quality Agreement: Its Past Successes and Uncertain Future* (Hanover, N.H.: Institute on International Environmental Governance, 1996). For more general accounts of international regimes dealing with water, see Genady N. Golubev, "Availability and Quality of Freshwater Resources: A Perspective from the North," in Oran R. Young, George J. Demko, and Kilaparti Ramakrishna, eds., *Global Environmental Change and International Governance* (Hanover, N.H.: University Press of New England, 1996), 107–22, and Thomas Bernauer, "Managing International Rivers," in Young, *Global Governance*, 155–95.

28. For a survey, see Levy, Young, and Zürn, "Study of International Regimes," esp. 290–308.

tors that appear to have some bearing on the effectiveness of regimes, at least in specific cases. But it has failed to yield robust generalizations about the relative importance of these factors, much less well-grounded propositions stating necessary or sufficient conditions for regimes to succeed as problem solvers or as process managers. Some analysts emphasize the nature of the problem to be solved and draw a distinction between benign and malign (or easy and difficult) problems.[29] Others differentiate among distinct social forces (for example, material conditions, interests, and ideas), seeking to sort out the relative importance of such factors as population growth, technology, decision-making procedures, and values as determinants of performance.[30] Another approach features a distinction between endogenous and exogenous factors. Those who look to endogenous factors focus on the role of various institutional attributes such as the nature of decision rules, revenue sources, and compliance mechanisms. Those who focus on exogenous factors, by contrast, tend to see regimes as relatively fragile structures influenced by societal forces ranging from material conditions such as technology to intangible conditions like the emergence of consensual knowledge. Yet another perspective emphasizes the extent to which individual regimes are embedded in larger institutional structures.[31] Partly, this is a matter of international or transnational linkages that can affect performance. In part, it is a matter of the extent to which regimes complement or clash with social institutions operating at the domestic and local levels. A particularly interesting suggestion relating to such matters is that effectiveness will often be a function of the compatibility between top-down approaches reflected in the content of international regimes and bottom-up approaches implicit in local or regional arrangements. The resultant issue of vertical interplay will be especially acute in such cases as climate change, in which the problem to be solved involves behavior reaching all the way down to the actions of individual users of motor vehicles or home appliances.

29. See, for example, Volker Rittberger and Michael Zürn, "Regime Theory: Findings from the Study of 'East-West' Regimes," *Cooperation and Conflict* 26 (1991), 165–83, and Steinar Andresen and Jørgen Wettestad, "International Problem-Solving Effectiveness: The Oslo Project So Far," *International Environmental Affairs* 7 (Spring 1995), 127–49.

30. On the distinctions among these clusters of social forces, see Robert W. Cox, "Social Forces, States, and World Orders: Beyond International Relations Theory," in Robert O. Keohane, ed., *Neorealism and Its Critics* (New York: Columbia University Press, 1986), 204–54.

31. For well-known examples, see John Gerard Ruggie, "International Regimes, Transactions, and Change: Embedded Liberalism in the Postwar Economic Order," in Krasner, *International Regimes*, 195–232, and John Gerard Ruggie, "Embedded Liberalism Revisited: Institutions and Progress in International Economic Relations," in Emanuel Adler and Beverly Crawford, eds., *Progress in Postwar International Relations* (New York: Columbia University Press, 1991), 201–34.

BROADER CONSEQUENCES OF REGIMES

Whether or not regimes succeed in solving or managing social problems, their presence can and often does have broader consequences for the social settings in which they operate. Some regimes produce spillover effects by influencing relations among members in functional areas beyond their nominal scope.[32] Regimes—especially those generally regarded as successful—can also generate demonstration effects by creating precedents that affect the thinking of both their own members and others as they confront new problems. Even more significant in the long run is the role that issue-specific regimes play as vehicles for the introduction of institutional innovations that diffuse throughout international society or global civil society in ways that have profound consequences for these social systems over time. Students of regimes have devoted relatively little attention to the analysis of these broader consequences.[33] We must invest more time and energy in their analysis if research on governance in world affairs is to flourish in the future.

It is important to avoid inflated expectations about the capacity of regimes to deal with the world's troubles. There may even be cases in which a preoccupation with problems amenable to treatment through the creation of regimes has the effect of diverting attention from larger or more pervasive concerns in international society and in global civil society. These include the resurgence of ethnic conflict that is leading to the breakdown or failure of multinational states; the steady growth of human population toward a level that raises questions about the Earth's carrying capacity; the surging tides of refugees, migrant workers, and illegal aliens that threaten to produce open conflict in a number of areas; and the spread of technologies that are leading human communities to expend the Earth's natural capital at an unprecedented rate. These problems are global not because they focus on systemic matters (such as the Earth's climate system) but because they involve large-scale processes that occur worldwide. Problems of this sort may be appropriate targets for the articulation of general international norms or broad principles of international law.[34] But it is difficult to see how they can be tackled effectively through the creation of issue-specific regimes.

---

32. Readers will recognize this idea as a familiar element in the logic of neofunctionalist integration theory. See, for example, Ernst B. Haas, *Beyond the Nation State: Functionalism and International Organization* (Palo Alto: Stanford University Press, 1964).

33. For a survey of what has been done so far, see Levy, Young, and Zürn, "Study of International Regimes," 308–12.

34. For a survey of recent thinking about international norms, see Gregory A. Raymond, "Problems and Prospects in the Study of International Norms," *Mershon International Studies Review* 41 (November 1997), 205–45.

Moreover, regimes at the international or transnational level have a limited capacity to alter the behavior within societies—the combustion of fossil fuels or the destruction of old-growth forests—that frequently underlies the problems to be solved. Partly, this results from the difficulties of gaining compliance with international or transnational rules.[35] In part, it stems from the fact that regimes are top-down arrangements whose ability to solve problems will be determined largely by the extent to which they complement bottom-up arrangements pertaining to the same issues. This is particularly true when the behavior in question is a matter of actions not on the part of regime members themselves but on the part of numerous actors—including individuals—operating below the level of regime members.

Consider climate change, especially as a result of the combustion of fossil fuels.[36] The emission of carbon dioxide from the burning of fossil fuels is a consequence of the actions of individuals operating automobiles, corporations using coal or oil to drive their production processes, municipalities relying on coal-fired power plants to generate electricity, and so forth. This does not mean that the 1992 Framework Convention on Climate Change (FCCC) is irrelevant or bound to prove ineffective. But the FCCC can achieve results only to the extent that it is coupled with effective efforts to influence behavior deep within the economic and social systems of the member states. Moreover, the behavior in question will be affected by values and local institutional arrangements that the FCCC—whose members are states—cannot alter in any direct sense. Under the circumstances, it is apparent that we need to think more systematically about institutional linkages and the interplay of institutions operating at different social scales.[37]

In more prosaic terms, both the creation and the operation of regimes are costly enterprises. This is partly a matter of direct costs—intangible as well as tangible—such as the expenditure of time and energy required to negotiate the terms of international agreements, the allocation of resources to pay for the operation of secretariats, or the restrictions that

35. For an account that explains why it is a mistake to overemphasize the distinction between domestic society and international society in these terms, see Abram Chayes and Antonia Handler Chayes, *The New Sovereignty: Compliance with International Regulatory Agreements* (Cambridge: Harvard University Press, 1995).
36. Ian H. Rowlands, *The Politics of Global Atmospheric Change* (Manchester: Manchester University Press, 1995).
37. Oran R. Young, "The Problem of Scale in Human/Environment Relationships," in Robert O. Keohane and Elinor Ostrom, eds., *Local Commons and Global Interdependence: Heterogeneity and Cooperation in Two Domains* (London: Sage, 1995), 27–45, and O. R. Young, "Science Plan for the Project on the Institutional Dimensions of Global Environmental Change," *IHDP Report*, no. 9 (Bonn: International Human Dimensions Programme on Global Environmental Change, 1999).

participation places on the freedom of individual members to do as they please. Looked at another way, it is also a matter of opportunity costs, because the expenditure of resources on any given regime ordinarily reduces the resources left to invest elsewhere. Particularly serious for less affluent societies, this problem underlies many of the criticisms of the climate regime by representatives of developing countries who are preoccupied with a range of other pressing concerns, such as food production and disease control. Beyond this, the creation and operation of regimes can sometimes produce perverse results by generating a false sense that certain problems have been taken care of and do not require additional attention or by giving rise to new problems in the process of solving old ones. To illustrate, a number of responsible observers have expressed concern about various chemicals that are being substituted for chlorofluorocarbons (CFCs) and about some sources of energy that may be substituted for fossil fuels. There is nothing unique about international or transnational institutions in these terms; exactly the same concerns arise at all levels of social organization. Yet it is well to temper enthusiasm for regimes with a healthy respect for the costs incurred in their formation and operation.

That said, let us focus explicitly on the question of the broader consequences that regimes engender, which entails two contrasting lines of thought. Some observers regard social institutions as conservative forces with respect to the societal settings in which they operate. Institutional arrangements are mechanisms of social control created by the dominant members of society to promote their own interests.[38] A liberal twist on this argument treats institutions as public goods that enhance the welfare of all members, even as they yield particularly beneficial results for the most powerful members of society. Familiar in studies pitched at all levels of social organization, this line of thinking has focused at the international level on trade regimes, which some regard as a means of institutionalizing neocolonialism, and on environmental regimes, which are sometimes viewed as a means of imposing the newly emerging environmental values of affluent societies on the rest of the world.[39] Needless to say, such arguments are contentious and difficult to resolve. In essence, the debate turns on three issues: the capacity of leading actors to impose institutional arrangements on others in the first place, the incidence of the benefits and costs of institutions once they become operational, and the extent to

38. Interestingly, both realists and marxists espouse arguments of this kind. For a prominent realist exposition, see Robert Gilpin, *The Political Economy of International Relations* (Princeton: Princeton University Press, 1987).

39. For an early and still influential account of the role of dominant actors in international trade regimes, see Charles P. Kindleberger, *The World in Depression, 1929–1939* (Berkeley: University of California Press, 1973).

which regimes acquire a life of their own over time which makes it difficult for leading actors to bend them to their will. Each of these issues raises profound concerns that students of international and transnational regimes will need to address in expanding their horizons to look at the broader consequences of institutional arrangements.

The other approach centers on the view that regimes are agents of social change in international society and probably in global civil society as well. Those seeking to reform international society have had little success in direct efforts to redefine its constitutive principles. Given the decentralized or nonhierarchical nature of international society, it is not easy even to see how to go about changing the general rules governing membership or relations among the members of this society. International law is essentially a set of rules which spell out the requirements for membership in a society of states and which guide their interactions with one another.[40] Yet today we face growing problems which are difficult to solve in the context of a states system and which have given rise to powerful pressures to alter the character of international society as we have known it. How is this to be done? The answer lies largely in efforts to introduce innovative arrangements at the level of specific regimes and then to take steps to encourage their diffusion through international society as a whole. Nowhere is this type of regime-based innovation more in evidence than in environmental arrangements formed during the last several decades. Not only do these regimes accord significant roles to nonstate actors, but they also introduce decision-making procedures designed to avoid the paralysis often associated with consensus rules and provide procedures to facilitate institutional growth and development.

Two distinct elements of this piecemeal approach to the reform of international society are worthy of particular notice. The first focuses on the activities of nonstate actors as catalytic agents in the creation and operation of international regimes.[41] The striking growth in the roles that environmental nongovernmental organizations (NGOs) play in a variety of regimes exemplifies this point. Today, representatives of these organizations are routinely included as members of national delegations engaged in negotiating and managing regimes. Meetings that were once closed (for example, the Antarctic Treaty Consultative Meetings) are now open so that NGOs can participate actively as observers. NGOs also provide the

40. Consider, for instance, the opening sentence of Brierly's well-known introduction to international law: "The Law of Nations, or International Law, may be defined as the body of rules and principles of action which are binding upon civilized states in their relations with one another" (J. L. Brierly, *The Law of Nations*, 6th ed. [New York: Oxford University Press, 1963], 1).
41. Paul Wapner, "Politics beyond the State: Environmental Activism and World Civic Politics," *World Politics* 47 (1995), 311–40.

brain trust for the participation of many smaller states in international regimes—such as the role of leading environmental groups in providing intellectual capital for the Alliance of Small Island States in connection with climate change.

Institutional initiatives that once would have gone through without controversy are now derailed and redirected in considerable part as a result of the efforts of environmental groups. Although Australia and then France became outspoken opponents of the 1988 Convention on the Regulation of Antarctic Mineral Resource Activities (CRAMRA), for example, a number of NGOs played significant roles in bringing pressure to bear on the governments of these countries to abandon this laboriously negotiated arrangement and to replace it with the Protocol on Environmental Protection of 1991, which bans the exploitation of minerals in Antarctica during the foreseeable future. The same can be said for the role of environmental NGOs in stalling the adoption and implementation of the Revised Management Procedures in the whaling regime and therefore barring any resumption of commercial or artisanal whaling sanctioned by the International Whaling Commission. Does all this signal the end of states as the most important members of international society? Certainly not. Does it mean that international society is undergoing significant change regarding the role of other types of players as a consequence of the creation and operation of an array of issue-specific regimes? It is hard to avoid an affirmative answer to this question.

A second element involves the constitutive principles governing the interactions among members of international society.[42] It is difficult to imagine a successful effort to redefine rules derived from the principle of sovereignty, for example, so long as this task is approached at the generic or societal level. Yet there is a widespread feeling that these rules are now evolving in ways that are likely to have profound consequences. How is this possible? Again, the engine of change emerges from a growing number of innovations introduced in connection with the creation and operation of issue-specific regimes. The idea that states are responsible for the external effects not only of their own actions but also of the behavior of various actors operating within their jurisdictions has been strengthened immeasurably as a consequence of the development of regimes concerned with marine pollution, transboundary air pollution, nuclear accidents, ozone depletion, and so forth. Given the traditional insistence on the right of

---

42. For an account that emphasizes the distinction between constitutive rules and regulative rules, see Nicholas Greenwood Onuf, *World of Our Making: Rules and Rule in Social Theory and International Relations* (Columbia: University of South Carolina Press, 1989).

states to use their natural resources and environmental systems as they see fit, this trend toward imposing restrictions on state sovereignty is a remarkable one. Similar observations are in order regarding the emergence of an obligation to share benefits derived from the use of such global commons as the deep seabed, the electromagnetic spectrum, and celestial bodies. In effect, the traditional view of sovereignty as a basis for the assertion of rights on the part of the members of international society is being joined by a complementary view that emphasizes the duties or obligations of sovereignty. The long-term consequences of this development—emerging largely in connection with the growth of an array of issue-specific regimes—are likely to be profound.

Generalizing the Environmental Experience

Many recent contributions to regime theory—including much of my work—focus on environmental issues as a source of empirical evidence and analytic insights. It is pertinent, therefore, to ask about the wider applicability of insights drawn primarily from the study of environmental or resource regimes. Numerous responses to this question are possible, ranging from the familiar idea that each case is unique to the equally familiar notion that outcomes flowing from environmental as well as other regimes are by and large a function of some master variable, like power in the structural or material sense. Little by little, however, more sophisticated insights regarding this matter are beginning to emerge.[43]

An examination of environmental cases serves to reinforce a number of observations that have arisen from the study of regimes more generally. Most regimes are driven by the need to deal with more or less acute problems, even though important differences exist with regard to the mix of regulatory, procedural, programmatic, and generative functions they perform. The extent to which members share a sense of community or a common discourse makes a difference not only to the process of forming regimes but also to their success in solving problems once they are in place. State capacity is an important determinant of the performance of regimes, but the capacity of states does not correlate well with simple measures of development or modernization. Although it is important to draw a distinction between regimes and organizations, there are significant roles for organizations to play in most issue areas both in the creation and in the operation of regimes.

43. Young, *Global Governance*.

Perhaps of greater interest is that drawing on the experience of environmental regimes leads to the identification of concerns that are less familiar but will warrant systematic examination in the future. Regime theory to date has been too state centric. Not only are we faced with the growth of transnational regimes whose members are not states at all, but we also need to pay more systematic attention to the participation of nonstate actors in international regimes. No matter how complex regimes become, they generally rest, in the final analysis, on a dominant vision or discourse.[44] These generative visions may center on any of a variety of ideas—achieving maximum sustainable yield from renewable resources; eliminating consumptive uses of living resources; taking a holistic view of large marine and terrestrial ecosystems; or focusing on the planet as a single system and directing attention to global environmental changes. And they typically have normative as well as analytic and empirical content.

Although it makes sense for certain purposes to study individual regimes in depth, individual regimes also exhibit complex linkages to other institutional arrangements. Often, it will prove helpful to think of institutional structures encompassing a number of regimes that deal with a broad range of functionally related issues such as trade or pollution.[45] The performance of international and transnational regimes will be affected, moreover, by their compatibility with other institutional arrangements that operate at the domestic and local levels. In other words, success is typically a matter of making the right connections between top-down arrangements and bottom-up arrangements operative in the same issue area. Regimes change continuously, and these changes are often nonlinear in character. Thus it is not acceptable to model regime dynamics in terms of analytic constructs that assume—explicitly or implicitly—linear processes.

To what extent are these concerns peculiar to environmental arrangements? Important differences exist both among regimes and among the problems they address. Coordination problems in which there is no incentive to cheat once an agreement is struck are clearly different from collaboration problems that occur when individual members can gain from cheating so that issues of compliance and the design of compliance mechanisms emerge as central concerns.[46] Regimes themselves differ markedly in their mix of regulatory, procedural, programmatic, and generative

44. See also Karen T. Litfin, *Ozone Discourses: Science and Politics in Global Environmental Cooperation* (New York: Columbia University Press, 1994).

45. See Konrad von Moltke, "Institutional Interactions: The Structure of Regimes for Trade and the Environment," in Young, *Global Governance*, 247–72.

46. Arthur A. Stein, "Coordination and Collaboration: Regimes in an Anarchic World," in Krasner, *International Regimes*, 115–40, and Lisa Martin, "Interests, Power, and Multilateralism," *International Organization* 46 (1992), 765–92.

provisions. Whereas compliance is a central concern for regulatory arrangements, decision-making processes constitute the primary concern in procedural arrangements, and the step-by-step development of common projects or substantive activities looms large from a programmatic perspective. The extent to which individual regimes are embedded in larger institutional structures is another important variable. There is a major difference, for example, between commodity regimes that are nested into the overarching arrangements governing trade, on the one hand, and regimes dealing with individual species (such as whales, seals, or polar bears) that are much more self-contained, on the other. Similar remarks pertain to the degree to which regimes anticipate pressures for change and incorporate orderly procedures for adjusting or adapting their provisions to changes in the nature of the problems they address and the demand for governance associated with them.

Yet the question remains: Do these differences vary systematically with a division of problems and institutional responses along functional lines (for instance, economic, environmental, human rights, and security problems and regimes)? Such a broad topic cannot be settled in the course of a single work. But a central theme of the analysis that I present in this book is the proposition that many features of problems and the regimes created to cope with them transcend conventional distinctions among social functions. To the extent that this is true, an examination of environmental cases can yield insights of a generic nature regarding both the demand for and the supply of governance in world affairs.

CHAPTER TWO

Regime Tasks and Types

Regime theory—as it has evolved over the last twenty years in the United States, Europe, and elsewhere—rests on the assumption that international institutions are relatively homogeneous with regard to the functions or tasks they are created to perform.[1] The origins of this assumption are not difficult to locate. Most thinking about international regimes is anchored squarely in the analysis of collective-action problems.[2] On this account, self-interested actors left to their own devices in an interdependent world will regularly choose courses which seem rational from a purely individualistic point of view but which lead to collective outcomes that are Pareto inferior in the sense that they are inferior to other feasible outcomes for all members of the group.[3] They will, under the circumstances, frequently fail to avoid joint losses, as in the well-known spirals we associate with arms races, trade wars, and tragedies of the commons. Similarly, they will often be unable to realize joint gains, as with familiar situations in which free-riding behavior undermines efforts to produce public or collective goods such as clean air or an effective world monetary system. Regimes take shape as devices that groups of actors create to avoid or ameliorate these collective-action problems. In essence,

---

1. See Stephen D. Krasner, ed., *International Regimes* (Ithaca: Cornell University Press, 1983), and Volker Rittberger, ed., *Regime Theory and International Relations* (Oxford: Clarendon, 1993).

2. Oran R. Young, *International Cooperation: Building Regimes for Natural Resources and the Environment* (Ithaca: Cornell University Press, 1989). Those looking at other levels of social organization have regularly adopted a similar approach. See, for example, Elinor Ostrom, *Governing the Commons: The Evolution of Institutions for Collective Action* (Cambridge: Cambridge University Press, 1990).

3. Thomas C. Schelling, *Micromotives and Macrobehavior* (New York: W. W. Norton, 1978).

they provide sets of rules or behavioral prescriptions designed to allow interdependent actors to avoid joint losses or to reap joint gains without going so far as to submit to the actions of a public authority of the sort we ordinarily think of as a government. In large measure, it is optimism engendered by regime theory about the effectiveness of such institutional arrangements in a variety of issue areas which has given rise to the widespread interest in the idea of "governance without government" among students of international relations.[4]

There is nothing wrong with this line of analysis. Many regimes do owe their existence to efforts to solve collective-action problems. And a strong case can be made for eschewing unnecessary subdivisions of a universe of cases, at least among those desiring to formulate propositions that are as powerful as possible in terms of their scope or the range of circumstances across which they apply. Yet it is equally important not to ignore differences among the members of a universe of cases when such differences make it difficult to generalize across the entire set and especially when subdividing the universe opens up prospects for generating significant new insights. In this chapter, I argue that regime theory today faces an issue of this sort. Much has been gained from the strategy of looking upon regimes as devices for solving collective-action problems. But it is increasingly clear that there are subsets of the overall universe of regimes that differ from one another in ways that have far-reaching implications for our efforts to make progress in understanding both the origins of institutional arrangements and the consequences that flow from their operation.

Specifically, I argue that we can and should differentiate among regimes in terms of the functions or tasks that they perform. Thus I sketch a taxonomy of institutional tasks. I do not claim that this typology is objectively correct or that it is the only way to organize thinking about institutional tasks. But I do contend that the introduction of this typology can help to illuminate important issues relating to the formation of regimes and to the effectiveness of regimes once they are in place. In this connection I focus first on the problem of regime formation and endeavor to show that the character of the process of regime formation will be affected in significant ways by the nature of the institutional tasks under consideration. I then present a parallel argument regarding regime effectiveness, suggesting that the key determinants of effectiveness will vary in terms of the institutional tasks performed by a regime.

The distinctions that I develop here regarding institutional tasks are analytic in nature. The same regime may perform two or more tasks or

4. James N. Rosenau and Ernst-Otto Czempiel, eds., *Governance without Government: Order and Change in World Politics* (Cambridge: Cambridge University Press, 1992).

functions at the same time, and regimes often evolve with regard to the priority they accord to one or another of these tasks. It follows that differentiating among regime types should not lead the unwary to assume that it is possible to assign actual regimes unambiguously to one category or another in the taxonomy of institutional tasks. Nonetheless, some regimes do deal primarily with a single task. There is much to be gained from working out the implications of analytically distinct types of regimes, even when actual regimes handle two or more tasks at the same time. And there is often scope for choice in defining the tasks to be performed by regimes— a point to which I will return. Self-interested actors engaged in designing these institutional arrangements can be counted on to be alert to a consideration of possible advantages and disadvantages of different options in thinking about the pursuit of their own objectives.

A TAXONOMY OF INSTITUTIONAL TASKS

Individual regimes can perform what I call regulatory, procedural, programmatic, and generative tasks or various combinations of these tasks. Because there is a tendency to focus, implicitly if not explicitly, on regulatory arrangements in the mainstream literature on regimes, I start with an account of regulatory tasks. But my purpose is to suggest that the other types of tasks included in the taxonomy are not only distinct but also more central to some problems leading to regime formation than is the classic task of regulation. A failure to grasp this point can only lead to confusion and frustration on the part of those seeking to understand the roles that institutions play in international society.

Regulatory Regimes

Regulation in international society is much like regulation in any other social setting: it centers on the framing and promulgation of rules or behavioral prescriptions whose purpose is to allow participating actors to reap joint gains or avoid joint losses in situations characterized by interactive decision making. Sometimes the subjects of these rules are states or governmental agencies acting on behalf of states, as in the partial nuclear test ban treaty's prohibition on the conduct of nuclear tests on land, under water, and in the atmosphere or the granting of most-favored-nation status under the terms of the General Agreement on Tariffs and Trade/World Trade Organization (GATT/WTO). In many other cases, the rules apply to the behavior of corporations, nongovernmental organizations, or individuals subject to the jurisdiction of states, even though the states themselves are the actual members of regimes. Thus, corporations producing chlorofluorocarbons are subject to the requirements of the ozone regime covering the phaseout of CFCs and a number of related chemicals. Businesses engaged in international trade are obligated to comply with rules prohibiting the dumping of goods on foreign markets. Tanker operators are expected to follow the rules covering the discharge of oily wastes at sea. As these examples suggest, regulatory arrangements may feature prohibitions (the partial ban on nuclear tests) or requirements (the phaseout of CFC production and consumption). To these categories, many analysts add permissions to cover actions that parties are neither required to take nor prohibited from taking.[5] Fisheries regimes, for example, often permit fishers to make their own choices about the boats they use in their efforts to harvest fish.

Some regulatory arrangements deal with relatively simple coordination problems; others address the more ambitious regulatory task of coping with collaboration problems.[6] The rules pertaining to the use of sea lanes, airspace, or even the electromagnetic spectrum, for instance, are largely matters of coordination in the sense that no one has any serious incentive to cheat once the relevant "rules of the road" are clearly defined and generally understood. New entrants desiring to join such arrangements are typically expected to accept the rules in place at the time they initiate the relevant activities. Rules of this sort are generally easy to administer. Regulatory arrangements dealing with collaboration problems (such as the nuclear nonproliferation regime or the regime covering trade in endangered species), on the other hand, are another matter. Because various actors stand to gain if they can violate these rules without provoking similar violations on the part of others, such arrangements require ongoing administrative apparatus to monitor the actions of their members, sort out disputes about alleged violations, and coordinate responses to the actions of violators. Needless to say, fulfilling these requirements poses a major challenge in a social setting lacking anything we would normally call a "government." Even so, arrangements concerning coordination problems and collaboration problems are similar in the sense that they regularly lead to the development of informal prescriptions intended to flesh out the formal rules set forth in constitutive agreements and because even the formal prescriptions typically evolve, becoming "rules in use" in contrast to the

5. On the distinctions among requirements, prohibitions, and permissions, see Ostrom, *Governing the Commons*.
6. Duncan Snidal, "Coordination versus Prisoner's Dilemma: Implications for International Cooperation and Regimes," *American Political Science Review* 79 (December 1985): 923–42.

initial formulas articulated in constitutive agreements.[7] Despite the complications that arise from the absence of government in international society, therefore, regulatory regimes in this setting are like their counterparts at other levels of social organization in that they require authoritative interpretation on a regular basis. The search for innovative ways to meet the need for authoritative interpretation in the absence of a formally constituted government represents one of the principal challenges of governance in international society.

Procedural Regimes

Regulatory arrangements prescribe actions that regime members are expected to take or to refrain from in more or less well-defined situations. The objective of procedural arrangements is to provide mechanisms that allow actors to arrive at collective or social choices regarding problems that arise in the issue areas covered by regimes. Such problems come in a variety of forms. There may be a need to deal with proposals to modify existing rules or to add new rules to the original set. Consider the creation of geographically defined whale sanctuaries in which all harvesting of whales is prohibited. The problem may involve making choices that in turn trigger the application of a set of rules already in place. The decision to place a species on appendix 1 of the convention on trade in endangered species, for example, brings into play a complex set of rules that do not apply to trade in species not listed on this appendix; similar in nature is the placement of pollutants on the blacklist of the Oslo Convention on the control of pollutants affecting the North Sea. Still other cases center on choices that must be made on a recurrent basis for a regime to function in a routine manner. Perhaps the classic instances deal with the setting of annual harvest or catch levels for living resources. At the same time, situations arise in connection with some regimes that are unique because they address one-time problems. The decision to add a compensation fund to the ozone regime as framed in the Montreal Protocol in order to draw in such important actors as China and India exemplifies this type of choice. Despite these variations in the nature of the problems they address, what sets procedural arrangements apart from regulatory arrangements is their focus on making collective choices that arise in connection with the operation of regimes in contrast to administering the sets of rules or prescriptions that constitute central features of regulatory arrangements.

In every case, procedural arrangements raise a number of important concerns that do not arise in connection with purely regulatory arrange-

7. On the idea of rules in use, see Ostrom, *Governing the Commons*.

ments. The first involves the character of the decision rule to be employed in making collective choices. Although casual observers sometimes assume that unanimity is the normal rule at the international level, regarding this requirement as a serious shortcoming of international governance systems, reality is considerably more complex than such arguments suggest. Not only are there many cases (such as whaling and trade in endangered species) in which some type of majority rule is in use, but international regimes also frequently operate under consensus rules that allow the parties to move forward so long as no member feels so strongly about an issue that it is prepared to go on record publicly as an opponent of actions espoused by the majority. Many regimes leave room for individual members to file reservations or objections that allow the majority to proceed with a collective choice, while the objector is free to exempt itself from any formal obligation to comply with the will of the majority. As whaling and trade in endangered species make clear, this option is often used by regime members to maintain a formal position at the same time as they accede to the will of the majority in de facto terms. Both Japan and Russia, for instance, have filed reservations from time to time regarding decisions of the International Whaling Commission, but in a number of instances they have then proceeded to alter their actual behavior to accord with the preferences of the majority. Beyond this, important questions arise over the nature of the obligation flowing from collective choices arrived at through the operation of procedural arrangements at the international level. At issue here is the extent to which decisions reached by a competent group, such as the conference of the parties, are binding on those who vote for them or, alternatively, require some process of ratification on the part of individual members to become binding on those operating under their jurisdiction. As the case of ozone depletion suggests, the status of decisions reached by the conference of the parties may depend on the issue at hand. Thus, decisions to extend the coverage of this regime to include additional chemicals (carbon tetrachloride, for example) are subject to ratification on the part of individual members. But decisions dealing with changes in phaseout schedules for chemicals already covered take affect without any requirement for further action on the part of individual members.

Programmatic Regimes

Classic examples of international governance systems typically feature the articulation of behavioral prescriptions and the establishment of procedures to allow parties to make collective choices on a regular basis. Yet many regimes are motivated, at least in part, by a desire to pool resources to undertake projects that for one reason or another cannot be carried out on a unilateral basis. Sometimes this involves setting up integrated monitoring and assessment programs designed to broaden and deepen common knowledge about the problems that regimes address. A striking case in point is the arrangement known as the Environmental Monitoring and Evaluation Programme (EMEP), which operates under the auspices of the Long-Range Transboundary Air Pollution (LRTAP) regime in Europe and which is widely credited with having played a key role in the transformation of this regime from a politically motivated gesture aimed at alleviating East-West tension to an influential social practice based on a growing understanding of the biological and chemical processes involved in what is popularly known as "acid rain." Programmatic arrangements are required as well when the members of a regime agree to establish and operate compensation funds, to set up procedures to implement agreements pertaining to technology transfers, or to explore options for joint implementation with respect to the fulfillment of obligations assumed under the provisions of regimes (for example, reductions of greenhouse gas emissions). A particularly interesting programmatic option centers on the establishment of joint development zones, which may only require agreements to harmonize production decisions, as with the unitization of oil and gas fields to maximize recoverable reserves. Here, the critical issue typically concerns the articulation of criteria for allocating the proceeds among the participants in such joint ventures. But collaborative efforts can assume considerably more far-reaching forms. A striking example is the Enterprise contemplated under the deep-seabed-mining provisions of the 1982 Convention on the Law of the Sea, which would have established an international operating authority capable of becoming a major producer of several important nonfuel minerals, including copper and nickel.

The issues that dominate discussions of programmatic regimes differ markedly from those which require attention in connection with regulatory and procedural arrangements. As the EMEP makes clear, it is often necessary to work out common research designs and adopt comparable methods of data collection and analysis to ensure that the results produced will be both powerful and acceptable to all parties concerned. Many programmatic arrangements also require more or less substantial organizational arrangements to administer the day-to-day efforts involved—think of the extensive network of observation stations used by EMEP and the administrative apparatus of the ozone compensation fund. Looming over all these organizational arrangements is the problem of finding the material resources needed to carry out programmatic tasks. Unlike regulatory and procedural tasks, which may be accomplished without incurring major costs except when noncompliance becomes a central issue, programmatic activities almost always require the provision of material resources

on a continuous basis. Such resources may take the form of in-kind contributions on the part of individual members (for example, the dedication
of monitoring stations located on national territory), funds contributed to
a common pool (such as the contributions of industrialized members to
the ozone compensation fund), or some distinct income stream subject to
the control of a regime's managers (such as fees levied in connection with
activities subject to regulation by the regime). Understandably, issues pertaining to material resources regularly become a bone of contention in
connection with programmatic regimes. Individual members are reluctant
to accord regimes the autonomy that goes with access to an independent
source of funds. Yet national contributions are often hard to come by and
subject to unpredictable fluctuations owing to the dynamics of domestic
political processes in which the fulfillment of international commitments
is not a high priority.

Generative Regimes

Regimes often perform tasks that are difficult to understand as ordinary
regulatory, procedural, or programmatic efforts but are of obvious importance nonetheless. These "generative tasks"—as I call them—center on
the development of distinctive social practices where none previously existed. Partly, this is a matter of defining or shaping the discourse in terms
of which problems are discussed and, in the process, setting agendas for
regime members to confront. Most successful regimes are built around
a central idea or guiding vision, and they often function as vehicles for
disseminating the discourse associated with that idea.[8] The operation of
regimes over time may also play a generative role in the sense of giving
birth to new ideas that subsequently become influential as determinants
of thinking about major problems. The early fisheries regimes, for example, both reflected and projected the set of ideas we associate with the pursuit of maximum sustainable yields (MSYs) from living resources. More recently created regimes for living resources, by contrast, typically rest on the
emerging notion of ecosystem management treated as a successor to MSY
which takes into account the complex interactions linking harvested species with other elements of the biotic and abiotic setting within which they
are embedded. Similarly, the emergence of the concept of critical loads is
widely interpreted as one of the major consequences flowing from the operation of LRTAP; it may in turn transform this regime from a loosely connected series of protocols concerning individual pollutants into an inte-

8. Karen T. Litfin, *Ozone Discourses: Science and Politics in Global Environmental Cooperation* (New
York: Columbia University Press, 1994).

31

grated approach to the broader problem of air pollution. Regimes often reflect broader currents of cognitive change, such as the shift from MSY to ecosystems management, and they may promote discourses based on generative ideas that ultimately prove of limited value. Some critics see the current movement toward incorporating the idea of sustainable development into international governance systems, for example, as an innovation we may live to regret. Still, regimes often do serve to frame the discourse that focuses the thinking of actors—including nonstate actors as well as states—both about the nature of problems to be solved and about strategies for solving these problems.

In part, the generative role of regimes involves the development of constituencies around various sets of problem-driven activities. At the official level, this often means that government agencies within member states incorporate the activities associated with specific regimes into their mission statements, forming mutually supportive alliances with their counterparts in other member states. The resultant networks can and often do survive the ups and downs of broader relationships among the states involved. Of even greater importance, in many cases, is the mobilization (or even the creation) of unofficial groups that take an interest in specific regimes and become cheerleaders, watchdogs, and, in some instances, sources of material support needed to make regimes successful. What some observers have described as the emergence of the Great Lakes community around the formal activities carried out under the provisions of the Great Lakes Water Quality Agreement constitutes a well-documented example.[9] The more recent literature on international regimes, based in considerable part on a study of environmental cases, has labeled these groups or coalitions "epistemic communities" on the assumption that the key contribution they make involves the formulation and dissemination of ideas.[10] But this perspective captures only one element of the phenomenon under consideration here. The essential point is that regimes can and often do become catalysts for the generation of both national and transnational groups that are united by a commitment to fostering the goals embedded in the regime itself. Strictly speaking, the existence of such a support group is probably not a necessary condition for the success of international regimes. But there is growing evidence from a variety of issue areas to suggest that such groups do provide critical backing in many cases and that the rise of these groups sometimes emerges as one of the most striking

9. Lee Botts and Paul Muldoon, *The Great Lakes Water Quality Agreement: Its Past Successes and Uncertain Future* (Hanover, N.H.: Institute on International Environmental Governance, 1996).

10. Peter M. Haas, ed., *Knowledge, Power, and International Policy Coordination* (Columbia: University of South Carolina Press, 1997).

consequences of the operation of regimes, regardless of their nominal focus on regulatory, procedural, or programmatic tasks.

Functional Combinations

As I noted at the outset, the distinctions among regulatory, procedural, programmatic, and generative functions are analytic in nature. Nothing prevents a single regime from taking on two, three, or even all four types of tasks at the same time. Many fisheries regimes, for example, spell out rules dealing with open and closed seasons, gear types, and licenses, while simultaneously establishing procedures to make annual decisions about total allowable catches (TACs) as well as more intermittent decisions about such matters as the suspension of harvesting to allow for the rebuilding of depleted stocks. Such regimes may also include provisions that mandate the mounting of observer programs or the initiation of collaborative research on the relative importance of various biophysical and anthropogenic factors affecting the size and behavior of fish stocks. Where these regimes are significant in generative terms owing to their role in changing the discourse associated with fisheries management (say, from an MSY to an ecosystems perspective), arrangements that are significant in terms of all four institutional tasks come into existence.

Yet such cases are exceptional in nature. More typically, regimes feature limited combinations of tasks in the effort to solve international problems. Some combinations seem intuitively more natural and are more common in practice than are others. Combining regulatory and procedural tasks, for example, makes obvious sense under a variety of conditions. In the whaling regime, the ozone regime, and the regime dealing with hazardous wastes, this task combination is accomplished by creating a conference of the parties (COP) or some functional equivalent and granting that body authority to make collective choices, including both choices that modify the regulatory rules and choices needed to structure the activities to which the regulatory rules apply. Yet this combination is by no means universal. Some regimes (for example, the polar bear agreement) feature regulatory arrangements that are not accompanied by procedural arrangements. Conversely, the climate change regime is an example of a relatively well-developed procedural arrangement that is not matched by a set of regulatory rules containing more than rudimentary content. Such regimes are often at an early stage of development and reflect limited success in the initial efforts of the parties to reach agreement on the content of more substantive regulatory rules. In such cases, the COP is apt to become an arena for concerted efforts to expand and tighten the regulatory component of the regime. Clearly, it would be a mistake to assume that regulatory and procedural arrangements always go together, a condition that would raise questions about the value of separating these tasks even in analytic terms. Yet functional combinations that feature regulatory and procedural arrangements are common in the world of international institutions.

Somewhat similar remarks are in order about links between programmatic and generative arrangements. Certainly, it is possible to think of situations in which programmatic activities loom large even when the nature of the problem is well understood. The operation of observer programs and the use of certificate-of-origin procedures in connection with the harvesting and marketing of living resources exemplify this class of situations. Yet programmatic arrangements often produce generative consequences, either because they are set up by actors desiring to initiate cooperation regarding problems that are poorly understood or because they initiate learning processes that lead to important changes in thinking about ways to solve problems or even about the nature of the problems themselves. The environmental protection regime for the Arctic set up under the Arctic Environmental Protection Strategy constitutes an interesting illustration. At its inception in 1991, most observers were inclined to dismiss the significance of the regime on the grounds that it had little to offer as either a regulatory or a procedural arrangement. But the regime has spawned a set of programmatic activities that have proven significant in generative terms both because they have contributed significantly to knowledge of the complex dynamics of Arctic systems and because they have fueled the emerging practice of treating the Arctic as a distinct region when it comes to the formulation of public policy.

Some functional combinations do not go well together and may even prove disruptive in institutional terms. When a problem is poorly understood and a programmatic arrangement is created for the express purpose of shedding light on the fundamental character of the problem, for instance, it would be premature and quite likely counterproductive to proceed with the articulation of an elaborate structure of regulatory rules. In this connection, it is easy to understand the thinking of those who decided to launch LRTAP in 1979 as a framework regime containing little regulatory content on the assumption that the work carried out by EMEP would facilitate efforts to work out the content of a series of regulatory protocols to be added to the basic framework over time. It makes sense for similar reasons to avoid inflexible procedural arrangements—that is, procedures for arriving at collective choices which make it difficult to alter or adjust institutional arrangements in connection with programmatic regimes intended to improve understanding of the character of the problem to be solved. Clearly, one of the strengths of the ozone regime lies in the capacity of the COP to make significant adjustments in some of the regime's provisions without triggering a requirement for ratification on the part of individual members. Somewhat similar thinking may well have led to the creation in 1995 of the Ad Hoc Group on the Berlin Mandate, a mechanism designed to encourage serious consideration of substantive adjustments in the content of the climate regime in the light of advances in scientific understanding of the problem to be solved and the accumulation of experience with the operation of the regime itself.

There are, finally, cases in which the advantages and disadvantages of linking institutional tasks are hard to evaluate or fundamentally indeterminate. At least two sets of circumstances can give rise to situations of this sort. First, in their zeal to produce concrete results, regime builders sometimes create organizations that are tangible and relatively easy to describe but are not clearly connected to institutional arrangements treated as social practices. The usual rule of thumb about form following function gets turned on its head, with the result that the process of regime formation eventuates in the creation of organizations in search of well-defined roles or missions. Something of this sort seems to have occurred in conjunction with the establishment of the Arctic Council in 1996. In such instances, there is an obvious need for the performance of generative tasks, but it is hard to say whether functional combinations involving regulatory, procedural, or programmatic tasks make sense. Second, similar complications can arise when regimes are expected to deal with two distinct problems at the same time. Current examples include the regimes dealing with hazardous wastes and biological diversity, in which an inner tension exists between the goals of protecting the environment and promoting or stabilizing international markets. Here, the combination of tasks that would make sense in terms of efforts to solve one problem may not make sense at all from the perspective of efforts to solve the other problem. The result is often an ongoing debate about the fundamental character of the regime which plays itself out in conflicts among interested parties framed in terms of different proposals regarding the regulatory, procedural, and programmatic tasks to be performed by the arrangement.

IMPLICATIONS FOR REGIME FORMATION

No matter how clever they are, taxonomies are of little use as ends in themselves. Their value rests on the contributions they make to the production of significant insights about the subject at hand. Thus what can be said about the usefulness of the distinctions among regulatory, procedural, programmatic, and generative tasks in thinking about international regimes? Consider first the issue of regime formation, or the processes through which institutional arrangements form in international society. Does the typology of institutional tasks yield notable insights regarding the establishment of international regimes?

The formation of regulatory regimes—even those which deal with co-ordination problems in contrast to collaboration problems—is typically dominated by a process that conforms well to the classic conception of bargaining as a mixed-motive process in which distributive concerns are well-defined and strongly represented in the thinking of the participants.[11] The actors involved in such situations, whether they are harvesters of fish, producers of CFCs, or users of the electromagnetic spectrum, are usually easy to identify, and these actors typically have interests in the problem at hand which are both clear and close to the surface. Under the circumstances, regime formation is apt to emerge as an interest-based process in which the emphasis falls on the negotiation stage and in which efforts on the part of individual participants to bring bargaining leverage to bear to achieve outcomes favorable to themselves dominate the process. This is not simply another way of saying that great powers—or actors in possession of large quantities of material resources—will usually get their way in this type of bargaining. As those who have worked to pin down the somewhat slippery notion of bargaining leverage have discovered, the sources of power in these interactive processes are almost always diverse and often quite subtle.[12] As experience in such areas as climate change and biological diversity suggests, even the United States as the sole remaining superpower cannot always call the shots in the creation of international regulatory regimes. Nonetheless, the central role of bargaining leverage stands out in efforts to understand the formation of regulatory regimes.

Not surprisingly, the stage of operationalization with regard to regulatory regimes will likely feature hard bargaining on the part of actors who are alive to the distributive implications of regulatory arrangements. The situation here bears a strong resemblance to the parallel process at the domestic level in which legislative enactments of a regulatory nature must be translated into much more detailed regulations to make them effective as determinants of behavior. In fact, because international society lacks a

---

11. For a seminal discussion of this type of bargaining, see Thomas C. Schelling, *The Strategy of Conflict* (Cambridge: Harvard University Press, 1960).

12. Oran R. Young, *International Governance: Protecting the Environment in a Stateless Society* (Ithaca: Cornell University Press, 1994), chap. 5.

government of its own and because many regulatory regimes prescribe rules concerning the behavior of actors (such as tanker or municipal power plant operators) acting under the jurisdiction of national governments, responsibility for operationalizing regulatory regimes often lies with the same agencies charged with operationalizing domestic rules. In the United States, for example, the Environmental Protection Agency is responsible for implementing the ozone regime with regard to American nationals, and the Commerce Department has similar responsibilities with regard to the regimes dealing with marine mammals and international fisheries. Thus the bargaining process does not come to an end with the signing or even the ratification of an international agreement containing a set of rules intended to solve or at least ameliorate a collective-action problem that transcends national boundaries.

The formation of procedural regimes, by contrast, centers on the design of collective-choice mechanisms intended to last for an indefinite period of time and to deal with issues that cannot be fully anticipated at the outset. In effect, the problem here is a microcosm of the one facing drafters of constitutions covering a wider range of issues. Here, too, the set of participants is apt to be clear-cut, and these participants will have incentives to promote their own interests. But the process of designing collective-choice mechanisms is greatly facilitated by what students of collective choice have called the "veil of uncertainty."[13] To the extent that those engaged in designing such mechanisms cannot predict with certainty the full range of issues that a procedural regime will be called on to handle or the content of the choices that the operation of such mechanisms will produce, they will have incentives to design arrangements that are unbiased or fair in the sense that they are not openly structured to favor the interests of specific actors or groups involved in the process. The thicker the veil of uncertainty becomes, the stronger the incentives of the participants to craft unbiased or fair arrangements will be. The designers of procedural regimes are certainly not disinterested parties motivated solely by a desire to devise arrangements that can be counted on to function in a manner that is efficient and equitable. Yet the resultant process of regime formation is likely to differ markedly from the process associated with efforts to hammer out the contents of regulatory arrangements.

At the same time, it is important to observe that those engaged in crafting procedural regimes at the international level are ordinarily constrained by the deep structure of international society in ways that do not

---

13. Geoffrey Brennan and James M. Buchanan, *The Reason of Rules: Constitutional Political Economy* (Cambridge: Cambridge University Press, 1985).

apply at the domestic level. Because states, which normally constitute the formal members of international regimes, are committed to principles of sovereignty which stipulate that they cannot be bound without their explicit consent, designers of procedural regimes have often felt compelled to create collective-choice mechanisms calling for consent on the part of all members. Yet there is more room for creativity in the process of regime formation than this constraint might appear to permit. The criterion of consent is not the equivalent of a rule of unanimity; acquiescence in the sense of the absence of an explicit protest is taken as a measure of consent in some cases. Many procedural regimes now allow for majority rule, on the understanding that any party seriously opposed to specific decisions can exempt itself from the obligation to comply with them by filing an objection or a reservation. In other cases, procedural regimes are granted the authority to make significant decisions that do not require any explicit process of ratification on the part of individual members to take effect. None of this means that international institutions are becoming increasingly analogous to governance systems operative in domestic societies. Yet reality is considerably more complex than might be expected in the face of blanket assertions regarding the principle of sovereignty, and those charged with designing procedural regimes at the international level have displayed considerable ingenuity in finding ways on a case-by-case basis to deal with the limitations imposed by the principle of sovereignty.

Programmatic regimes feature another pattern of regime formation. Negotiating the terms of these regimes is a somewhat open-ended affair that is more like the process of forming a limited partnership or building a coalition to solve a particular problem than the process of bargaining over the distribution of a fixed pool of assets. In the typical case, the formation of a programmatic regime will launch a coordinated project that is expected to produce benefits for all the participants in the long run but whose payoffs cannot be calculated with any certainty at the outset. This is particularly true of cases such as EMEP, in which the project centers on joint initiatives designed to improve understanding of the underlying problem. But similar remarks are in order about programmatic initiatives involving joint development zones, which provide no guarantee of any payoffs; international enterprises (such as that for deep seabed mining), in which volatile markets make it impossible to predict outcomes; or joint implementation initiatives, in which all partners reap benefits from the same set of activities. This does not mean that all the partners in programmatic regimes are equal in terms of the resources they contribute to such arrangements, the rewards they expect to gain, or the liabilities they assume as parties to the partnerships. Like partnerships at the domestic level, programmatic arrangements in international society can assume a wide variety of forms. But in most cases, the process of forming such arrangements will involve a more substantial element of what is often called "integrative" or "productive" bargaining than we would expect to encounter in negotiations focused on hammering out the provisions of regulatory regimes.[14]

As is true in other social settings, however, it is important to draw a distinction between international programmatic arrangements dealing with ordinary private goods and those which aim at the production of collective or public goods. A joint development zone created to unitize an oil or gas field, for example, is a relatively straightforward affair. The parties can negotiate an agreement about their respective contributions to the partnership and concur that they will receive benefits proportional to their contributions. Yet when it comes to arrangements designed to yield products which are pure collective goods or which exhibit some of the essential properties of collective goods such as nonexcludability (the preservation of species or protection of the Earth's climate system), classic free-rider problems begin to surface.[15] Why should individual actors contribute to programs designed to protect habitat important to endangered species, for example, when they hope to benefit from the contributions of others to such projects without cost to themselves? Under the circumstances, we should expect efforts to devise programmatic regimes dealing with collective goods to be characterized by hard bargaining over the terms of cost-sharing mechanisms. As is true in other settings, such bargaining is apt to become more difficult as the size of the group increases. Thus, we would expect it to be harder to work out the terms of what are called "policies and measures" in the climate regime than the terms of bilateral arrangements to protect shared lakes or rivers. Such negotiations are also likely to be complicated when they are influenced by judgments about responsibility for the occurrence of the relevant problems in the first place. The emphasis that countries such as China and India have placed on forcing Western, industrialized countries to acknowledge responsibility for the problem of climate change and to take the lead in dealing with the problem is entirely understandable. But it does not alter the fact that the behavior of these developing countries will play a critical role in the protection of the Earth's climate system during the foreseeable future.

In some ways, the process involved in the formation of generative regimes is quite distinct from the analogous processes in the cases of regu-

---

14. Richard E. Walton and Robert B. McKersie, *A Behavioral Theory of Labor Negotiations: An Analysis of a Social Interaction System* (New York: McGraw-Hill, 1965), and John G. Cross, *The Economics of Bargaining* (New York: Basic, 1969).

15. Mancur Olson Jr., *The Logic of Collective Action* (Cambridge: Harvard University Press, 1965).

latory, procedural, and programmatic regimes. For one thing, the process is much harder to interpret as a matter of conscious design on the part of well-defined sets of participants. Of course, central ideas—much less coherent discourses—do not emerge and permeate processes of regime formation all by themselves. Ideas are never neutral, and those involved in processes of regime formation are apt to be well aware of the significance of influencing the terms of the debate. It will come as no surprise, therefore, that interest groups and social movements regularly work hard to control the characterization of problems and to set the terms in which solutions to relevant problems are discussed. There is an understandable tendency, therefore, to assume that those who have power in the material sense will normally find ways to control the content of the discourse used to address problems. Yet the diffusion of ideas is a complex process that involves a variety of players and is difficult to capture within the confines of a well-defined bargaining process. Ideas appeal to people for various reasons, and their diffusion tends to involve a gathering of momentum that is difficult to stop once it gets under way. In thinking about the formation of generative regimes, therefore, we can expect to focus more on the stage of agenda formation than on the stages of negotiation and operationalization and to find ourselves paying attention to a far wider range of players than those who show up as representatives of states and other major actors in formal negotiating sessions.

Thus I suggest that the process of forming generative regimes has a strong bottom-up component. This is not to deny the importance—even in the context of generative regimes—of reaching agreement on constitutive principles that can be articulated in the form of conventions, treaties, or ministerial declarations. But regimes treated as social practices rather than as sets of rules typically arise from the development of a community or a collection of groups that join forces around the effort to promote a particular set of activities. Many students of regimes have endeavored to capture this phenomenon in terms of the idea of "epistemic communities." Useful as it is, however, this concept does not capture several important aspects of the phenomenon under consideration here. As commentators have pointed out, the groups driving the process of regime formation need not be limited to those composed of scientists or, more broadly, specialists in ideas. Moreover, these groups are often better understood in terms of the notion of social movements than in terms of ordinary interest groups.[16] Social movements do not figure as players in the negotia-

16. Thomas E. Princen and Matthias Finger, *Environmental NGOs in World Politics: Linking the Local and the Global* (London: Routledge, 1994), chap. 3.

tions giving rise to regulatory or procedural regimes. They are not organized to focus on the ins and outs of various formulations to be considered for inclusion in the texts of constitutive documents. Yet as the spread of defining ideas—such as ecosystems management, sustainable development, and global environmental change—suggests, social movements may loom large in efforts to account for generative arrangements that influence the course of affairs more by structuring the way parties think about problems than by laying down regulatory rules or setting up collective-choice mechanisms.

Once again, the distinctions I discuss here are analytic in nature. In many regimes, such as those concerning trade in endangered species and ozone depletion, the parties seek to spell out systems of regulatory rules and devise collective-choice mechanisms at the same time. A particularly interesting feature of the more recent experience in building regimes dealing with atmospheric issues—transboundary air pollution, ozone depletion, climate change—is the tendency to begin with the development of a generative or programmatic regime and then to proceed to develop regulatory and procedural arrangements on that foundation over time.[17] The interactions between these functional initiatives under real-world conditions open up numerous opportunities for negotiation on the part of actors seeking to promote their own interests. They can also produce situations in which miscommunication leading either to stalemate or to the development of misshapen agreements is a common occurrence. Under the circumstances, it seems especially important to grasp the differences in the processes of regime formation associated with regulatory, procedural, programmatic, and generative arrangements when several of these processes are involved at the same time.

•

IMPLICATIONS FOR REGIME EFFECTIVENESS

Equally important is a consideration of the implications of differentiating between regulatory, procedural, programmatic, and generative tasks for thinking about the effectiveness of regimes—that is, the extent to which they succeed in solving the problems which motivate actors to create them. Studies of effectiveness focus on a variety of matters, including implementation, ongoing administration, funding, compliance, imple-

17. See Marvin S. Soroos, *The Endangered Atmosphere: Preserving a Global Commons* (Columbia: University of South Carolina Press, 1997).

mentation review, and dispute resolution, consideration of which is important in asking about the effectiveness of regimes in handling different tasks. Work on the effectiveness of international institutions has also directed attention toward the causal mechanisms through which regimes are able to affect the behavior of both the members themselves and a wider variety of subjects involved in the relevant activities.[18] This subject too deserves consideration in thinking about the links between specific tasks and effectiveness.

Regulatory regimes, once again, raise the classic issues that center on implementation, compliance, and the treatment of noncompliant behavior. Some of the most interesting work on international regimes deals with these issues. To what extent does it make sense to adopt a management approach to compliance, which focuses on helping subjects to understand regulatory requirements and to acquire the capacity to adjust their behavior to conform to these requirements, in contrast to an enforcement approach, which emphasizes the development of monitoring systems to enhance transparency and the use of sanctions to influence the behavior of subjects?[19] When regime members disagree about the actions required to comply with an arrangement's rules, how can authoritative interpretations of these rules be generated in the absence of a public authority of the sort ordinarily thought of as a government?[20] What sorts of sanctions are likely to prove effective in international society? Is it best to concentrate on actions designed to affect the utilitarian calculations of actual or potential violators, or is there something to be said for sanctions that work through other behavioral mechanisms, such as triggering feelings of shame in the minds of key decision makers? More recent studies dealing with such subjects as the framing of rules to facilitate compliance and the development of noncompliance procedures to resolve disagreements about what regime rules require in the absence of allegations of wrongful behavior seem

18. Marc A. Levy, Oran R. Young, and Michael Zürn, "The Study of International Regimes," *European Journal of International Relations* 1 (September 1995), 267–330. For a more extended account of the operation of various causal mechanisms in the specific cases, see Oran R. Young, ed., *The Effectiveness of International Environmental Regimes: Causal Connections and Behavioral Mechanisms* (Cambridge: MIT Press, 1999).

19. On the differences between management and enforcement models of compliance, see Abram Chayes and Antonia Handler Chayes, *The New Sovereignty: Compliance with International Regulatory Agreements* (Cambridge: Harvard University Press, 1995), and George W. Downs, David M. Rocke, and Peter N. Barsoom, "Is the Good News about Compliance Good News about Cooperation?" *International Organization* 50 (Summer 1996), 379–406.

20. For a study that deals with this issue in relation to the climate change regime, see Jacob Werksman, "Designing a Compliance System for the UN Framework Convention on Climate Change," in James Cameron, Jacob Werksman, and Peter Roderick, eds., *Improving Compliance with International Environmental Law* (London: Earthscan Publications, 1996), 85–112.

particularly important in this regard.[21] They speak directly to central issues that pertain to the effectiveness of regulatory regimes.

Although questions of compliance may arise in connection with the operation of procedural regimes, this is not the central concern regarding the effectiveness of such arrangements at the international level. By contrast with domestic societies, procedural regimes at the international level frequently require some form of consensus, typically allow individual parties to exempt themselves from the impact of collective choices by filing objections or reservations, and are limited by the principle of sovereignty, even in the absence of specific provisions allowing for exemptions. What this means is that participants who know that they would experience strong pressure to ignore or reject the outcomes produced by collective-choice mechanisms are likely to act to prevent these mechanisms from producing substantive outcomes in the first place. Under the circumstances, the key issues arising in connection with procedural regimes have to do with the productivity of collective-choice mechanisms and the effort to persuade individual participants to refrain from entering objections or reservations in specific cases. Many observers suggest that these problems are so severe that they will prevent procedural regimes from becoming effective in international society, except in connection with relatively unimportant or marginal concerns. But while the problem is real, it is easy to overdo this argument. Consensus rules differ fundamentally from unanimity rules. Many significant regimes now allow weighted majorities to make important decisions. Even parties that enter reservations or objections often bow to political pressure to conform to the will of the majority, using the legal device of filing objections or reservations more as a face-saving measure than as a real barrier to behavioral change.

Programmatic regimes, by contrast, raise a number of questions regarding effectiveness which differ from those outlined in the preceding paragraphs. In essence, these questions center on project design, the provision of adequate funding on an ongoing basis, and the maintenance of effective commitments on the part of line agencies within member governments. Programmatic efforts require line agencies with authority over the issue at stake—environment ministries, agencies responsible for land management, and so on—to engage in conscious coordination with their counterparts in other member states and to work together to fulfill com-

---

21. For a helpful survey, see Ronald B. Mitchell, "Compliance Theory: An Overview," in Cameron, Werksman, and Roderick, *Improving Compliance*, 3–28. On the specific case of the ozone regime, see David G. Victor, "The Early Operation and Effectiveness of the Montreal Protocol's Non-Compliance Procedure," Executive Report ER-96-2, International Institute for Applied Systems Analysis, 1996.

mon goals on an ongoing basis. This need not require the creation of an international administrative body, as experience with the management of international or transboundary parks and protected natural areas makes clear. But given the influence of standard operating procedures within line agencies, it can be extremely difficult for the relevant agencies to devise a common discourse, much less to achieve the ability to work in consort with one another. Contemporary experience with efforts to harmonize the procedures different countries have developed to conduct environmental impact assessments constitutes a dramatic case in point. It is important also to emphasize that joint projects typically call for the investment of material resources, including the time of agency personnel as well as financial resources, on a continuing basis. Consider projects involving the development of infrastructure such as roads or irrigation systems or the protection of wildlife habitat as illustrations. In a setting marked by increasingly serious financial stress, international commitments of this sort tend to be particularly vulnerable. As a result, meeting programmatic commitments will sometimes prove more problematic than will complying with regulatory rules that have passed into standard practice.

As usual, generative regimes differ significantly from their regulatory, procedural, and programmatic counterparts when it comes to the determinants of effectiveness. The diffusion of key ideas and the rise of social movements are processes that are more spontaneous than the operation of collective-choice mechanisms or the implementation of joint projects. It is especially difficult to regulate or control the spread of ideas. Some attractive ideas fail to catch on, despite vigorous efforts on the part of their proponents to publicize their virtues. Others (for example, the concept of sustainable development) spread like wildfire, despite—or perhaps because of—serious ambiguities regarding their application to concrete situations. It may well be that epidemiological or tipping models are needed to understand this phenomenon.[22] It is difficult to have new ideas taken seriously, especially where orthodox ways of thinking are solidly entrenched. But once new ideas reach a point of takeoff, they are apt to spread rapidly, regardless of the desires of actors whose interests will be affected by such developments. Even actors in possession of ample material resources often find it frustratingly difficult to spread some new ideas and virtually impossible to stop the spread of others once they reach the takeoff point. Undoubtedly, social movements have something to do with the spread of new ideas. This is especially true of the current era in which modern technology allows ideas and the social movements that espouse them to spread

22. Schelling, *Micromotives*.

from one end of the planet to the other with extreme rapidity. Under the circumstances, generative regimes are likely to differ from one another dramatically in terms of their success in spreading ideas and stimulating the development of significant social practices. But the processes involved in every case will be particularly hard for governments or, for that matter, specific interest groups to control.

Let me turn now to some observations about the causal mechanisms through which various types of regimes affect the behavior not only of their members but also of other actors involved in the relevant issue areas.[23] Regulatory regimes constitute the classic case considered by those whose thinking is rooted in the collective-action paradigm. Assuming that the identity of the relevant actors is known at the outset and that the interests of these actors are more or less fixed, the central idea behind this approach is that institutions enhance cooperation by coordinating behavior around equilibrium points, raising costs of defection or free-riding behavior, increasing transparency, and lowering transaction costs.[24] But there are good reasons to question the assumptions underlying this way of thinking in analyzing many collective-action problems that arise at the international level. In some cases, regulatory regimes work by shifting the focus from actors, such as tanker operators, whose compliance with key rules (discharge standards) is difficult or impossible to monitor, to a different set of actors, such as shipbuilders, whose compliance with somewhat different rules (equipment standards) is much easier to monitor.[25] In other cases, regulatory regimes give the same actors new roles or redefine the roles they played before the establishment of the relevant regimes. The creation of Exclusive Economic Zones adjacent to the territory of coastal states, for instance, has allowed these states to assume a variety of new roles that are now accepted without serious question by other members of international society. This has had striking consequences, to cite one example, for both the creation and the effectiveness of a number of regulatory regimes dealing with marine living resources.

For their part, procedural regimes rely heavily on an acknowledgment of the legitimacy or authoritativeness of the collective choices they produce. This is especially true at the international level, given extreme limits on the capacity of bodies created to administer regimes meant to pres-

---

23. See also Young, *Effectiveness of International Environmental Regimes.*

24. Robert O. Keohane, *After Hegemony: Cooperation and Discord in the World Political Economy* (Princeton: Princeton University Press, 1984), and Kenneth Oye, ed., *Cooperation under Anarchy* (Princeton: Princeton University Press, 1986).

25. Ronald B. Mitchell, *Intentional Oil Pollution at Sea: Environmental Policy and Treaty Compliance* (Cambridge: MIT Press, 1994).

sure members to accept collective choices, as well as the usual practice of allowing individual members to exempt themselves from the application of specific choices made in any case. Yet it would be wrong to overdo the distinction between international regimes and domestic institutions on this basis. If municipal governments had to rely routinely on coercion or the threat of enforcement actions to compel individuals and corporations to accept the collective choices they make, they would soon go out of business or turn into unusually nasty police states. Under the circumstances, the maintenance of a widespread sense that its decisions are legitimate products of authoritative processes is one of the most important assets any public authority can possess. Given the conditions that prevail at the international level, such as specific regimes unsupported by an overarching public authority or the scarcity of material resources, the role of authoritativeness in connection with procedural regimes is simply enhanced. This is not to say that the utilitarian arguments mentioned in the preceding account of regulatory regimes are of no importance in connection with procedural regimes. Individual actors may be motivated to accept the results produced by procedural regimes, in part at least, because they cannot reject them covertly and the transaction costs of starting over again are high. But the importance of authoritativeness as a mechanism through which procedural regimes produce behavioral impacts seems beyond doubt.[26]

Programmatic regimes are apt to produce effects through a combination of learning, role definition, and the creation of domestic constituencies within member states. Often, the projects that programmatic regimes undertake generate new knowledge about a certain problem that becomes a force leading to the evolution of the regime itself. Consider the role of the Great Lakes Water Quality Agreement in shifting attention from individual pollutants to ecosystems perspectives or the role of EMEP in directing attention to critical loads in connection with air pollution as examples. When they really take root, moreover, programmatic regimes generally stimulate the growth of a sense of ownership on the part of line agencies that assume responsibility for their administration or management on an ongoing basis. In effect, such agencies come to see the operation of programmatic regimes as a significant component of their identity as actors in domestic political systems. Of course, this does not mean that such agencies will be immune from capture on the part of outside interests or that they will always hold a strong hand in the bureaucratic politics characteristic of domestic political arenas. But it does mean that they are apt to become committed advocates on behalf of the programmatic regimes that

26. Thomas M. Franck, *The Power of Legitimacy among Nations* (Oxford: Oxford University Press, 1990).

belong to their portfolio. And it often leads to the development of allies in legislative bodies and among nongovernmental interest groups who are able to help defend the joint projects mounted by programmatic regimes. When the maintenance of the regime is costly to other interest groups, as in projects that subsidize the activities of particular sets of actors, the existence of strong allies in various quarters can prove critical to the effectiveness of programmatic regimes.

At one level, generative regimes are apt to produce effects through the development of domestic constituencies and the resultant realignment of political forces within member governments. Whether they are epistemic communities seeking to influence the thinking of administrators working in line agencies or social movements endeavoring to bring pressure to bear on legislative committees, the forces responsible for the spread of ideas and the development of social practices invariably work to promote their causes in a variety of political settings. But generative regimes can also produce results by facilitating learning processes and inducing key actors to alter the way they think about their roles. A manager located in a fish and wildlife agency and concerned only with traditional ideas of maximum sustainable yield, for example, is apt to ignore completely a variety of species that will seem of considerable interest to a manager in the same agency who adopts the perspective of ecosystems management. Similarly, the introduction of the discourse of sustainable development makes it difficult to ignore the continuing role of human users in protected natural areas and encourages representatives of public authorities to see themselves as participants in comanagement arrangements rather than as outside agents mainly concerned with enforcing rules on resistant subjects. In effect, discourses are important not only because of their impact on the ways in which parties frame problems and think about solutions but also because of the effects they have on the interpretation of the roles actors play in the associated social practices.

IMPLICATIONS FOR INSTITUTIONAL DESIGN

Let me conclude with some observations about the implications of this discussion of institutional functions or tasks for the efforts of those charged with designing new international regimes or modifying existing regimes to deal with changing circumstances. Both the construction of new regimes and the adjustment of existing arrangements are messy processes. They typically involve hard bargaining, a fact that means the results are apt to take the form of compromises required to allow negotiations to succeed rather than reflecting coherent institutional designs. There is often an element of spontaneous development in the process of regime formation as well; thus some elements of regimes are normally products of interactive processes that are essentially unplanned.[27] It would be a mistake, therefore, to exaggerate the role of institutional design in the processes involved in the creation of international regimes.

Even so, opportunities exist to steer these processes, and much can be said for thinking carefully about such opportunities in advance in order to make the most of them when they do arise. In this connection, the main lesson to be drawn from the preceding account of institutional functions or tasks is that it is important to differentiate clearly among these tasks for purposes of institutional design and to think about each in its own terms. Where the emphasis falls on regulation, for instance, the critical questions for institutional design involve such matters as framing rules in a manner that ensures that their behavioral requirements are as clear as possible; they are directed toward easily identifiable actors whose behavior is not difficult to monitor, and they can be adjusted in a straightforward way to meet changing needs as the relevant human activities evolve. In the case of procedural arrangements, by contrast, the problem is to design systems that are productive in the sense that they have decision rules which allow them to avoid outcomes of gridlock, while minimizing the likelihood that the results will prove ineffectual because they are lacking in substantive content or trigger the filing of objections or reservations on the part of key members. For their part, the design questions arising in connection with programmatic arrangements center on the identification of agencies within member governments that are able and willing to make an ongoing commitment to carry out joint projects, and on the establishment of funding mechanisms capable of generating the material resources required to do the job. These are distinct concerns; a failure to separate them explicitly in thinking about institutional design can only lead to trouble.

At the same time, it is essential to bear in mind that many specific regimes encompass two or more of the institutional tasks discussed in this chapter. In such cases, the components of compound regimes which deal with specific tasks must be designed such that they interlock or fit together properly. For a regulatory regime that concerns a poorly understood problem or is subject to rapid change, it is important to create a collective-choice mechanism that makes it relatively easy to adjust or alter the rules to meet evolving needs. Similarly, when procedural arrangements trigger the application of relatively elaborate rules, there must be clarity regarding the exact nature of the rules that are triggered and the circumstances under which one or another cluster of rules comes into play as a result of

27. Young, *International Cooperation*, chap. 4.

collective choices made under the provisions of these regimes. Obviously, the design of such packages of institutional arrangements covering two or more distinct tasks and the connections between them calls for a level of sophistication that is at least an order of magnitude higher than the design of arrangements that involve only a single task. What is more, the effects of compromises arising from the bargaining process are likely to cause particularly serious distortions in connection with compound regimes. Yet these design questions are not only challenging in intellectual terms, but their treatment is also likely to have especially far-reaching consequences for the significance of regimes as a means of meeting the demand for governance in world affairs.

CHAPTER 3

The Problem of Problem Structure

Some problems that make their way onto the international political agenda are more difficult to solve than others, a fact that readily explains the growth of interest in the concept of problem structure among students of international regimes. Few would contest the proposition that controlling emissions of greenhouse gases, which are associated with core activities of advanced industrial economies, is a more complex and challenging task than developing substitutes for chlorofluorocarbons, which are important in only a few economic sectors. Similarly, we would expect to encounter greater difficulties in protecting the ecosystems that make up the Great Lakes Basin, an area that is home to millions of people pursuing highly diverse interests, than in avoiding or managing problems arising in Antarctica, a sparsely populated area that has not become a focus of intense interest on the part of influential groups of human users. Much the same can be said of the difference between the regulation of international air traffic, an example of what analysts often call coordination problems, in which no one has an incentive to cheat once the rules of the game are in place, and the regulation of marine fisheries, an endeavor which poses collaboration problems and in which there is a constant temptation for individual participants to increase their own gains at the expense of others by becoming free riders.

So far, so good. Yet efforts to take the next step—devising an integrated or generic measure of the difficulty or hardness of governance problems to use in assessing issues that find their way onto the international political agenda and in comparing and contrasting these problems in ways that would prove helpful to policymakers—regularly run into trouble. The attractions of constructing a generic index of problem structure are easy to understand both in analytic terms and in terms of policymaking. For the theoretically inclined, problem structure is a variable of obvious interest in the sense that there are compelling reasons to formulate hypotheses linking the locus of problems on a scale from easy to hard to solve, on the one hand, and various measures of success in regime formation and effectiveness in regime operation, on the other. For the practitioner, an ability to determine the locus of problems on such a scale would be equally useful, providing a basis for estimates of the amount of resources required to assure success in problem-solving efforts. It might prove useful as well in picking and choosing among problems to tackle during any given time period. Thus, it is not difficult to understand the frustrations experienced by those who have struggled to come to grips with the problem of problem structure.

What can we do to alleviate these frustrations? That is the central concern of this chapter. I first examine efforts to devise a general measure or index of problem structure, spelling out the obstacles that these efforts have encountered—I do not hold out much hope for the construction of a satisfactory scale in this realm during the foreseeable future. I then consider problem structure from a different angle, arguing that we can identify and evaluate a variety of factors that make problems more or less difficult to solve, even if we are not able to develop a single scale in terms of which it is possible to represent them all. While not as useful as a generic index, a knowledge of these factors can take us a considerable way toward understanding the issues raised by the problem of problem structure. Finally, I split the problem of problem structure into two subproblems: one concerning the formation of regimes, and the other dealing with the operation of existing regimes. I contend that what makes it difficult to reach agreement on the creation of a regime in the first place may differ significantly from what makes it difficult to operate a regime successfully once it is in place. In effect, the things that make life difficult for those engaged in institutional bargaining may differ sharply from the headaches encountered by these responsible for implementing the terms of existing regimes.

GENERAL APPROACHES TO PROBLEM STRUCTURE

The construction of an index of problem structure requires, first and foremost, the selection of a single dimension by which to rank the difficulty or hardness of individual problems or, alternatively, the specification of a common metric or some similar device that can be used to combine several separate dimensions of hardness into a single scale. The challenge here is much like that facing those who formulated the idea of gross national product (GNP) as an aggregate measure of the size of an economy and as a device allowing analysts both to measure rates of change in individual economies and to compare and contrast different economies in terms of their size and growth rates. As this example suggests, it is important to be able to operationalize the factors included in such scales or indexes, which explains why measures of GNP rely on monetary calculations rather than on some underlying scale of utility. Although utility is conceptually preferable in the sense that it encompasses money and includes other sources of welfare too, no one has figured out a way to measure utility in a manner that makes it a useful vehicle for empirical research.

With regard to the problem of problem structure, two approaches to index construction are prominent in the literature. One, generally associated with the work of Volker Rittberger and his colleagues at the University of Tübingen, focuses on conflict and seeks to rank problems in terms of the nature and intensity of the conflicts occurring among the parties involved. The other, arising from the work of Arild Underdal and his colleagues in Oslo and Seattle, looks to interests or preferences and directs attention to game-theoretical constructs as a source of insights for those seeking to formulate an index of problem structure. How exactly do these approaches endeavor to solve the problem of index construction referred to in the preceding paragraph, and how successful are they in producing a measure of problem structure that works in practice?

The Tübingen Approach

The Tübingen group begins its analysis "by introducing a problem-structural approach which contends that the properties of issues (or conflicts) (pre)determine the ways in which they are dealt with."[1] The group conceptualizes regime formation as a method of solving conflicts, which directs attention to the intensity or severity of conflict as a means of rating problems in terms of what is called "regime conduciveness." This leads in turn to the construction of a taxonomy of conflict types including conflicts about values, conflicts about means, conflicts of interest about relatively assessed goods, and conflicts of interest about absolutely assessed goods. Deploying this taxonomy, the Tübingen group hypothesizes that "conflicts about values are the most difficult to regulate whereas conflicts of interest about relatively assessed goods are the second most difficult. Conflicts about means are believed to be relatively easily amenable to regime formation whereas conflicts of interest about absolutely assessed goods

---

1. Volker Rittberger and Michael Zürn, "Regime Theory: Findings from the Study of 'East-West' Regimes," *Cooperation and Conflict* 26 (1991), 171.

are most conducive to regulated conflict management."[2] Taken together, these hypotheses yield an ordinal scale of regime conduciveness in which problems that feature value conflicts are expected to be most resistant to regime formation, and problems that involve conflicts of interest about absolutely assessed goods are regarded as the easiest to solve through the establishment of regimes.

Several points of clarification about this approach are in order at the outset. The Tübingen approach involves an effort to construct an integrated scale based on two separate dimensions of conflict. One dimension arises from the distinction between ends and means and includes dissensual conflicts in which the "actors disagree about what is desirable, not just for each of them individually but for all of them collectively."[3] The other dimension encompasses consensual conflicts in which the "actors are confronted with a situation of scarcity in which each actor desires the same valued object but cannot fully be satisfied because there is not enough for everybody."[4] Thus, when problems result from these different types of conflict, questions arise over the procedure of ranking them on a single scale ranging from easy to solve through the creation of regimes, to difficult to solve in this way. Value conflicts are generally thought to be especially hard to solve. But the logic of treating value conflicts as uniformly more difficult to solve than conflicts about relatively assessed goods, in which the parties care more about their standing with respect to each other than about their position in absolute terms, is far from clear.[5] Even more problematic is the proposition that conflicts about absolutely assessed goods are always easier to solve than conflicts about means, which also lacks the intuitive appeal of the idea that value conflicts are particularly intractable. In short, the construction of a single typology of conflicts based on two unrelated dimensions raises a variety of questions whose answers are anything but self-evident.

Three additional observations of a general nature will help to clarify the Tübingen approach to problem structure. First, as Thomas Schelling and others have taught, most specific conflicts are embedded in larger mixed-motive or competitive/cooperative relationships.[6] Even value conflicts are apt to seem more or less serious to the parties involved depending on whether the larger relationships within which they occur are marked by a dense network of cooperative links or by an array of conflicts pertaining to

2. Ibid., 171–72.
3. Ibid., 168.
4. Ibid.
5. For a number of perspectives on the problems associated with efforts to maximize relative gains, see David Baldwin, ed., *Neorealism and Neoliberalism: The Contemporary Debate* (New York: Columbia University Press, 1993).
6. Thomas C. Schelling, *The Strategy of Conflict* (Cambridge: Harvard University Press, 1960).

other matters. Thus, groups of actors that have developed a habit of co-operation over a long period of time may have less trouble dealing with value conflicts than actors lacking such a habit experience in dealing with conflicts over means. Second, the Tübingen approach applies mainly to issues of problem structure as they relate to regime formation, rather than to the operation of regimes once they are in place. Thus, it makes good sense to think about the problems that lead to processes of regime forma-tion in terms of the nature of the conflicts embedded in them. As we shall see, this is also a hallmark of the game-theoretic constructs underlying the Oslo/Seattle approach. But this approach makes much less sense when it comes to analyzing the performance of regimes that are already in place. This is not to say that managing regimes is a process that is completely free from conflict. There are often disagreements, for example, regarding the meaning of various provisions of a regime's constitutive principles or about appropriate ways to implement the provisions of a regime within the ju-risdictions of individual regime members. But there is no obvious way to characterize these differences in terms of the typology of conflicts which underlies the Tübingen approach.

A third general observation concerns the process of mapping the sub-stantive problems that appear on the international political agenda onto the analytic typology of conflicts associated with the Tübingen approach. Consider the high-profile international problems relating to ozone deple-tion, climate change, and the loss of biological diversity in this connection. Where do these problems belong in terms of the fourfold typology of con-flicts? Because an intact ozone layer, a stable climate system, and a high level of biological diversity are in large measure collective or public goods, they do not turn on the problems of scarcity that underlie consensual con-flicts.[7] Nor are they classic value conflicts. No one is opposed to the pro-tection of the ozone layer, the stabilization of the climate system, or the maintenance of biological diversity, though it is certainly fair to say that some actors place a higher value than others on these conditions. Per-haps, then, these problems are simple matters featuring conflicts of means. Yet such an interpretation does not seem helpful when it comes to think-ing about the processes involved in negotiating a phaseout schedule for ozone-depleting substances or an agreement regarding targets and time-tables relating to reductions of greenhouse gas emissions. I do not mean to suggest that problems such as ozone depletion, climate change, and the loss of biological diversity are not sources of serious conflicts. But it is hard

7. A defining characteristic of collective or public goods is nonrivalness. This means that the consumption or use of such goods by one member of a group does not diminish the supply available for consumption by others. For a seminal account, see Mancur Olson Jr., *The Logic of Collective Action* (Cambridge: Harvard University Press, 1965).

to see any simple or clear-cut way to map these problems onto the typology of conflicts that lies at the heart of the Tübingen approach, and there is no reason to regard these examples as unusual or peculiar cases.

I turn now to some comments that pertain to each of the four categories that together form the Tübingen group's typology of conflicts. As leading members of the group recognize, serious value conflicts "are not negotiable, especially if the value differences concern the relationship between individuals and the state."[8] What this means is that "the classification of an issue area as dominated by a conflict about values is an almost sufficient condition for the absence of regimes."[9] For all practical purposes, then, value conflicts are intractable, and thus regime formation will not occur in connection with problems that are framed so as to highlight conflicts of this type. Although this may seem discouraging at first, it leads to the additional observation that different ways often exist to frame problems which emerge on the international political agenda and that decisions about framing can have far-reaching consequences for efforts to solve problems through a process of regime formation.[10] The problem of climate change, for example, may be treated as a northern concern to be solved exclusively through behavioral changes in the north that lead to substantial reductions in greenhouse gas emissions. Similarly, the problem of biological diversity may be regarded as a matter of forcing a number of southern countries to take measures to protect moist tropical forests located within their jurisdictions. Such perspectives highlight the conflictual elements of these problems. But it is also possible to frame the same concerns more as issues requiring exercises in cooperative problem solving in the form of activities featuring technology transfer, financial assistance, capacity building, and joint implementation. The point to ponder here is this: while value conflicts are not realistic candidates for regime formation, there is room to frame almost any issue in such a way that it does not become a value conflict, if the parties have the desire to do so.

Analyses of problems featuring conflicts of interest about relatively assessed goods or "relative gains" have become a cottage industry in recent years.[11] Not surprisingly, the proposition that such conflicts constitute the norm in international society has quickly become a mainstay of realist and neorealist arguments about the "false promise of institutionalism."[12] No doubt, there are situations in which actors are concerned with their rank-

8. Rittberger and Zürn, "Regime Theory," 176.
9. Ibid.
10. For a seminal account of issue framing in domestic settings, see John W. Kingdon, *Agendas, Alternatives, and Public Policies,* 2d ed. (New York: Harper Collins, 1995).
11. Some examples can be found in Baldwin, *Neorealism.*
12. John J. Mearsheimer, "The False Promise of International Institutions," *International Security* 19 (Winter 1994/95), 5–49.

ing in the international standings. But it is easy to overdo these arguments. Partly, this is a matter of determining the extent to which actors in international society actually do approach their dealings with others in these competitive terms, a matter that cannot be resolved by assertion. In part, it arises from a weakness in the logic of arguments that emphasize the role of relative gains. To understand this weakness, consider a highly simplified situation in which two relative-gains maximizers—A and B—are negotiating about the formation of a bilateral regime intended to solve some common problem (managing a shared natural resource or regulating bilateral trade in some particular product). Suppose also that the collaboration will produce an initial gain of 200 units for A but only 100 of the same units for B. According to the usual argument regarding relative gains, these circumstances are not regime conducive, because B will focus more on the prospect of falling behind A in relative terms than on the prospect of making a gain of 100 units in absolute terms. But, there is room for bargaining here over the distribution of the second hundred units initially accruing to A from the formation of the regime. Any allocation of the units from 101 to 200 accruing to A would leave both parties better off by a wide margin in absolute terms than they would be in the absence of an agreement to form the regime. An even split of these units would also preserve their relative positions vis-à-vis each other. Assuming normal—rational and self-interested—behavior on the part of A and B, this case collapses into a conventional conflict of interest about absolutely assessed goods. It follows that this category in the Tübingen typology, much like the category of value conflicts, is of only limited interest from the perspective of understanding regime formation.

With regard to conflicts about means, a little reflection suggests that such matters are either conducive to technical solutions or harbor distributive issues giving rise to conflicts of interest about absolutely or relatively assessed goods. In some cases, disagreements about means are largely matters of uncertainty concerning the merits of different methods of achieving common ends. Much of the current debate about policies and measures to adopt in the effort to reduce emissions of greenhouse gases, for instance, involves differences of opinion of this sort.[13] So long as such matters do not produce easily identifiable distributive consequences, they constitute suitable subjects for experts (scientists, economists, policy analysts) to tackle, and there may well be room for the initiation of a variety of experiments or pilot projects designed to clarify the merits of adopting different policy instruments. Yet the selection of policy instruments (such

13. See, for example, Committee on Science, Engineering, and Public Policy, *Policy Implications of Greenhouse Warming* (Washington, D.C.: National Academy Press, 1991).

as systems featuring charges or tradable permits as methods for regulating greenhouse gas emissions) frequently becomes controversial precisely because the actors involved believe that choices among such instruments will have significant distributive consequences. To take a familiar example, the most severe conflicts over systems of taxation have to do with what is known as the "incidence of the taxes"—that is, who pays what—not questions about the ability of various taxes to solve the regulatory or programmatic problems that trigger moves to levy taxes in the first place. But in all these cases, the nub of the problem lies in conflicts of interest about absolutely or relatively assessed goods rather than in conflicts about means, a fact that undermines the distinction between these categories in the Tübingen typology of conflicts.

This leaves the category of conflicts of interest about relatively assessed goods as the mainstay of the Tübingen approach. But this conclusion is unsatisfactory for at least two reasons. To begin with, the larger the proportion of the overall universe of cases that falls into a single category, the greater the need to devise a mean of differentiating among these cases by some measure of intensity of conflict. But the Tübingen approach offers no way of differentiating or ranking conflicts of interest about absolutely assessed goods in terms of regime conduciveness. Nor is it easy to think of a way to accomplish this task that can be grafted onto the Tübingen approach. It does not follow, to consider an obvious possibility, that there is any simple relationship between the length of the contract curve in a given situation and the severity of the conflict of interest involved.[14] Beyond this, some important problems on the international political agenda do not fit comfortably into this category in the conflict typology, even though there is no place for them in any of the other categories. Consider ozone depletion in this connection.[15] Deciding how to deal with ozone depletion is much more than a simple matter of selecting the right means to solve a common problem. Yet fundamentally it is not an issue that can be characterized as a value conflict. It is true, of course, that elements of conflict are embedded in the problem of ozone depletion, which is why it took the creation of the Multilateral Fund and the addition of provisions for technology transfers to persuade such countries as China and India to become members of the ozone regime. Even so, casting the problem as a simple conflict of interest about either relatively or absolutely assessed

14. The concept of a contract curve is central to economic models of bargaining going back to the work of Edgeworth. For a survey, see Oran R. Young, ed., *Bargaining: Formal Models of Negotiation* (Urbana: University of Illinois Press, 1975), pt. 2.

15. For a good overview of the international effort to regulate and ultimately to phase out ozone-depleting substances, see Edward A. Parson, "Protecting the Ozone Layer," in Peter M. Haas, Robert O. Keohane, and Marc A. Levy, eds., *Institutions for the Earth: Sources of Effective International Environmental Protection* (Cambridge: MIT Press, 1993), 27–73.

goods would also leave a very distorted impression of the problem of ozone depletion.

In the final analysis, then, the Tübingen approach to the construction of a generic index of problem structure breaks down. The approach produces a tendency to converge on the single category of conflicts of interest about relatively assessed goods in seeking to determine when regime formation is a realistic prospect. Moreover, many problems that find their way onto the international political agenda cannot be captured properly on a scale based exclusively on a typology of conflicts. Put another way, the sorts of problems that lead to regime formation at the international level tend to be multidimensional. They often do involve an element of conflict. But at the same time, they involve other dimensions that cannot be ignored in any effort to explain or predict whether they will give rise to active efforts to form regimes and whether these efforts will succeed or fail.

The Oslo/Seattle Approach

A second approach to the construction of an integrated scale by which to rank collective-action problems focuses on the preferences of the actors involved and takes its inspiration from the theory of games. The result is a system in which problems are rated on a scale running from benign situations, which are easy to solve, to progressively more malign problems, which pose increasingly serious challenges to those looking for solutions. As Arild Underdal puts it, the degree of malignancy exhibited by a problem is "conceived of primarily as a function of the configuration of actor interests and preferences which it generates. According to this conceptualization, a perfectly 'benign' problem would be one characterized by identical preferences. The further we get from that state of harmony, the more 'malign' the problem becomes."[16]

Turning to familiar game-theoretic constructs, it is relatively easy to illustrate the basic idea on which this approach to problem structure rests.[17] Thus, a coordination problem which has a unique equilibrium and involves no conflict of interest among the participants exemplifies the idea

16. Arild Underdal, "Patterns of Effectiveness: Examining Evidence from Thirteen International Regimes," paper presented at the annual convention of the International Studies Association, Toronto, March 1997, 11–12. See also Edward L. Miles et al., *Explaining Regime Effectiveness: Confronting Theory with Evidence* (Cambridge: MIT Press, forthcoming).

17. See Arthur Stein, "Coordination and Collaboration: Regimes in an Anarchic World," in Stephen D. Krasner, ed., *International Regimes* (Ithaca: Cornell University Press, 1983), 115–40, and Lisa L. Martin, "The Rational State Choice of Multilateralism," in John Gerard Ruggie, ed., *Multilateralism Matters: The Theory and Praxis of an Institutional Form* (New York: Columbia University Press, 1993), 91–121.

of a perfectly benign problem. Somewhat more malign are problems, such as the game known as battle of the sexes, in which there are multiple equilibria and the participants have divergent preferences regarding these equilibria. More difficult still are situations, like the game of chicken, in which the preferences of the actors diverge and there is no equilibrium at all. Particularly malign situations are problems, such as prisoner's dilemma, in which there is an equilibrium but it is suboptimal (possibly disastrous) for all parties concerned. As many analysts have observed, there is a special malignancy associated with prisoner's dilemma because the choice of dominant strategies leads to outcomes that are undesirable for all the participants and because efforts to improve the situation through cooperation are always vulnerable to cheating or defection on the part of individual actors seeking to exploit the goodwill of others for their own benefit.[18]

Presented in such general terms, this approach is easy to grasp and intuitively appealing. Problems become more malign as the incentives of the parties to seek and abide by cooperative solutions decline or, conversely, the incentives they experience to maximize their own payoffs through uncooperative behavior increase. At this level, however, the approach is largely illustrative or heuristic. As a result, Underdal and his colleagues have sought to refine their approach into a more operational system for ranking collective-action problem according to their degree of malignancy. As they now characterize the procedure, "problem 'malignancy' [is] a function of incongruity, asymmetry and cumulative cleavages. We consider incongruity as the principal criterion for classification; the other two are aspects which tend to increase further the political intractability of incongruity problems."[19] What defines incongruity in turn "is that the cost-benefit calculus of an individual actor is systematically 'biased' in favor of either the costs or the benefits of a particular course of action."[20] Such biases may occur for objective reasons, as in the familiar upstream-downstream situation in which one side has much less incentive to cooperate than the other, or for subjective reasons, as in competitive situations in which the participants evaluate outcomes on the basis of a measure of relative gains. This description suggests that a number of issues remain to be resolved in moving the Oslo/Seattle approach from the overarching concept of malignancy to a procedure for ranking individual problems on

18. For an influential argument that prisoner's dilemma need not always prevent the growth of cooperative relationships, see Robert Axelrod, *The Evolution of Cooperation* (New York: Basic, 1984).

19. Underdal, "Patterns of Effectiveness," 19.

20. Ibid., 13.

a malignancy scale that is fully specified in analytic terms. Still, the basic character of the approach as a ranking system that directs attention to the interests or preferences of well-defined actors and seeks to assess the degree to which these interests diverge is clear.

Bearing in mind that the Oslo/Seattle approach remains a work in progress, we can nonetheless consider some of the limitations of this effort to construct a general index of problem structure. The approach carries with it the analytic baggage of the theory of games with respect to the assumptions it makes about the participants in collective-action problems and the information required to specify the nature of specific problems. Thus, the participants are regarded as unitary actors possessing utility functions which they bring to collective-action problems and which they use in evaluating the range of outcomes that can emerge from processes of interactive decision making. Similarly, the outcome that would flow from any particular combination of choices on the part of the participants is assumed to be known and not subject to change as a consequence of the interactive process itself. The attractions of this approach in terms of analytic tractability are, of course, well known. But so also are the problems the approach poses, especially for those interested in conducting empirical research relating to the sorts of problems that make their way onto the international political agenda. How might we go about mapping such problems as climate change or the loss of biological diversity onto an analytic framework of this sort? Accomplishing this transition will require heroic assumptions (for example, that states are unitary actors, the strategies available to individual actors are finite in number, or the outcomes associated with combinations of strategies are easy to specify) under the best of circumstances. Even then, it is difficult to know where to start in thinking about how to locate problems of this type on a scale ranging from perfectly benign to perfectly malign problems.

These comments lead to three additional observations about limitations inherent in the Oslo/Seattle approach to problem structure. The first has to do with the role of ideas or cognitive factors as opposed to interests in the determination of problem structure.[21] There is no denying that actors can frame the same problems in different ways and that choices made in framing a problem can have far-reaching consequences for the nature of the interactive decision making associated with the problem. Consider, for instance, the issue of whether to approach fisheries management as a problem of achieving maximum sustainable yields from individual species

---

21. For a collection of essays seeking to revive interest in the role of ideas in international affairs, see Judith Goldstein and Robert O. Keohane, eds., *Ideas and Foreign Policy: Beliefs, Institutions, and Political Change* (Ithaca: Cornell University Press, 1993).

or stocks, a problem of maximizing combined yields from multiple species, or a problem of managing large marine ecosystems on a more holistic basis.[22] Obviously, the choice among these perspectives will determine both the identity of the sets of actors involved in collective-action problems and the range or breadth of the issues to be included in any efforts to agree on cooperative solutions. Or, consider the question of whether the problem of climate change should be approached as a matter of managing the use of a common pool resource or as a matter of regulating transboundary externalities. Whereas a focus on common pool resources leads to an effort to devise rules that are symmetrical in that they apply to the actions of all members of the group, an emphasis on transboundary externalities leads to a concern with asymmetrical relations and the development of liability principles. The point here is not to determine whether one or another of these perspectives is objectively correct in dealing with any given collective-action problem. Rather, the message is that ideas play a critical role in determining how we conceptualize such problems. Among other things, this means that individual actors can and often do interpret the same problem quite differently.

The second observation concerns matters that have been discussed repeatedly under the heading of "two-level games."[23] The essential point is that the unitary actor assumption common to most approaches inspired by game theory abstracts away all the inner workings that affect the behavior of the actors in international society. Consider, once again, such problems as ozone depletion, climate change, and the loss of biological diversity. How can we explain developments like the confusing crosscurrents surrounding the American position on reductions of greenhouse gas emissions or the sharp shifts in the American position regarding the acceptability of the Convention on Biological Diversity without resorting to an analysis of domestic bargaining processes taking place within the United States? These comments regarding two-level games apply just as well to the behavior of nonstate actors as they do to the behavior of states that ordinarily become the formal members of international regimes. To illustrate, many observers have sought to reconstruct the inner workings of the DuPont Corporation that eventuated in its striking switch in early 1987 from opposition to the phaseout of ozone-depleting substances to a position of active support for what became the core of the Montreal Protocol.[24] None

22. James R. McGoodwin, *Crisis in the World's Fisheries: People, Problems, and Policies* (Stanford: Stanford University Press, 1990).

23. Robert D. Putnam, "Diplomacy and Domestic Politics: The Logic of Two-Level Games," *International Organization* 42 (Summer 1988), 427–60.

24. Richard E. Benedick, *Ozone Diplomacy: New Directions in Safeguarding the Planet*, rev. ed. (Cambridge: Harvard University Press, 1998).

of this implies that it is never appropriate to treat the players involved in the formation and operation of international regimes as unitary actors. But the importance of two-level games in this setting does make it clear that any approach to problem structure that relies exclusively on a unitary actor assumption will leave out a number of factors that can loom large as determinants of the malignancy of specific problems.

Finally, there is the issue of problem dynamics or change over time. Like most game-theoretically inspired constructs, the Oslo/Seattle approach to problem structure is somewhat static—that is, the approach seeks to rank problems on the benign-malign scale on the assumption that individual problems will not shift around on this scale over time. Of course, the assumption that problems stay put in terms of their malignancy is a helpful one from the perspective of analytic tractability. But many of the problems that emerge on the international political agenda are highly dynamic with regard to their level of malignancy. A number of forces, operating individually or together, can and often do lead either to objective changes in the character of specific problems or to changes in the way in which relevant actors perceive them. Problems may deepen or become increasingly malign as a result of delays in taking effective action to address them. Thus, for example, the problem of dealing with severely depleted fish stocks, such as cod in the Northwest Atlantic, is fundamentally different from the problem of initiating regulatory measures when the first signs of stock depletions appear. Social learning can produce striking changes in the understanding of problems over time.[25] Consider the shift from the focus on transboundary fluxes of individual pollutants to the concept of critical loads in thinking about air pollution in Europe as a case in point. Integrative or productive bargaining—in contrast to conventional distributive bargaining—can lead parties to redefine problems in more cooperative terms or open up new opportunities for cooperation during the course of interactive decision making.[26] The emerging interest in the use of incentive-based mechanisms (such as joint implementation) as options for solving problems exemplifies this prospect. What is more, exogenous events can produce profound effects on the dynamics of specific situations that involve interactive decision making. Striking illustrations include far-reaching changes in the domestic political systems of one or more of the key participants, as with the collapse of the Soviet Union, and the impact

25. On social learning in connection with international governance systems, see William C. Clark, J. van Eijndoven, and Jill Jaeger, eds., *Learning to Manage Global Environmental Risks: A Comparative History of Social Responses to Climate Change, Ozone Depletion, and Acid Rain* (Cambridge: MIT Press, forthcoming).

26. Richard E. Walton and Robert B. McKersie, *A Behavioral Theory of Labor Negotiations: An Analysis of a Social Interaction System* (New York: McGraw-Hill, 1965).

of exogenous shocks or crises, such as the onset of a serious recession or economic downturn. In all these cases, the point to ponder is the same: a problem that is malign to start with may become more benign over time as a result of either objective or subjective change or vice versa. This line of thinking does not call into question the fundamental proposition that some problems are more malign, or more difficult to solve, than others. But it does demonstrate the hazards of seeking to pinpoint the location of a problem on the benign-malign scale at one time and then assuming that it will stay put at that location over time.

Like the Tübingen approach, the Oslo/Seattle approach to problem structure has significant strengths. The idea of focusing on configurations of the preferences of participating actors and measuring how far the configurations depart from a state of harmony in specific cases is appealing. So also is the use of familiar game-theoretical constructs to illustrate the underlying character of the approach. But serious difficulties arise when it comes to using this approach in an operational rather than a heuristic mode. Some of these difficulties have to do with operationalizing key concepts for empirical research; they are familiar to all those who have worked with game-theoretical constructs in one setting or another. Other difficulties are more analytic and more specific to the Oslo/Seattle approach in character. They arise from the assumptions embedded in the approach about such matters as the sources of actor behavior and the extent to which the defining elements of problem structure can be expected to remain unchanged over time. At this stage, at least, there is no avoiding the conclusion that the Oslo/Seattle approach cannot provide us with a generic index of problem structure that is usable in arriving at practical judgments about the malignancy or difficulty of current issues on the international political agenda.

Future Prospects

What are the prospects for constructing a general index of problem structure during the foreseeable future, either by building on one of the existing approaches or by devising some alternative approach? The value of being able to locate specific problems on an integrated scale ranging from problems that are easy to solve to those which are hard to solve is undeniable. As a result, it surely makes sense to continue investing time and energy in index construction in this area; high potential payoffs can justify investments even when the probability of success in such an endeavor is low. But at this juncture, I am not optimistic about the prospects for success. The fact that problem structure encompasses a number of distinct dimensions makes it necessary to devise a common metric or to come up with some other integrating device in order to develop a general scale. The influence of subjective factors on the thinking of actors about specific problems is difficult to capture, even through the use of conceptual devices such as preference structures or utility functions. What is more, the dynamic character of the problems on the international political agenda makes it risky to assume that we can assess the difficulty of individual problems on a one-shot basis. Under the best of circumstances, therefore, it would be necessary to monitor problems on an ongoing basis to track shifts in their location on a scale of hardness or malignancy. This conclusion suggests the desirability of launching some more-limited or modest efforts to improve our understanding of problem structure, even while some analysts continue to search for a generic measure of hardness or difficulty. In the remaining sections of this chapter, I offer some points of departure for such efforts.

DIMENSIONS OF PROBLEM STRUCTURE

The absence of a generic index of problem structure does not mean that progress cannot be made toward understanding the factors that render some problems harder to solve than others. In this section, I examine a variety of dimensions of problem structure that are known to play a role in determining how hard it is to solve problems at the international level through the formation and operation of regimes. This effort is preliminary; I do not claim that the dimensions of problem structure which I discuss here are either exhaustive or mutually exclusive. It is perfectly possible that additional work in this area will allow us to supplement this taxonomy or even to replace it altogether with some improved conceptual framework. Nonetheless, this discussion should suffice to convey some sense of an approach to the problem of problem structure that is useful, even though it is certainly not a substitute for the construction of a generic index of problem structure. For ease of exposition, I group the factors I consider into four clusters: problem attributes, actor characteristics, asymmetries, and social setting.

Problem Attributes

A logical place to begin this inquiry is with an examination of various attributes of the problems themselves. The nature of the task(s) a regime is required to perform, for instance, is an important factor in determining how hard a problem is to solve. With respect to regulatory tasks, hardness is largely a function of the degree of difficulty encountered in eliciting compliance with essential rules from both member states and nonstate actors or even individuals operating under the jurisdiction of members. As a result, assessments of the ability of regulatory regimes to solve problems center on issues of capacity building, monitoring, implementation review, and the availability of appropriate sanctions.[27] In the case of programmatic tasks, the key to hardness is likely to revolve around the availability of the material resources needed to carry out joint projects. For their part, procedural tasks are difficult to perform to the extent that regime members insist on using consensus rules in making collective choices or refuse to give up the option of entering objections or reservations as a means of opting out of the application of specific collective choices to themselves. Another factor, which cuts across the dimension of regime tasks, involves the depth of intervention in the domestic affairs of regime members needed to solve problems. In general, the deeper the intervention required, the harder a problem is to solve.[28] Thus, a regulatory arrangement that calls for deep penetration into the domestic systems of regime members, as does controlling emissions of greenhouse gases, will rank high on the scale of hardness. By contrast, a programmatic regime that deals only with borderlands or is limited to activities taking place outside the jurisdiction of individual regime members, such as human activities in Antarctica, will rank low on a scale of hardness.

A number of other problem attributes also play a role in determining the hardness of international problems. Problems featuring relationships expected to continue into the indefinite future are widely regarded as relatively easy to solve owing to the impact of the shadow of the future.[29] In effect, knowing that it will be necessary to interact with fellow regime members over the long run serves to inhibit uncooperative or disruptive behavior in the present. The presence of uncertainty, however, usually makes problems more difficult to solve. Some types of uncertainty can actually contribute to problem solving by increasing the thickness of the "veil of uncertainty." But uncertainty about the nature or the seriousness of the problem will make it difficult for parties to reach agreement on a common formulation of the issues at stake. Uncertainty about the nature or the consequences of proposed solutions will complicate efforts to reach agree-

27. Edith Brown Weiss and Harold K. Jacobson, eds., *Engaging Countries: Strengthening Compliance with International Environmental Accords* (Cambridge: MIT Press, 1998), and David G. Victor, Kal Raustiala, and Eugene B. Skolnikoff, eds., *The Implementation and Effectiveness of International Environmental Commitments* (Cambridge: MIT Press, 1998).

28. See George W. Downs, David M. Rocke, and Peter N. Barsoom, "Is the Good News about Compliance Good News about Cooperation?" *International Organization* 50 (Summer 1996), 379–406.

29. Kenneth A. Oye, "Explaining Cooperation under Anarchy: Hypotheses and Strategies," in Oye, ed., *Cooperation under Anarchy* (Princeton: Princeton University Press, 1986), 1–24.

ment on the constitutive provisions of regimes. Transparency, too, is an attribute that is relevant to assessing the hardness of problems. Of course, transparency is particularly important in efforts to solve regulatory problems. But there is a sense in which openness regarding the behavior of regime members makes all international problems easier to solve, which is why technological advances, such as the use of satellites to facilitate nonintrusive monitoring of compliance with arms control agreements or with agreements concerning fishing in exclusive economic zones, sometimes make it possible to create effective regimes where the parties were previously unable to agree even on the content of constitutive agreements.

As these observations suggest, actors may find that opportunities exist to frame problems or design solutions in ways that make problems more or less difficult to solve. Wherever possible, for example, it makes sense to focus on the behavior of a small number of actors whose identity is clear and whose behavior is easy to monitor. That it is easier to monitor the behavior of the producers of CFCs than of the consumers of these chemicals or the behavior of the builders of tankers rather than their operators has not been lost on those responsible for building regimes to deal with these problems.[30] Similarly, arrangements featuring outright prohibitions are generally easier to operate than arrangements allowing certain activities, say harvesting marine mammals or using various pesticides, to proceed on a highly regulated basis.[31] When an activity is banned altogether, there is no need to enter into protracted debates about the extent to which specific actions conform to prevailing regulations. This is not to say that there are always ways to frame problems which make them relatively easy to solve. What is more, it is generally difficult to persuade parties to adopt a new way of thinking about a problem once they have reached agreement on a particular approach to the issues involved. Yet there is much to said for devoting substantial time and energy to such matters in the interests of devising approaches to problems which minimize the difficulties involved in finding workable solutions.

Actor Characteristics

Just as the attributes of the problems themselves are important to assessments of hardness, so also are various characteristics of the actors whose behavior is at stake. The most familiar proposition about the actors is that

---

30. Benedick, *Ozone Diplomacy*, and Ronald B. Mitchell, *Intentional Oil Pollution at Sea: Environmental Policy and Treaty Compliance* (Cambridge: MIT Press, 1994).

31. Steven Lewis Yaffee, *Prohibitive Policy: Implementing the Federal Endangered Species Act* (Cambridge: MIT Press, 1982).

problems become harder to solve as the number of stakeholders increases and, therefore, as the number of distinct interests that must be taken into account in developing solutions grows.[32] The logic of this argument is simple. It rests on the presumption that regime formation in international society ordinarily proceeds under a consensus rule, together with the observation that transaction costs rise as a direct function of the number of players involved in efforts to reach consensus on the terms of agreements. Thus, one of two things is likely to occur. Institutional bargaining may become protracted, as in recent experiences with the law of the sea, in which case problem solving becomes a slow and costly process.[33] Or the parties may sacrifice substantive content in the interests of arriving at some agreement quickly, as with the framework convention on climate change, in which case regimes—at least in their initial form—will have little capacity to solve the problems they are intended to address.[34]

This argument clearly has merit. Yet two factors serve to mitigate the degree to which increases in the number of relevant actors make international problems harder to solve. Often, the number of distinct actors or interests involved in the bargaining process is sharply reduced through the formation of negotiating blocs or groups. In the case of ozone depletion, for example, the essential problem was to find a solution acceptable to a bloc led by the United States, another encompassing the European Community, and a third based on the Group of 77. Although individual states obviously retain the right to accept or reject the final texts arising from processes of institutional bargaining, the pressures to accept the terms of consensus texts are great. In addition, it is possible in many efforts to solve international problems to leave much of the bargaining to individual regime members in their dealings with actors operating under their jurisdiction. To take the case of ozone depletion again, the parties were able to adopt a general phaseout schedule at the international level, leaving all the details regarding the implementation of the schedule within individual members to the governments of those states.[35] Certainly, these considerations do not obviate the argument that the hardness of a problem is a func-

32. Oye, "Explaining Cooperation."

33. Robert L. Friedheim, *Negotiating the New Ocean Regime* (Columbia: University of South Carolina Press, 1993).

34. Irving M. Mintzer and J. A. Leonard, eds., *Negotiating Climate Change: The Inside Story of the Rio Convention* (Cambridge: Cambridge University Press, 1994).

35. Kenneth Hanf and Arild Underdal, "Domesticating International Commitments: Linking National and International Decision-Making," in Underdal, ed., *The International Politics of Environmental Management* (Dordrecht: Kluwer Academic Publishers, 1995), 1–20, and Kal Raustiala, "Domestic Institutions and International Regulatory Cooperation: Comparative Responses to the Convention on Biological Diversity," *World Politics* 49 (July 1997), 482–509.

tion of the number of actors involved. But they go some way toward preventing international problems from becoming intractable.

A preoccupation with the issue of numbers should not lead us to ignore other actor-related matters that play a role in determining how hard it is to solve international problems. Some of these have to do with the degree to which the relevant actors are homogeneous or heterogeneous along several important dimensions. It seems reasonable to conclude, for example, that states possessing similar political systems, such as groups of democracies, or similar economic systems, such as groups of advanced market economies, will find it easier to reach mutually agreeable solutions to problems than would actors that are more heterogeneous in these terms. The same can be said with regard to cultural homogeneity.[36] Thus, states that share a common cultural heritage (for example, Indo-European societies) are likely to find it easier to negotiate the terms of constitutive contracts designed to solve problems than are states that are heterogeneous in these terms; they may even find it easier to devise a common or mutually comprehensible discourse by which to frame the problem for purposes of regime formation.[37] Another significant factor involves the nature of state/society relations and the distinction between strong states and weak states.[38] Homogeneity with respect to state/society relations is likely to facilitate efforts to solve problems, especially when the key actors all have strong states that can be trusted to deliver on the commitments or promises they make during processes of regime formation. A well-known and important problem in this regard concerns the role of the United States, a powerful actor whose participation in many regimes is essential to problem solving but one which has a relatively weak state that sometimes proves incapable of meeting international commitments requiring significant behavioral change at the domestic level.[39]

The role of nonstate actors is worthy of note in this discussion as well. Sometimes nonstate actors (consider producers of CFCs or operators of power plants) are the ultimate subjects of the substantive provisions of international regimes. In such instances, hardness is a function of the

36. On the influence of cultural factors in international negotiations, see Guy Olivier Faure and Jeffrey Z. Rubin, eds., *Culture and Negotiation* (Newbury Park, Calif.: Sage, 1993).

37. The influence of discourses in processes of regime formation is explored in Karen T. Litfin, *Ozone Discourses: Science and Politics in Global Environmental Cooperation* (New York: Columbia University Press, 1994).

38. On the distinction between strong states and weak states, see Joel Migdal, *Strong Societies and Weak States: State-Society Relations and State Capabilities in the Third World* (Princeton: Princeton University Press, 1988).

39. For an account that discusses the implications of this situation, see Konrad von Moltke, "Institutional Interactions: The Structure of Regimes for Trade and the Environment," in Oran R. Young, ed., *Global Governance: Drawing Insights from the Environmental Experience* (Cambridge: MIT Press, 1997), 247–72.

sources of their behavior and the capacity of member states to induce these actors to make the necessary behavioral changes. As experience to date with the climate change regime makes clear, for example, redirecting the behavior of large, powerful, and resistant corporations can be a tall order. In other cases, nonstate actors (such as environmental advocacy groups) can emerge as allies in the efforts of states to solve international problems, either by becoming active in designing innovative solutions to problems or by becoming vocal as pressure groups or watchdogs in connection with efforts to implement the terms of constitutive contracts once they are adopted. Sometimes this leads to adversarial relations in which groups such as Greenpeace attempt to bring pressure to bear on reluctant governments to accept more far-reaching commitments than they would otherwise adopt. As the Great Lakes Water Quality Agreement illustrates, however, nonstate actors can also play important roles in nurturing the development of a concerned community that becomes an integral part of the evolving social practice which grows up around the formal provisions of a regime.[40]

Asymmetries

There is a pronounced tendency to assume—implicitly if not explicitly—that international problems and the relationships among the parties involved in them are symmetrical in thinking about ways to solve problems that emerge on the international political agenda. Partly, this tendency results from such paradigmatic examples as prisoner's dilemma and battle of the sexes which we habitually use to facilitate the analysis of such matters. In part, it stems from the idea that the members of international society are equals in legal and political terms, despite their obvious differences in other respects. Yet numerous asymmetries are associated with international problems, and some of them make a difference with respect to how hard it is to solve specific problems. Perhaps the most familiar examples involve structural asymmetries, such as the well-known upstream-downstream problem.[41] Thus, the allocation of limited supplies of water is apt to prove especially difficult where the upstream state can simply divert water to meet its own needs, with or without the consent of the downstream state. Similarly, problems of transboundary air pollution are difficult to solve in situations where there are marked asymmetries between those states which are sources and those which are victims of pollution.

40. Lee Botts and Paul Muldoon, *The Great Lakes Water Quality Agreement: Its Past Successes and Uncertain Future* (Hanover, N.H.: Institute on International Environmental Governance, 1996).
41. See, for example, Miriam R. Lowi, *Water and Power: The Politics of a Scarce Resource in the Jordan River Basin* (Cambridge: Cambridge University Press, 1993).

Somewhat analogous concerns arise from economic asymmetries between producers and consumers of goods and from geopolitical asymmetries involving exposure to military threats. A consumer who can obtain the same product from any of a number of suppliers, for instance, is in a situation very different from that of a consumer who must do business with a single supplier or go without the product. A country that shares a border with a potential aggressor has more to worry about than one that is protected by intervening land masses or water bodies.

Other asymmetries that can make international problems easy or difficult to solve arise from differences in the roles that relevant players occupy in contrast to structural asymmetries among them. The traditional distinction among flag, port, and coastal states, coupled with the presumption that only flag states were authorized to apprehend and sanction vessels flying their flags, for instance, long served as an obstacle to solving problems involving the harvest of fish and marine mammals or the control of vessel-source pollution. This explains the significance of recent developments that accord coastal states increased authority over activities occurring in their exclusive economic zones (EEZs). Somewhat similar observations pertain to differences in the roles of nuclear weapon states and nonnuclear weapon states. A factor contributing to the hardness of the problem of preventing nuclear proliferation arose from the fact that in agreeing to the terms of the Nuclear Nonproliferation Treaty (NPT), nonnuclear-weapon states were being asked to accept an asymmetrical arrangement that would have the effect of making their disadvantage permanent.[42] Not all asymmetries regarding roles make problems more difficult to solve. In some instances, such as role differences arising from natural resource endowments, asymmetries in the roles states occupy may facilitate problem solving. But the general point is clear. It is important to consider asymmetries that relate to roles in any effort to assess how difficult international problems are to solve.

The effects of these asymmetries are usually reflected in the bargaining leverage of the actors involved in the formation and operation of international regimes.[43] Sometimes bargaining leverage is directly related to asymmetries in material conditions. Even weak states can drive hard bargains in cases where behavioral changes on their part are essential to solving problems that others care about deeply. Any serious effort to solve

42. Roger K. Smith, "Explaining the Non-Proliferation Regime: Anomalies for Contemporary International Relations Theory," *International Organization* 41 (Spring 1987), 253–81.

43. For a general account of bargaining leverage in regime formation, see Oran R. Young, *International Governance: Protecting the Environment in a Stateless Society* (Ithaca: Cornell University Press, 1994), chap. 5.

problems associated with the loss biological diversity, for instance, cannot succeed without accommodating the needs of such countries as Brazil, Indonesia, and Malaysia which contain habitat essential to an unusually large number of species. In other cases, important normative asymmetries underlie bargaining leverage. To the extent that the "polluter pays" principle achieves universal acceptance, for example, it will become more and more costly for states that are sources of transboundary air or water pollution to hold out against the pressures which victims bring to bear on them to change their ways and to compensate for damages already incurred. This also explains the concerted effort on the part of developing countries to establish clearly the responsibility of the advanced industrial states for increases in levels of carbon dioxide and other greenhouse gases residing in the Earth's atmosphere. Once these states—roughly the set of OECD members—acknowledge responsibility, the problem of climate change will become easier to solve through the addition of substantive protocols to the existing framework convention.

Social Setting

Problems that find their way onto the international political agenda do not exist in a vacuum. On the contrary, there are typically linkages among different issues and, as a result, among the institutional arrangements devised to cope with them. To understand how hard it will be to solve a particular problem, then, it is important to ask how it is linked to other problems. Sometimes these linkages are of a material nature. Because CFCs are greenhouse gases, for example, phasing out the use of these chemicals constitutes a positive step in addressing the problem of climate change, making it an easier problem to solve in the process. Other linkages are more political in nature. Thus efforts to deal with such problems as climate change may tax the problem-solving capacity of states in a manner that requires other problems to be set aside for a period of time. As these examples suggest, linkages among discrete problems can cut either way in terms of making it easier or harder to solve individual problems. Conscious efforts to exploit such linkages by addressing two or more problems at once can facilitate problem solving by enabling the negotiation of package deals in which participants make trade-offs that help to solve several problems at the same time.[44] But if the package becomes too large, as with the law of the sea, the result may be a tendency for the bargaining process

44. James K. Sebenius, "Negotiation Arithmetic: Adding and Subtracting Issues and Parties," *International Organization* 37 (Spring 1983), 281–316.

to bog down or for the implementation of the whole package to be held hostage to disagreements over a few specific issues. Much the same is true of interactions among distinct regimes once they are put in place.[45] The existence of multiple regimes may facilitate problem solving by creating economies of scale with respect to such matters as implementation and the development of effective noncompliance procedures. But when institutional congestion leads to overlaps and interference among regimes that address different problems, the existence of multiple regimes may make individual problems more difficult to solve.[46]

Moreover, broader societal conditions and trends play a significant role in making international problems more or less difficult to solve. A few examples will suffice to illustrate this proposition. Advances in technology that occur for reasons having nothing to do with efforts to solve international problems often affect the hardness of specific problems. The development of high-endurance stern trawlers, for instance, greatly complicated problems of fisheries management at the international level.[47] Conversely, the development of earth-orbiting satellites enabled the solution of some problems by increasing transparency and allowing actor behavior to be monitored in an efficient and nonintrusive manner. The privatization movement and initiatives featuring the devolution of political authority to subnational units of government, to take another example, has complicated efforts to solve a variety of international problems by making it more difficult for the governments of member states to assume commitments and to deliver on those promises they do make during the course of institutional bargaining. Economic trends are of similar importance in this connection. Behavioral changes that appear acceptable during periods of prosperity are apt to seem out of reach when the economies of member states are experiencing severe recessions. While international problems may be more or less difficult to solve in their own terms, the larger social setting in which they unfold can make intrinsically difficult problems considerably easier to solve or intrinsically easy problems much harder to solve.

Let me reemphasize several points introduced at the beginning of this section. Problem structure is a multidimensional phenomenon, which

45. Oran R. Young, "Institutional Linkages in International Society: Polar Perspectives," *Global Governance* 2 (January–April 1996), 1–24.

46. For a discussion of these issues phrased in terms of the idea of treaty congestion, see Edith Brown Weiss, "International Environmental Law: Contemporary Issues and the Emergence of a New World Order," *Georgetown Law Review* 81 (March 1993), 675–710.

47. William W. Warner, *Distant Water: The Fate of the North Atlantic Fisherman* (Boston: Little, Brown, 1983).

helps explain why efforts to devise a generic index of the hardness of international problems have not met with great success. There is no difficulty in identifying specific factors that make international problems more or less difficult to solve. The taxonomy employed in this section is suggestive of the range of relevant dimensions. I do not claim that this taxonomy encompasses these dimensions in a mutually exclusive and exhaustive fashion. Rather, my conclusion is that the problem of problem structure constitutes an important challenge for students of international institutions and that we have a long way to go in our efforts to solve this problem in a satisfactory way.

PROBLEMS OF REGIME FORMATION AND REGIME EFFECTIVENESS

In this chapter I have addressed the problem of problem structure in holistic terms. Treating regimes as arrangements created to solve more or less well-defined problems that make their way onto the international political agenda, I have examined efforts to make overall assessments of the locus of specific problems on an integrated scale ranging from problems that are quite easy to solve at one extreme to those that are unusually difficult to solve at the other. This led in turn to a more disaggregated approach featuring a search for distinct dimensions of problem structure without seeking to come up with a generic index by which to rank problems on a scale from easy to difficult to solve. These are certainly appropriate strategies to adopt as a point of departure; devising procedures for scoring or ranking international problems in terms of a generic concept of hardness would be a major accomplishment.

Yet the harder one tries to reach this goal, the more difficult it seems to arrive at such overall judgments. Thus, it is desirable to explore other approaches to the problem of problem structure. One promising approach involves subdividing problem structure into several distinct components. Perhaps the most obvious line of attack here arises from the distinction between regime formation and regime effectiveness. Simply put, what makes it difficult to succeed in efforts to create a regime in response to a particular problem may not be the same as what makes it hard to operate the regime effectively as a problem-solving device once it is up and running. Cases in which regimes formed with high hopes turn out to be outright failures or even dead letters are by no means uncommon. Even when they do prove effective, regimes in operation often diverge in fundamental ways from the vision articulated in their constitutive documents.

Regime Formation

Regime formation is primarily a process of institutional bargaining.[48] The factors that make regime formation hard, therefore, are bargaining impediments—conditions that make it difficult for participants to engage in constructive bargaining or to reach closure on the terms of constitutive contracts once the bargaining process gets under way. Some such impediments arise from attributes of the problem or the attitudes of the parties toward it; they affect problem solving even before the process of institutional bargaining begins. In extreme cases, these impediments may make it impossible to proceed with an organized effort to form an international regime. While all parties concerned may agree that a problem exists, for instance, there are often striking differences among them with respect to problem definition. Even when some measure of consensus exists regarding the nature of the problem, the parties may not share a discourse in terms of which to organize thinking about ways to solve the problem. Beyond this, there are often substantial differences in the priority that various parties attach to the problem. Some may be unwilling to invest time and energy in developing a solution, even when others are most anxious to address the problem. When some parties regard the management of living resources as a problem of maximizing sustainable yields while others treat the problem as one of eliminating all consumptive uses, for instance, the prospects for regime formation will be bleak. The breakdown of the familiar discourse associated with the generative idea of maximum sustainable yield and the failure to devise an alternative discourse that is both operational and widely accepted have greatly complicated many efforts to develop management regimes dealing with fish and marine mammals. Similarly, many developing countries rank such problems as climate change and the protection of biological diversity low on their scale of priorities, leading to difficulties in drawing them into serious negotiations as active participants. Just as the advanced industrialized countries are becoming genuinely concerned about problems of global environmental change, important developing countries such as Brazil, China, and India are preoccupied with securing safe drinking water, feeding growing populations, and raising material standards of living for their citizens.

Even when negotiations do get off the ground, impediments affecting the process of institutional bargaining can make problems more or less difficult to solve. The balance between integrative bargaining and distributive bargaining, for instance, typically influences the prospects for success. Problems that give rise to win-win situations in which there is ample

48. Young, *International Governance*, chap. 4.

scope for expanding the frontier of social welfare are much easier to solve through the negotiation of constitutive contracts than problems featuring distributive bargaining where the scope for mutual gains is small. At the same time, the rules governing the bargaining process can make the same problem more or less hard to solve. Thus, the extent to which the parties are committed to using a consensus rule and therefore endeavoring to arrive at constitutive agreements that appeal to the coalition of the whole is a factor that affects the likelihood of success in regime formation. When the parties are committed to assembling a coalition of the whole—either because they believe it is needed to solve the problem at hand or because prevailing social norms require it—even small players can make large demands, and the likelihood increases that negotiations will end in stalemate. To be sure, powerful actors can make concerted efforts to overcome this impediment by offering side payments to bring holdouts into the coalition or threatening them with various types of sanctions. But it is easy to see that a combination of the invocation of consensus rules and the prominence of distributive bargaining can produce situations that rank high on a scale of hardness with regard to regime formation.

Regime Effectiveness

What makes a regime hard to operate successfully, by contrast, is a matter of conditions that influence whether the behavior of regime members and other relevant actors will change in response to the regulatory, procedural, and programmatic measures initiated under the terms of the regime. Clearly, a number of conditions can play important roles in this context.[49] To begin with, there are questions regarding whose behavior must change and how much behavioral change is needed to solve a problem. Is the change a matter of altering the practices of a specific government agency, as with most arms control arrangements, or of redirecting the behavior of private actors, as with the ozone depletion and climate change regimes? Where the behavior of private actors is the source of the problem, is it essential to alter the actions of large numbers of consumers, as in the case of climate change, or of a small number of producers, as in the case of ozone depletion? Can substitutes be developed and adopted without undue delay or cost, or is there a need to make changes that will intrude more deeply into the lives of affected actors? In general, the greater the behavioral changes required and the larger the number of actors

49. For an account that stresses the role of different behavioral mechanisms, see Oran R. Young, ed., *The Effectiveness of International Environmental Regimes: Causal Connections and Behavioral Mechanisms* (Cambridge: MIT Press, 1999).

whose behavior is affected, the harder it will be to operate a regime effectively. But it is easy to see that a wide range of factors may determine these conditions in specific cases.

Another approach to hardness at the level of regime operation directs attention to conditions affecting the success of efforts to implement the provisions of regimes within the domestic systems of regime members. As those who have studied the implementation of public policies in domestic settings have demonstrated, there is ample room for slippage in moving from paper to practice in the effort to operationalize regimes.[50] In extreme instances, regimes—like other regulatory arrangements—can be captured by those whose behavior they are intended to regulate. But other—less dramatic—problems are common as well. The material resources needed for effective implementation may not be forthcoming. Actors whose interests are affected may drag their feet, necessitating legal action to force them to alter their behavior in extreme cases. Internal tensions within agencies responsible for implementing the provisions of regimes may cause delays in taking the initiative with regard to implementation. The policy instruments chosen may be poorly designed or ill-suited to dealing with the problem at hand. Shifts in thinking about the relative merits of policy instruments—for example, the recent growth of interest in incentive systems in contrast to command-and-control regulations—may make it difficult to translate the provisions of regimes into operational procedures in a straightforward manner. Under the circumstances, it is apparent that no matter how well the constitutive provisions of regimes are crafted, political complications affecting the implementation process may make them extremely hard to operate successfully. The fact that these difficulties may be more severe within some regime members than others only adds to the complexity of assessing hardness along this dimension.[51]

Problems of compliance constitute yet another source of hardness in connection with the operation of regimes. Some regimes are able to tolerate a higher level of violations than others without becoming ineffective. Most trade regimes, for instance, are more tolerant of violations than are arms control regimes, especially those involving nuclear weapons or strategic delivery vehicles. In general, the higher the level of compliance required for effectiveness, the harder the problem of regime operation becomes. Beyond this lies the realm of factors affecting how difficult it is to elicit compliance, particularly from those actors whose activities are cen-

---

50. For a classic example, see Jeffrey L. Pressman and Aaron Wildavsky, *Implementation: How Great Expectations in Washington Are Dashed in Oakland*, 2d ed. (Berkeley: University of California Press, 1973).

51. For a wealth of examples, see Weiss and Jacobson, *Engaging Countries*.

tral to the problem at hand.[52] It is reasonable to assume, for example, that parties are more likely to comply with the requirements of regimes in the absence of conventional enforcement measures when they feel a strong sense of ownership regarding the arrangement; when there is a strong informal network or community of regime supporters to serve as a watchdog and booster; and when key government agencies define their missions, at least in part, in terms of responsibilities associated with operating the regime. Numerous other factors undoubtedly play a role in this connection as well. But given the decentralized character of international society, it seems reasonable to conclude that the higher the level of compliance with a regime's provisions in the absence of formal or official sanctions, the more effective the arrangement will be in operational terms.

INTUITIVELY, IT SEEMS self-evident that some problems on the international political agenda are more difficult to solve than others and that problem structure is therefore an important determinant of success or failure in efforts to solve these problems through the creation of international regimes. This has led, understandably, to efforts to assess individual problems in terms of such criteria as benign or malign and—even more ambitiously—to devise an integrated scale by which to rank the universe of problems with respect to how hard it is to solve them. Success in this endeavor would be a major accomplishment. The most prominent efforts to construct integrated scales of hardness, which I have characterized as the Tübingen approach and the Oslo/Seattle approach, leave a great deal to be desired. Moreover, I am not sanguine about the prospects for overcoming the limitations of these approaches during the foreseeable future. Problem structure is a multidimensional phenomenon, and there is no procedure in sight in terms of which to aggregate the most important dimensions into a single ordinal scale, much less to attach numerical values to them in the interests of constructing an interval scale of hardness.

Still, we are not completely helpless when it comes to differentiating among problems with respect to how hard they are to solve. In this chapter, I have explored, in a preliminary fashion, two approaches of a more modest nature to the problem of problem structure. One involves identifying a number of distinct dimensions of problem structure and examining them individually. This effort yielded a taxonomy made up of four clusters of dimensions, which I have labeled problem attributes, actor characteristics, asymmetries, and social setting. It is also helpful, in my

---

52. Abram Chayes and Antonia Handler Chayes, *The New Sovereignty: Compliance with International Regulatory Agreements* (Cambridge: Harvard University Press, 1995), and Downs, Rocke, and Barsoom, "Good News about Compliance."

view, to consider subdividing the problem of problem structure in order to illuminate sources of hardness that pertain mainly to the process of regime formation and other sources of hardness that come into focus in connection with the operation of regimes once they are in place. Whereas hardness during regime formation is essentially a matter of conditions affecting the process of institutional bargaining, hardness during regime operation centers on issues related to behavioral change. These approaches to the problem of problem structure do not constitute a substitute for a generic scale of hardness, and they should not be allowed to detract from continuing efforts to devise such a scale. But they do add significantly to our understanding of the problem of problem structure, especially in a setting in which no generic or integrated scale is available to guide our assessment of problems giving rise to a demand for governance in world affairs.

CHAPTER 4

Is Enforcement the Achilles' Heel
of International Regimes?

A common reaction among laypeople to the central propositions of
regime theory is epitomized in the following question: how can regimes
prove effective in solving problems arising in international society in the
absence of a higher authority endowed with both the capacity and the will
to enforce their essential rules? Nor is this concern confined to laypeople.
It underlies much of the long-standing debate among lawyers and legal
scholars about the extent to which the rules of international law are *law-
ful* in the ordinary sense of the term.[1] In a characteristic statement, Jacob
Werksman observes that "the absence of institutions empowered to enforce international obligations by compulsorily settling disputes between
states has often been cited as the Achilles' heel of the international legal
system."[2] Some political scientists have joined this debate as well, express-
ing concerns of a similar nature. George Downs and his colleagues, for example, have developed an interesting argument that links the need for enforcement with what they call the "depth of cooperation" or the extent to
which international agreements capture available collective benefits. As
they put it, "the deeper the agreement is, the greater the punishments required to support it."[3]

The logic embedded in such arguments about the importance of en-

1. For a convenient collection stressing alternative perspectives on the nature and status of
rules at the international level, see Robert J. Beck, Anthony Clark Arend, and Robert D. Van-
der Lugt, eds., *International Rules: Approaches from International Law and International Relations*
(New York: Oxford University Press, 1996).

2. Jacob Werksman, ed., *Greening International Institutions* (London: Earthscan Publications,
1996), xvi.

3. George W. Downs, David M. Rocke, and Peter N. Barsoom, "Is the Good News about Compliance Good News about Cooperation?" *International Organization* 50 (Summer 1996), 386.

forcement is simple, resting on three linked propositions. First, effectiveness requires compliance. Achieving compliance, in other words, is a necessary condition for international regimes to become successful in the sense of solving or managing the problems that motivate their creators to establish them. Second, compliance requires enforcement—that is, the availability of credible enforcement mechanisms is necessary to gain high levels of compliance, especially where the behavioral adjustments required to capture collective benefits are extensive. Third, enforcement requires government. A duly constituted public authority or a "government" is necessary for the creation and operation of enforcement mechanisms that work well. It is understandably difficult for those who subscribe to all three propositions to take regime theory seriously. Even the combination of the first two propositions is sufficient to raise searching questions about the significance of international regimes. No doubt, regimes will sometimes prove capable of solving simple coordination problems or even making small improvements with regard to more complex collaboration problems. But the promise of "governance without government,"[4] which regime theorists have been proclaiming in a variety of forums, will surely prove a chimera when it comes to solving really difficult or "malign" collective-action problems in international society.[5]

What should we make of this argument? I do not claim that the logic outlined in the preceding paragraph is entirely lacking in merit; there are surely good reasons why governments allocate substantial resources to the operation of enforcement mechanisms in domestic social settings. Yet this logic is by no means as straightforward or as compelling as it may seem at first glance. In this chapter, I examine this logic critically from a number of distinct but related angles. In the process, I show that there are situations to which the logic does not apply in any unambiguous way and that the individual propositions that make up the logic are of doubtful validity under a variety of circumstances. The result is not a total denial of the role of enforcement in connection with the operation of international regimes. Rather, my analysis suggests that enforcement is more important under some conditions than others and that circumstances exist in which enforcement mechanisms can operate effectively in the absence of anything we would normally call a "government."

4. For a particularly prominent expression of the fundamental idea underlying the phrase "governance without government," see James N. Rosenau and Ernst-Otto Czempiel, eds., *Governance without Government: Order and Change in World Politics* (Cambridge: Cambridge University Press, 1992).

5. For a discussion of the benign/malign distinction, see Steinar Andresen and Jørgen Wettestad, "International Problem-Solving Effectiveness: The Oslo Project So Far," *International Environmental Affairs* 7 (Spring 1995), 127–49.

The heart of my argument consists of a series of observations about the role and sources of compliance in connection with the sorts of problems that give rise to the formation and operation of international regimes.[6] These observations allow me to probe both the nature of the problems and the roots of the behavior of those actors engaged in efforts to address them. What emerges is a more complex picture which suggests both that the relevance of compliance is a variable to be analyzed with care and that compliance is often better treated as a matter of management or facilitation than as a matter of enforcement.[7] As is well known, moreover, enforcement mechanisms can and often do produce negative externalities, whatever their results in terms of promoting compliant behavior.[8] But I pass over these concerns in this discussion in favor of an effort to unpack the links between regime effectiveness, on the one hand, and compliance and enforcement, on the other.

EFFECTIVENESS WITHOUT COMPLIANCE

Each of my observations focuses on one of the links in the argument sketched in the preceding paragraphs. I first offer two observations that raise questions about the nature of the link between compliance and effectiveness.

Regime Tasks and Types

Although compliance is a central concern in connection with regulatory tasks, regimes often perform other tasks with respect to which compliance is of lesser importance or even irrelevant. International regimes perform a variety of functions. While many regimes are designed to carry out two or more functions at the same time, others specialize in one particular type of task. Given the deep roots of the new institutionalism in international

6. Although private regimes or arrangements whose members are nonstate actors are subject to growing interest among students of regimes, in this chapter I focus on the classic cases in which the members of regimes are states. I do, however, address the increasingly important roles that nonstate actors play in these classic cases.

7. The management/enforcement distinction is articulated with particular clarity in Abram Chayes and Antonia Handler Chayes, *The New Sovereignty: Compliance with International Regulatory Agreements* (Cambridge: Harvard University Press, 1995). See also Ronald B. Mitchell, "Adversarial and Facilitative Approaches to On-Site Inspection in Arms Control and Environmental Regimes," paper presented at the annual meeting of the International Studies Association, Minneapolis, March 1998.

8. Oran R. Young, *Compliance and Public Authority: A Theory with International Applications* (Baltimore: Johns Hopkins University Press, 1979), chap. 8.

relations in the study of collective-action problems,[9] it is understandable that work in this field has placed a heavy emphasis on regulatory regimes or arrangements that center on rules or behavioral prescriptions specifying actions which those subject to the regimes are expected to take or to refrain from taking under various circumstances. Rules dealing with the prohibition on nuclear testing everywhere except underground,[10] the maintenance of the civil rights of citizens of one country who reside in another, the protection of intellectual property, and the regulation of consumptive uses of living resources by season and gear type are well-known cases in point. As these examples suggest, regulatory arrangements can be directed toward governmental agencies, such as defense establishments or trade offices, or toward actors operating under the auspices of member states, such as fishers or corporations responsible for emitting pollutants. But in every instance, the rules emphasize behavior that is expected of various groups of subjects with regard to more or less well-defined classes or categories of situations.

Important as these regulatory arrangements are, they do not exhaust the range of tasks that international regimes are expected to perform. Consider the distinctive features of procedural, programmatic, and generative regimes. Procedural regimes are arrangements designed to produce collective or social choices regarding matters in which a number of stakeholders have a legitimate interest. Unlike regulatory arrangements, which feature explicit rules intended to govern the behavior of subjects in well-defined and recurrent situations, procedural arrangements establish mechanisms that allow groups of actors to make collective choices about matters that are irregular, unique, and often unforeseen by a regime's creators. For their part, programmatic regimes involve the development and execution of joint projects in situations where individual actors are not in a position or do not have the resources to carry out important projects alone. These arrangements deal with such concerns as the conservation of migratory species that move from one jurisdiction to another, the development of reserves of nonrenewable resources that straddle jurisdictional boundaries, and the production of knowledge when it is desirable to obtain observations from many sources. Generative regimes, finally, feature coordinated activities that lead to new understandings of common problems and, often, to new ways of organizing efforts to deal with these prob-

9. Oran R. Young, *International Governance: Protecting the Environment in a Stateless Society* (Ithaca: Cornell University Press, 1994).

10. The partial nuclear test ban treaty of 1963 prohibits tests above ground, under the sea, and in outer space. Recent efforts have produced a comprehensive test ban agreement. But this agreement is not yet in force.

lems. In such instances as the emergence of the concepts of critical loads, ecosystems management, or large marine ecosystems, these efforts can give rise to a central idea that constitutes the basis for a distinctive discourse among those engaged in the activities in question.[11]

Compliance emerges as the central issue only in the case of regulatory regimes. The primary concern about procedural regimes centers on the capacity of international institutions to produce collective choices which are substantive in nature and which the participants will accept and implement within their own jurisdictions. Given the tendency at the international level to rely on consensus rules and the existence of an option for individual participants to file reservations or objections where majority-rule procedures are in use, there is a recurrent problem in connection with the operation of procedural arrangements of steering a middle course between toothless decisions that fail to address problems effectively and far-reaching decisions that fail to solve problems because key players choose to opt out.[12] But none of this is a matter of *compliance* in the ordinary sense of the term.

When it comes to programmatic regimes, the standard challenge is to persuade participants to set up the organizational apparatus needed to carry out joint projects and to find ways to generate needed resources (especially money and materiel). In many cases, member states—including those which have the wherewithal to do so—are reluctant to enter into binding agreements regarding contributions, and individual members are not above shirking on the commitments they do make. This is one reason for the growing interest in options for devising regimes that have the capacity to generate resources of their own.[13] Generative regimes produce consequences by promoting the development of ideas and triggering the diffusion of new ways of thinking about international problems. While such consequences may seem limited relative to the scope or magnitude of the problems to be solved, they are apt to be difficult—even impossible—

---

11. On the role of discourses in shaping the character of the negotiations regarding international issues, see Karen T. Litfin, *Ozone Discourses: Science and Politics in Global Environmental Cooperation* (New York: Columbia University Press, 1994).

12. The filing of a reservation or an objection normally exempts a member from any formal legal obligation to comply with decisions made by the majority. As the regimes for endangered species and whaling suggest, however, members may find it expedient for political reasons to conform to the preferences of the majority, even after filing a reservation or an objection. In such instances, regimes can give rise to behavior that has significant consequences, though the issue is not one of compliance in the legal sense.

13. As the cases of the failed Antarctic minerals regime and the failed deep seabed mining provisions set forth in part 11 of the 1982 Convention on the Law of the Sea suggest, however, states often prefer not to accept arrangements that would provide regimes with revenue sources of their own.

for actors to control whether or not they like the effects such cognitive forces produce.[14] In the long run, these somewhat intangible processes can lead to consequences that are at least as far-reaching as those we associate with regulatory arrangements. Nevertheless, the essential point is that compliance and, by extension, enforcement are concerns which are peripheral to some international regimes, even though they are central to others.

Violation Tolerance

Regulatory arrangements at the international level differ greatly in the extent to which they can tolerate violations without becoming ineffective. There is a tendency in many discussions of compliance to start, whether explicitly or implicitly, by positing a standard of perfection and then to see signs of serious trouble on the horizon whenever this standard is not met. But the use of such a standard can easily become an impediment to thinking constructively about problems of compliance in every social setting, including international society. Although they do exist, cases in which it is essential to achieve perfect compliance are rare. More common are regulatory arrangements that can tolerate a certain amount of violation or cheating without endangering the performance of their social functions. On reflection, it seems clear that violation tolerance is a variable that requires consideration on a case-by-case basis. In most social settings, the gap between the ideal and the actual is significant. But the size of this gap and the consequences that flow from it will vary in response to a number of different conditions.

At the international level, there are at least two kinds of situations in which perfect compliance or something approaching it seems important. In some instances, even a single violation will seem intolerable in terms of its direct consequences. Rules proscribing the use of biological weapons, chemical weapons, nuclear weapons, or any other weapons of mass destruction exemplify this class of situations. Quite apart from the spiral of destruction that the use of such weapons may touch off, the harm caused by even a single use will seem unacceptable to many—perhaps most—policymakers and observers. Moreover, there are cases in which seemingly small departures from a standard of perfect compliance are likely to initi-

14. Sheila Jasanoff, "Contingent Knowledge: Implications for Implementation and Compliance," in Edith Brown Weiss and Harold K. Jacobson, eds., *Engaging Countries: Strengthening Compliance with International Environmental Accords* (Cambridge: MIT Press, 1998), 63–87.

ate sequences of actions and reactions that can lead, sometimes quickly, to the collapse of important social institutions. Such concerns surely underlie the thinking of many who worry about escalating violence, trade wars, and tragedies of the commons. A small spark may ignite a large and uncontrollable conflagration, a suggestion that points to the importance of avoiding even minor violations of regulatory arrangements that perform critical social functions.[15]

Even so, evidence from domestic and international cases alike makes it clear that some level of violations is both commonplace and not a cause for great concern in many situations. Minor infractions of rules dealing with nuclear explosions (such as the occurrence of venting in connection with underground tests) have not called into question the effectiveness of the test ban regime.[16] Tanker owner/operators can be expected to incorporate required equipment into the design of new vessels if a few of the most important port states (the United States and several Western European states) insist that they do so, regardless of the behavior of others with respect to the relevant rules.[17] Marginal violations of rules dealing with the harvesting of living resources are not likely to cause severe disruptions, so long as they do not impinge on the calculations of most harvesters. But the consequences here are likely to be sensitive to the population dynamics of the species in question. Even minor violations of rules dealing with the harvesting of species that are slow to regenerate (such as most great whales) cause greater worry than do more substantial violations of rules relating to species that can bounce back in a short period of time (as do herring or capelin).

Thus a good deal of variation exists in what may be termed *break points*— that is, points at which levels of violations begin to become intolerable. A key issue regarding compliance is the need to identify such break points with regard to specific issues and to ensure that the incidence of violations remains within the tolerable zone on a case-by-case basis rather than squandering scarce resources on unnecessary campaigns to achieve perfect compliance in every case. For obvious reasons, it is awkward to state in public that some level of noncompliance is acceptable regarding any given regulatory arrangement. But the fact that this is so is ordinarily well understood by all parties concerned in the context of specific regimes.

---

15. It is important not to exaggerate this concern. Thus, there is no basis for concluding that the 1998 nuclear tests carried out by India and Pakistan will wreck the nuclear nonproliferation regime.

16. Young, *Compliance and Public Authority*.

17. Ronald B. Mitchell, *Intentional Oil Pollution at Sea: Environmental Policy and Treaty Compliance* (Cambridge: MIT Press, 1994).

COMPLIANCE WITHOUT ENFORCEMENT

A second set of observations, which constitute the heart of my argument, raises questions about the link between compliance and enforcement. Without denying the role of enforcement under some circumstances, these observations make it clear that the achievement of compliance is a more complex problem than simple arguments about enforcement make it out to be.

Social Conventions

Some regulatory arrangements generate few, if any, incentives for individual members to cheat, a condition that makes compliance easy and enforcement largely irrelevant. An assumption underlying the concerns of those who worry about enforcement is that individual regime members will invariably have an incentive to cheat or to violate the rules, at least when there is some hope that they can do so without triggering similar behavior on the part of others. But this does not always hold true. The familiar distinction between coordination problems and collaboration problems, articulated with particular clarity in the theory of games but applicable to a wide range of situations, rests squarely on this insight.[18] Thus, the emergence of an equilibrium point—or an outcome that leaves none of the participants with any incentive to change its behavior unilaterally—ensures that there will be no temptation to cheat once the participants succeed in coordinating their behavior around that point. Sometimes, as in the paradigmatic situation known as "assurance," there is a unique equilibrium point yielding satisfactory outcomes. Such cases are uncomplicated and easy to handle. In other situations, such as battle of the sexes, there are two or more equilibria, which yield differential payoffs to the players involved. When this condition occurs, it may be difficult to reach agreement initially on the character of cooperative arrangements. But once they are in place and an equilibrium outcome has emerged, the parties will experience no incentive to cheat or to violate the agreed-on rules. In still other cases, such as prisoner's dilemma, there is an equilibrium outcome, but it yields payoffs for all participants that are inferior to those

---

18. Arthur Stein, "Coordination and Collaboration: Regimes in an Anarchic World," *International Organization* 36 (1982), 299–324; Duncan Snidal, "Coordination versus Prisoner's Dilemma: Implications for International Cooperation and Regimes," *American Political Science Review* 79 (1985), 923–42; and Lisa L. Martin, "Interests, Power, and Multilateralism," *International Organization* 46 (Autumn 1992), 765–92.

associated with at least one other feasible outcome. These situations have understandably become a focus of intense concern. Because the equilibrium outcome is suboptimal for all participants and the optimal outcome is blighted by incentives to cheat, it is difficult to find any simple solution to interactions of this sort.[19]

If we call rules that generate no incentive to cheat *social conventions* and move from the world of game theory to everyday situations, it is easy to demonstrate that regulatory regimes featuring such arrangements are both common and important.[20] Often-cited examples concern conventions related to telling time, driving on roadways, or using language in comprehensible ways.[21] But it is not hard to find examples that are of obvious relevance to international affairs, such as the rules covering numerous aspects of marine shipping and air traffic. The emerging conventions concerning electronic communication and especially the phenomenal growth of the World Wide Web are notable as well. The character of these conventions reflects the preferences of those who took the lead in the development of shipping, air transport, and electronic communications. But the point here is that there is nothing to be gained and a good deal to be lost from unilateral or isolated violations of these social conventions. We can safely assume that no need exists for enforcement to ensure compliance with regulatory arrangements of this type.

How pervasive are these social conventions marked by an absence of incentives to cheat? A large and rapidly growing core of international interactions—especially in the areas of commerce and communications—fit this description.[22] Yet we tend to overlook the significance of these social conventions, and for understandable reasons. It is safe to assume that social conventions will do their job in a reasonably effective manner, whether we pay much attention to them or not. Collaboration problems characterized by incentives to cheat, by contrast, are not only difficult to solve in the first instance but also require continual attention to be sure that individual parties do not succumb to the incentive to violate rules they have accepted at the outset. Perhaps this is a helpful way to think about the distinction between what students of international relations frequently call "high" politics and "low" politics. Such a distinction explains why we de-

19. Robert Axelrod, *The Evolution of Cooperation* (New York: Basic, 1984).

20. David K. Lewis, *Convention: A Philosophical Study* (Cambridge: Harvard University Press, 1969).

21. H. Peyton Young, "The Economics of Convention," *Journal of Economic Perspectives* 10 (Spring 1996), 105–22.

22. This may be one of the reasons why writers such as Henkin regard compliance as the normal state of affairs in international society. See Louis Henkin, *How Nations Behave: Law and Foreign Policy* (New York: Praeger, 1968).

vote so much of our attention to solving problems located in the realm of "high" politics. But it also makes it clear that the realm of "low" politics is both broad and essential to the operation of a society at the international level.[23]

Contingent Punishments versus Rewards

Not all rules are the same with regard to the problems involved in persuading subjects to comply with them.[24] Some rules feature what I call "contingent punishments." They say, in effect, abide by a prohibition or fulfill a requirement or risk being exposed as a violator or even becoming a target of sanctions imposed by some authorized agent. Many familiar rules, including those involving respect for property and the civil rights of individuals, take this form. Other rules spell out requirements that must be met to qualify for "contingent rewards." Many licensing rules are of this type. They say, in essence, we will grant you a license to drive or to practice law or medicine, but only after you have demonstrated to the satisfaction of an authorized agent that you are qualified to engage in the activity in question and, more often than not in today's world, that you have the necessary insurance to meet applicable liability standards. When we start to think about rules, we tend to come up with examples of the first type, and these are undoubtedly the classic cases. But there is much to be said for the proposition that rules featuring contingent rewards are increasingly important in many walks of life.

This observation seems just as applicable to international society as to other social settings. Consider some concrete illustrations. The shift from discharge standards to equipment standards in the case of oil pollution at sea essentially constituted a shift from contingent punishments to contingent rewards.[25] Whereas discharge standards command operators not to engage in behavior that is very difficult to monitor, equipment standards make it clear that owners and operators of tankers cannot gain the approval of classification societies and obtain insurance coverage unless they conform to the rules covering such things as segregated ballast tanks. Similar comments apply to debt restructuring and related macroeconomic re-

---

23. Most writers approach the distinction between "high" and "low" politics in functional terms, treating security issues as the realm of "high" politics and economic issues as the domain of "low" politics. What I am suggesting is an approach that ties this distinction to differences in problem structure rather than to functional attributes.

24. For a helpful distinction between prohibitions, requirements, and permissions, see Elinor Ostrom, *Governing the Commons: The Evolution of Institutions for Collective Action* (Cambridge: Cambridge University Press, 1990).

25. For an extended and sophisticated account of this case, see Mitchell, *Intentional Oil Pollution at Sea.*

quirements in connection with World Bank development loans or International Monetary Fund (IMF) stabilization loans.[26] In both cases, there are substantial rewards to be reaped, but they cannot be had unless the recipient can demonstrate in a reasonably convincing manner that it is fulfilling the requirements of various rules administered by the bank or the IMF. Much the same is true of the world trade regime, under which countries cannot be sure of receiving and retaining most-favored-nation-treatment unless they comply with a variety of rules governing international trade, as spelled out in GATT and the other components of the regime set forth in the 1994 World Trade Organization agreement.[27]

When it comes to eliciting compliance, a fundamental difference exists between rules featuring contingent punishments and those involving contingent rewards. Whereas rules of the first type pose the classic problems of enforcement, those responsible for the administration of rules of the second type can simply threaten to withhold the desired reward as a means of securing compliance. This is particularly true for rules such as those spelling out equipment standards for oil tankers. Unlike catalytic converters on automobiles, which can be disabled by determined violators, there is no going back on the use of segregated ballast tanks once a tanker is constructed to meet such requirements. This observation on rules applies both to the actions of states as the formal members of regimes and to the actions of various nonstate actors (tanker owners, chemical producers, airlines) operating under the jurisdiction of states. In many cases, states will find it attractive to devise rules featuring contingent rewards to minimize the costs of obtaining compliance from actors who operate under their jurisdiction and whose behavior they have agreed to regulate under the terms of some international regime. In fact, as the tanker case illustrates, states may even shift the burden of administering rules onto such other actors as classification societies and insurance companies.

Framing the Rules

Opportunities often exist to frame regulatory rules in ways that make it easier or harder to induce subjects to comply with them. As I have sug-

---

26. See Benjamin J. Cohen, "Phoenix Risen: The Resurrection of Global Finance," *World Politics* 48 (January 1996), 268–96, for a review of more recent thinking about the evolving character of the international financial system that forms the backdrop for World Bank and IMF measures. The essays in Stephan Haggard and Robert Kaufman, eds., *The Politics of Economic Adjustment* (Princeton: Princeton University Press, 1992), offer a range of perspectives on the pressures involved in economic adjustments.

27. The WTO agreement, produced at the conclusion of the Uruguay Round, incorporates the GATT as one of several components of the overall trade regime.

gested, there are differences among regulatory arrangements with respect to the problems they present for those in charge of compliance, an observation that extends well beyond the distinction between contingent punishments and rewards. Again and again, policymakers find that there are alternative ways to cast the rules included in regulatory arrangements and that choices made at this stage have far-reaching implications for the prospect of compliance with rules. Consider some illustrations relating to contemporary international issues. The number of actors involved is often a key variable. Thus, it is easier to regulate the actions of a relative handful of producers of ozone-depleting substances than to regulate the behavior of millions of consumers of products using these chemicals, even though it is the consumption of CFCs and several groups of related chemicals that ultimately causes the depletion of stratospheric ozone.[28] In fact, this case has another feature that makes the control of production a particularly attractive regulatory target. Not only are the producers small in number, but most of them are also integrated corporations that produce numerous other products and do not rely on ozone-depleting substances for a large proportion of their total income stream. Unlike large corporations that are heavily dependent on a single family of products, therefore, these corporations can be expected to find it easier to comply with bans on the production of specific chemicals than to use their considerable influence to resist the regulatory process in various political arenas to the bitter end. Compare this example with the problem of regulating carbon dioxide emissions to prevent climate change, in which it is hard to find an approach that focuses on controlling the behavior of a small number of actors.[29]

Another factor centers on the degree to which rules are framed so as to maximize the transparency of the behavior of those to whom they apply.[30] In cases like harvesting fish in marine ecosystems, discharging oily wastes at sea, or distinguishing between legal and illegal ivory, it is hard to frame rules in such a way as to achieve transparency. The result is the mounting of costly enforcement operations (for instance, the U.S. Coast Guard's fisheries enforcement program), which nonetheless yield disappointing results.[31] Situations of this kind can sometimes be avoided by recasting the

28. Richard E. Benedick, *Ozone Diplomacy: New Directions in Safeguarding the Planet*, rev. ed. (Cambridge: Harvard University Press, 1998).

29. See also James K. Sebenius, "Designing Negotiations toward a New Regime: The Case of Global Warming," *International Security* 15 (Spring 1991), 110–48.

30. Robert O. Keohane, *After Hegemony: Cooperation and Discord in the World Political Economy* (Princeton: Princeton University Press, 1984).

31. Oran R. Young, *Natural Resources and the State: The Political Economy of Resource Management* (Berkeley: University of California Press, 1981), chap. 4.

rules to make it easier to achieve transparency. I have already referred to the shift from discharge standards to equipment standards in the oil pollution example. But worth consideration are approaches that involve the use of gear restrictions, observers, and certificate-of-origin requirements for fisheries regimes, as well as total bans—possibly accompanied by compensation procedures—rather than selective bans in the case of ivory. Under the Convention on International Trade in Endangered Species of Wild Fauna and Flora (CITES), a provision exists for including "like species" in appendix 1 listings, precisely in order to avoid the problems of transparency that result from the need to make difficult distinctions between closely related species.

Yet another issue involving the framing of rules to minimize problems of compliance centers on the idea of pressure points. Collective-action problems frequently involve a chain of behavior that can be cut into at a number of places in the interests of achieving regulatory success. The typical production process, for example, entails the extraction of raw materials, the fabrication of manufactured goods, the shipment of goods to market, and the consumption of goods on the part of purchasers. Regulatory efforts may focus on any or all of the links in this chain, which often opens up opportunities to frame rules in such a way as to maximize the prospect of compliance. Again, the example of equipment standards for tankers is illustrative in that it is virtually impossible to cheat once segregated ballast tanks have been installed. But other cases are also relevant, such as bans on the production of supersonic transports (SSTs) and requirements that pipelines carrying crude oil to markets meet certain easily verifiable construction standards.

Domesticating Compliance

The individual members of international regimes frequently take steps to domesticate the rules of these arrangements, thereby giving international rules the same legal status as ordinary domestic rules. The procedures that states have devised to fulfill obligations they assume under the provisions of international regimes vary considerably not only in nature but also in the consequences they produce. In countries that follow monist precepts, obligations assumed under the terms of international conventions or treaties automatically become the law of the land and take precedence over preexisting laws or regulatory systems. When countries adopt dualist precepts, the situation is less clear-cut, and international obligations may or may not be regarded as trumps in relation to municipal rules.[32] Nonetheless, many states that become members of international regimes proceed to pass implementing legislation that not only gives international obligations the status of domestic law but also assigns responsibility for carrying out these obligations to specific agencies and articulates a set of procedures for them to follow in doing so.[33] In the United States, for example, the Clean Air Act Amendments of 1990 include—among other things—provisions implementing the rules of both the LRTAP regime and the ozone regime;[34] domestic legislation has been passed on a number of occasions as a means of implementing the regulatory provisions added to the trade regime in successive rounds of trade negotiations, as with the Uruguay Round, finally completed in 1994. Even comparatively obscure international regimes exhibit a similar pattern, as in provisions included in the Marine Mammal Protection Act to implement the rules of the Agreement on the Conservation of Polar Bears.

The passage of implementing legislation clearly does not ensure that there will be no concerns regarding a country's compliance with the provisions of regulatory regimes.[35] For example, a responsible agency, such as the U.S. Environmental Protection Agency (EPA) with regard to the ozone regime, will encounter more or less serious problems in its efforts to control the behavior of those whose behavior is at the root of the problem (producers or consumers of CFCs). Situations exist in which the responsible agency is captured by the actors whose behavior it is intended to regulate or populated by officials who are overly sympathetic to the concerns of subjects for one reason or another. In other cases, as with most arms control regimes, the behavior in question is a matter of the actions of public agencies themselves rather than of private actors whose activities are subject to regulation by public agencies. Of course, legislatures often engage in oversight activities intended to ensure that agencies carry out their mandates. In some political systems—the United States today, for instance—there is also the possibility of initiating citizen suits to force public agencies to live up to their mandates. But agencies that are unenthusiastic about their roles have many ways to drag their feet when it comes to implementation of legislative mandates. In some cases, legislatures even

32. Whereas the priority accorded to legally binding international commitments is unambiguous in monist systems, there may be considerable debate in dualist systems about what to do when international commitments conflict with domestic laws. See Urban G. Whitaker, *Politics and Power: A Text in International Law* (New York: Harper and Row, 1964).

33. Kal Raustiala, "The Domestication of International Commitments," Working Paper WP-95-115, International Institute for Applied Systems Analysis, 1995.

34. Gary Bryner, *Blue Skies, Green Politics: The Clean Air Act of 1990* (Washington, D.C.: CQ Press, 1993).

35. Certainly compliance is a major problem with many domestic regulatory arrangements that have nothing to do with international obligations.

undermine their own directives by failing to appropriate the resources that public agencies would need to do a serious job of carrying out legislative mandates.[36]

These are serious concerns; they often lead to mediocre or poor performance in connection with regulatory arrangements. But the point I wish to stress is that no significant distinction exists between the rules of international regimes and the rules of purely domestic regimes once the international rules have been domesticated through the passage of implementing legislation. As I have already said, it is more difficult to achieve compliance with some regulatory arrangements than with others, and there is sometimes scope for framing the rules in ways that make compliance more or less easy to achieve. A particularly complex class of cases in this regard are those involving resources, such as migratory species, that regularly cross national borders, thus making it necessary for responsible public agencies in two or more countries to join forces to fulfill the requirements of regulatory regimes. The Lusaka Agreement, under which game managers in a number of southern African countries have joined forces to administer the rules of CITES, is an especially interesting example here.[37] But the central point remains: once international rules are domesticated, the distinction between international regimes and domestic or municipal regimes with respect to compliance washes out.

Building Domestic Constituencies

Success in the pursuit of compliance generally depends on building and sustaining constituencies within members that stand to benefit from the achievement of compliance. It is a mistake to think that regulatory arrangements, whether international or domestic, exist in a vacuum and that subjects comply with their requirements as a matter of course in the absence of a supportive context. We cannot do without systems of well-defined rules. They provide authoritative focal points around which the efforts of a variety of constituencies can coalesce. Yet rules that do not give rise to associated communities—usually including both public and private participants—have little chance of becoming vibrant social practices

36. For a comparative study of these matters, see David Vogel and Timothy Kessler, "How Compliance Happens and Doesn't Happen Domestically," in Weiss and Jacobson, *Engaging Countries*, 19–37.

37. Farhana Yamin and Annabella Gualdoni, "A Case Study of a Regional Approach to Compliance with CITES in Southern Africa," in James Cameron, Jacob Werksman, and Peter Roderick, eds., *Improving Compliance with International Environmental Law* (London: Earthscan Publications, 1996), 185–203.

that make a difference in the world.[38] This point underlies the growing realization that successful practices usually feature both top-down and bottom-up components or, to put it another way, that links between political systems (the state in domestic settings) and civil society constitute a key to the success of regulatory arrangements.[39]

With respect to international regimes, two distinct comments about the role of supportive constituencies are in order. Regimes ordinarily become the property of specific public agencies within governments rather than of the government as a whole. Consider the EPA in the case of air pollution agreements, the National Marine Fisheries Service with regard to agreements dealing with fish and whales, and the Department of Commerce with respect to trade agreements. In successful situations, the agency in question acquires a sense of ownership with regard to the regimes it administers and is willing both to fight other agencies promoting actions incompatible with these regimes and to work hard to obtain appropriations from the legislature needed to carry out their mandates. Typically, the agency comes to regard the importance of the regimes it administers as an article of faith that does not require reexamination on a day-to-day basis. Such advocacy may go a long way toward ensuring that the behavior of both public and private actors conforms to the requirements of international regimes. Yet several conditions may limit the effectiveness of these processes in solving compliance problems. Formally responsible agencies may never bond with regimes assigned to their care. Relevant agencies may be unusually weak when it comes to defending their interests at the bureaucratic level or at the legislative level. What is more, agencies may come under the influence of nongovernmental forces that are hostile to the goals of specific regulatory arrangements.

As a result, the existence of an outside constituency that can serve as a watchdog and as a pressure group on behalf of a regime often emerges as a critical determinant of levels of compliance with regulatory arrangements. Such groups—increasingly described as "communities"—may include public officials among their members. But they ordinarily emerge as nongovernmental organizations or coalitions of such organizations that define their goals in terms of the larger objectives of the regimes with which they are associated. Recent work has revealed the role of such an NGO community in connection with the North American Great Lakes wa-

---

38. Lee Botts and Paul Muldoon, *The Great Lakes Water Quality Agreement: Its Past Successes and Uncertain Future* (Hanover, N.H.: Institute on International Environmental Governance, 1996).

39. Oran R. Young, ed., *Global Governance: Drawing Insights from the Environmental Experience* (Cambridge: MIT Press, 1997).

ter quality regime,[40] and there is every reason to expect that detailed research on other successful regimes will turn up similar findings. Some analysts, impressed with the role of scientists or of specialists in knowledge more generally, have described these groups as "epistemic communities."[41] But it seems increasingly evident that epistemic communities constitute a special case of a larger class of groups that play important roles in connection with the operation of social practices. Most important, such groups, whatever the glue that holds them together and whether or not their existence is acknowledged in the international agreements that establish regimes, play critical roles in building and energizing constituencies which make it impossible to forget about regimes or to shunt them aside through attitudes of benign neglect.

Soft Compliance Paths

Many problems of compliance are better treated as matters of management than as matters of enforcement. Mainstream thinking about compliance in international society has generally approached noncompliance as a product of willful violations. That is, those subject to the rules in question are regarded as competent, clear-thinking actors who for one reason or another prefer to violate the rules than to behave in conformity with them. Enforcement in the sense of threatening or imposing sanctions, it is assumed, is the only way to deal with the "wrongful" behavior of these actors. Yet this picture of the noncompliant actor has been subjected to relatively severe criticism on the part of those who believe that many cases of noncompliance are better understood and dealt with as forms of "good faith" noncompliance—that is, behavior that does not constitute willful violations of rules that are clear-cut and well understood by all members of the relevant subject group.[42] The result is a growing interest in various soft compliance paths that seek to increase levels of compliance through a variety of initiatives designed to help those who are acting in good faith and to strengthen the hand of those desiring to comply with international

40. For a particularly compelling account of the Great Lakes case, see Botts and Muldoon, *Great Lakes Water Quality Agreement.*

41. Peter M. Haas, ed., *Knowledge, Power, and International Policy Coordination* (Columbia: University of South Carolina Press, 1997).

42. The concepts of "good faith" noncompliance and "wrongfulness" are developed in Ronald B. Mitchell, "Compliance Theory: An Overview," in Cameron, Werksman, and Roderick, *Improving Compliance*, 3–28, and Jacob Werksman, "Designing a Compliance System for the UN Framework Convention on Climate Change," in Cameron, Werksman, and Roderick, *Improving Compliance*, 85–112.

rules in their interactions with other factions in various political arenas.[43] A number of initiatives at the international level during the 1990s have grown out of this way of thinking about compliance.

One strand of this approach to compliance emphasizes matters of capacity or the possession of the resources needed to comply with international rules without sacrificing other high-priority values. In such cases as the efforts of developing countries to fulfill their obligations with respect to the protection of the stratospheric ozone layer or biological diversity, this problem centers on the availability of financial resources, appropriate technologies, and technical knowledge. The Multilateral Fund created under the 1990 London Amendments to the Montreal Protocol and the Global Environment Facility (GEF) created to help developing countries cope with obligations regarding climate change and biological diversity are examples of efforts to build capacity for compliance.[44] So also are various arrangements calling for technology transfers and at least some of the ideas now lumped together under the heading of "joint implementation." Originally considered with the circumstances of the developing countries in mind, problems of capacity in one form or another are widespread with regard to the issue of complying with international rules. For example, it is now generally accepted that the countries of Eastern Europe and the former Soviet Union cannot be expected to comply with such rules in the absence of substantial assistance.

Another strand of this management approach to compliance stresses the extent to which troublesome behavior is a product of simple misinterpretations of (sometimes ambiguous) rules or understandable disagreements among participants regarding the meaning of rules articulated in international agreements. Such matters resemble familiar problems associated with the pursuit of compliance at the domestic level, and the appropriate response according to those who espouse soft compliance paths should be much the same as well. A number of contemporary developments reflect this way of thinking.[45] The dispute panels organized on a case-by-case basis to deal with claims regarding violations of the provisions of the GATT and other elements of the international trade regime constitute one straightforward example. A somewhat more innovative response to this perspective on compliance is reflected in the noncompli-

43. The most comprehensive statement of this perspective is to be found in Chayes and Chayes, *New Sovereignty*.

44. Andrew Jordan and Jacob Werksman, "Financing Global Environmental Protection," in Cameron, Werksman, and Roderick, *Improving Compliance*, 247–55.

45. Philippe Sands, "Compliance with International Environmental Obligations: Existing International Legal Arrangements," in Cameron, Werksman, and Roderick, *Improving Compliance*, 48–81.

ance procedures (NCPs) which have come into existence in the ozone regime and which are beginning to emerge in conjunction with the climate regime.[46] In contrast with conventional dispute settlement procedures (DSPs), which become relevant when one actor formally charges another with noncompliance, NCPs are intended to sort out understandable disagreements regarding matters of compliance that do not cast one party in the role of plaintiff and another in the role of defendant. On the assumption that parties are behaving in good faith in the sense that they are not willful cheaters or violators, procedures of this sort are designed to work toward mutually acceptable interpretations of rules that are acknowledged to be ambiguous as stated.

The management approach and the enforcement approach to compliance should not be viewed as requiring an either/or choice. It is perfectly possible to argue that soft compliance paths have great potential with regard to regulatory regimes without denying that there is a hard core of noncompliance that will not yield to such treatment.[47] What is more, it is important to bear in mind that compliance is a continuous variable rather than one that is essentially dichotomous. There are many situations in which improving compliance is a worthy achievement even when the outcome does not reach the level of perfect compliance.[48] But the essential message of this line of thought with regard to the issue addressed in this chapter is clear: to the extent that compliance with international rules can be improved through the deployment of various managerial procedures, it would be wrong to see the absence or weakness of enforcement mechanisms in international society as a fatal flaw.

Rule-Following Behavior

Even in the context of international society, it is a mistake to treat actors exclusively as self-interested utility maximizers responding only to calculations of costs and benefits in contrast to other sources of behavior that have different implications for compliance. From a methodological point of view, the idea of starting from the assumption that the actors in international society are unitary and self-interested utility maximizers makes perfectly good sense. Models of interactive behavior based on this assump-

---

46. Werksman, "Designing a Compliance System," and David G. Victor, "The Early Operation and Effectiveness of the Montreal Protocol's Non-Compliance Procedure," Executive Report ER-96-2, International Institute for Applied Systems Analysis, 1996.

47. See Downs, Rocke, and Barsoom, "Good News about Compliance," for a helpful corrective to the views of those who have developed unrealistic expectations regarding the efficacy of the management approach.

48. Young, *Compliance and Public Authority*.

tion are comparatively tractable in analytic terms, and they have contributed substantially to our understanding of a number of international phenomena. Yet it is apparent that such models abstract away a variety of sources of behavior which are pervasive in international society and which have important implications for compliance. The problem lies with both components of the utility-maximizing assumption. International actors frequently engage in nonutilitarian behavior, and they often exhibit internal processes that cannot be captured in models which assume the presence of unitary actors. Once the assumption of unitary utility maximizers is relaxed, it becomes possible to focus on a variety of other behavioral mechanisms that have important implications for the achievement of compliance at the international level.

Why, then, do subjects of international regimes follow the rules in many cases without bothering to go through some sort of utilitarian calculation regarding their actions? Just as socialization is a source of compliance among individuals, routinization can go a long way toward explaining compliance among public agencies and corporate entities. In effect, the rules become embedded in standard operating procedures that are seldom questioned by those who are responsible for day-to-day operations.[49] Related to this is the idea of conditioning, which produces what some have termed a "habit of obedience" among individuals and which can generate similar responses among subjects of international regimes.[50] In effect, actors often obey or comply with regulatory rules without giving the matter any conscious thought; levels of compliance are high because it does not occur to relevant actors to think about doing anything else on a day-to-day basis. Beyond this, officials responsible for the actions of public agencies or corporate entities are by no means immune from the force of norms or the sense that authoritative rules ought to be complied with because they are legitimate and because compliance with legitimate rules is the right and proper thing to do.[51] Moreover, the task of complying with particular rules is often assigned to specific agencies within governments (such as the EPA or the Arms Control and Disarmament Agency within the U.S. government) or well-defined units within corporations (such as the Environment and Safety Departments of many large corporations), and these units regularly identify with the rules and come to feel that it is their mission to fight for compliance within the larger decision-making systems of

49. Roger Fisher, *Improving Compliance with International Law* (Charlottesville: University Press of Virginia, 1981).
50. H. L. A. Hart, *The Concept of Law* (Oxford: Oxford University Press, 1961).
51. Thomas M. Franck, *The Power of Legitimacy among Nations* (Oxford: Oxford University Press, 1990).

which they are a part. These units will face opposition from time to time, and they may well lose the battle in specific cases. Still, the existence of a unit that becomes an advocate for compliance within the larger system can tip the balance toward compliant behavior under some conditions.

This is only a quick and superficial sketch of sources of rule-following behavior not captured in models that begin by assuming unitary utility maximizers.[52] Yet it will suffice to point up that analyses of compliance which do not go beyond such models leave much to be desired. What is more, these observations tend to heighten interest in the management approach to compliance in contrast to the enforcement approach. They suggest, for example, that it is often helpful to assign the task of compliance to a designated unit within a larger organization and then to devise a system of standard operating procedures that will lend a kind of automaticity to compliant behavior. They suggest as well that there is a place for normative arguments in this realm and that some policymakers will respond to arguments framed in terms of "shoulds" and "oughts" in contrast to arguments about the benefits and costs associated with particular options. The more recent literature on the role of ideas in international society only reinforces this assertion that utilitarian calculations linked to well-defined interests cannot explain all the variance in international behavior.[53] I do not mean to suggest that calculations of costs and benefits relating to well-defined interests are marginal or unimportant at the international level. Rather, the point is that the opposite view or the assumption that utilitarian calculations are all that count runs the risk of missing a number of factors that have substantial implications for the pursuit of compliance in international society.

ENFORCEMENT WITHOUT GOVERNMENT

Even when enforcement does emerge as a critical determinant of regime effectiveness, it is not always necessary to create a government to enforce the regulatory provisions of international institutions. My final observation involves options relating to the deployment of sanctions in a society that has no *government*.

---

52. For more general discussions of these matters, see Malcolm Rutherford, *Institutions in Economics: The Old and the New Institutionalism* (Cambridge: Cambridge University Press, 1994), and W. Richard Scott, *Institutions and Organizations* (Thousand Oaks, Calif.: Sage, 1995).

53. Judith Goldstein and Robert O. Keohane, eds., *Ideas and Foreign Policy: Beliefs, Institutions, and Political Change* (Ithaca: Cornell University Press, 1993).

Decentralized Sanctions

Whatever the significance of nonutilitarian sources of compliance and the role of soft compliance paths, it is naïve to think that enforcement will never be needed to achieve adequate levels of compliance with the rules of international regimes. Thus the question is, Does any substitute exist for the creation of a government to devise enforcement mechanisms and to administer the sanctions that constitute the essential tools of such mechanisms? The authoritativeness we usually associate with the actions of governments is undoubtedly advantageous in this connection. The use of sanctions by other entities inevitably raises questions about the extent to which they are simply exploiting difficult situations as a means of promoting their own interests and therefore about the legitimacy of more decentralized processes of enforcement. Nonetheless, reality is less clear-cut than this observation suggests. In many social settings, governments are little more than instruments of entrenched ruling elites, and some agents in more decentralized settings are motivated by a desire to promote or protect some universal value, such as order or justice. To make progress in thinking about decentralized sanctions in international society, it is helpful to consider the activities of three different types of agents: international organizations, states, and nongovernmental organizations.

International organizations are notoriously weak when it comes to using sanctions to promote compliance with international rules. In many cases, they lack the authority to make and execute decisions about the use of sanctions. Frequently, they do not have the capacity to do so, even when authority is not a problem. Yet some organizations created to administer international regimes are able to take actions that regime members cannot ignore in making decisions about compliance with the requirements of regulatory arrangements. Sometimes this involves nothing more than exposing noncompliant behavior and ensuring that it does not go unnoticed by others, a role that has been played by the GATT panels established to deal with issues arising under article 20 of the agreement.[54] In other cases, such as the operation of the IMF or the Multilateral Fund of the ozone regime, international organizations can withhold or cut off funding as a means of bringing pressure to bear on violators. Obviously, these procedures are limited by comparison with the actions of governments. But they are not trivial.

---

54. For a broader account of enforcement in relation to the GATT, see Robert E. Hudec, *Enforcing International Trade Law: The Evolution of the Modern GATT Legal System* (Salem, N.H.: Butterworth, 1993).

Given the limited capacity of international organizations to deploy sanctions, it is not surprising that member states sometimes take matters into their own hands with regard to the use of sanctions to improve compliance with international rules. This has occurred with the approval of a regime's governing body—the Lusaka Agreement, in which wildlife law enforcement officials from a number of southern African countries have joined forces in an effort to improve compliance with the rules of CITES, appears to be an example. In other instances, individual members act unilaterally and without formal approval to exert pressure on actual or potential violators. The use of the Pelly and Packwood Amendments on the part of the United States to bring pressure to bear on a number of states to abide by decisions of the International Whaling Commission constitutes a well-known example of this type of action.[55] Such unilateral efforts have a number of drawbacks. They inevitably raise questions of legitimacy; they often go beyond what is required by the rules themselves; and they sometimes fail even when the disparity in terms of power in the material sense is great (as with U.S. efforts to influence Iceland's actions regarding whaling). Still, such unilateral measures would be completely intolerable if they could not be justified more or less persuasively as actions taken in the interests of enforcing legitimate international rules. Even a hegemon, such as the United States in the case of whaling, cannot get away with unilateral enforcement measures unless they can be portrayed in some reasonably convincing manner as actions required to deter or punish violations of authoritative rules.

Nongovernmental organizations have also begun to take actions intended to sanction violators of international rules. Such measures range from physical actions, such as the sinking of Icelandic whaling boats, to commercial actions, like organizing boycotts of products coming from offenders, and efforts to shame violators by exposing their behavior and publicizing it in influential circles. There are some obvious complications associated with the efforts of NGOs to enforce international rules. They generally lack the authority to intervene legitimately in the affairs of regime members in this way; they are under no obligation to differentiate between actions required to comply with rules in force and actions required to promote their own goals; and they are not always above initiating campaigns that are better understood as means of raising funds to support their own operations than as actions designed to enforce authoritative

55. Gregory Rose and George Paleokrassis, "Compliance with International Environmental Obligations: A Case Study of the International Whaling Commission," in Cameron, Werksman, and Roderick, *Improving Compliance*, 147–75.

rules in a decentralized social system. Under the circumstances, the growing role of NGOs as players interested in compliance with international rules is by no means an unmixed blessing. But this should not lead us to ignore a phenomenon which is already important and which can be expected to become increasingly significant in the years to come.[56]

THE PROBLEM OF AUTHORITATIVE INTERPRETATION

These observations about compliance in international society should suffice to raise serious questions about the views regarding enforcement I outlined at the beginning of this chapter. Yet in one area, often neglected by skeptics and believers alike, international society is undeniably at a disadvantage in comparison with the political and legal systems that prevail in most domestic societies—the need for recognized procedures that can be counted on to provide a dependable stream of authoritative interpretations concerning the meaning of regulatory rules as applied to specific situations. Societies differ with regard to the means they devise to handle this need. Some, such as the United States, rely heavily on the courts to perform this task and set great store by the development of common law as a means of fleshing out the meaning of generic or loosely worded rules. Others, such as the United Kingdom, turn to administrative procedures, which sometimes take on a quasi-judicial character, to give operational meaning to general rules. Still others, like Canada and Japan, have developed processes that feature negotiations between public agencies and subjects to arrive at mutually acceptable interpretations of the rules. Of course, most societies make use of a combination of these processes at the same time. But no system can escape the need to provide a dependable stream of authoritative interpretations without becoming ineffectual and ultimately irrelevant.

There are at least three reasons for this need, which are just as applicable to international society as to any other society. At best, rules are framed in general terms, whereas the situations to which they apply are specific and contextually distinctive. This is why agencies charged with administering rules typically find it necessary to promulgate voluminous regulations to spell out the meaning of the rules under a variety of circumstances, a process that is a predictable focus of contention among those whose interests are likely to be affected by the content of regulatory ar-

56. James Cameron, "Compliance, Citizens, and NGOs," in Cameron, Werksman, and Roderick, *Improving Compliance*, 29–42.

rangements. Additionally, rules are normally products of institutional bargaining—whether it occurs in a legislature in domestic society or in a legislative conference in international society—a process that ensures that they are often framed in ambiguous terms owing to sloppy drafting or, more often, the pressure to devise formulas that are acceptable to a variety of parties at the same time. This is especially true in settings, such as international society, in which the frequent use of consensus rules makes it necessary to find formulas that are acceptable to all the major players or factions engaged in the process of regime formation.[57] Beyond this, circumstances change, often rapidly, whereas rules are articulated at particular points in time. As a result, there is a constant need to interpret rules in the light of circumstances that their framers did not consider and frequently could not have foreseen. This problem is a universal one, but it is particularly apparent in areas, such as environmental protection, where biophysical systems—or our understanding of the dynamics of these systems—are changing rapidly.

The problem to be solved in this context is that international society is poorly endowed with recognized and widely accepted procedures for meeting the demand for authoritative interpretations on an ongoing basis. Whereas courts are major sources of such interpretations in many domestic systems, international courts (with the partial exception of the European Court of Justice) have not succeeded in acquiring the authority or the capacity to play this role effectively. There is an understandable tendency to avoid creating new administrative entities at the international level, largely as a result of antipathy to the real or alleged behavior of international bureaucracies. Yet this limits the prospects for devising administrative mechanisms capable of articulating authoritative interpretations in international society. The parties to international negotiations often focus so intensively on what are essentially distributive concerns that any idea of arriving at authoritative interpretations through some process of negotiation is one that has only limited application. The result is a profound challenge for those concerned with promoting compliance with international rules. In every social setting, compliance is at least as much a matter of resolving legitimate differences regarding meanings assigned to rules in connection with specific situations as it is a matter of identifying violators and bringing pressure to bear on them to alter their behavior. But the decentralized character of international society limits sharply the availability of some of the standard procedures that domestic societies employ to come to terms with such issues.

57. Young, *International Governance.*

Under the circumstances, it is of great interest to observe the evolution of a number of procedures aimed at filling this gap at the international level.[58] Some of these procedures focus on improving understanding of the underlying problems to which rules apply in the interests of eliminating or reducing differences about the applicability of rules that arise from factual disagreements. A striking example is the role of the Intergovernmental Panel on Climate Change (IPCC), a mechanism whose purpose is to provide common ground regarding the processes involved in the greenhouse effect and the probable trajectory of climate change on a decadal scale. Other procedures are designed to clarify and flesh out the terms of international agreements in cases where the drafting process left major ambiguities or changing circumstances require reinterpretations of provisions accepted at any earlier stage. The GATT/WTO panels I referred to earlier in this chapter provide a means for applying general rules to the circumstances prevailing in specific situations. When it comes to supplementing existing arrangements, the case of climate change is again instructive. Thus, the Ad Hoc Group on the Berlin Mandate (AGBM), established by the conference of the parties to the Climate Convention at its first meeting in 1995, took on the task of interpreting and expanding the commitments of the developed countries in preparation for the adoption of a protocol to the convention at the third meeting of the COP which convened in Kyoto, Japan, in December 1997.

These are significant developments. But three other procedures seem even more promising as institutionalized means of overcoming the deficit in authoritative interpretation that plagues international regimes. In a number of cases, the COP, meeting on a regular basis, has acquired the authority to interpret and even to extend regulatory arrangements without triggering a requirement for ratification on the part of individual members for decisions to take effect. Several of the most significant developments in the ozone regime, for instance, have been hammered out at COP meetings and have come onstream in the absence of a time-consuming ratification process.[59] Equally important is the growth of NCPs intended to resolve legitimate differences between parties regarding the regulatory provisions of rules rather than to track down and punish wrongdoers. Exemplified by the procedures already in place in connection with the ozone regime and the emerging procedures associated with the climate regime,

58. Fisher, *Improving Compliance*, addresses these issues under the heading of "second-order compliance." In my own work, I have found it more helpful to draw a distinction between compliance as such and authoritative interpretation.

59. Edward A. Parson and Owen Greene, "The Complex Chemistry of the International Ozone Agreements," *Environment* 37 (March 1995), 16–20 and 35–43.

such arrangements hold out the prospect of introducing an institutionalized method for arriving at authoritative interpretations of ambiguous
provisions of international regimes.[60] Yet another development of interest
in this connection centers on the growth of systems for implementation
review (SIRs).[61] Although not designed explicitly with the problem of authoritative interpretation in mind, SIRs frequently lead to the identification of ambiguities in the provisions of regimes and can stimulate processes
of clarification that do not require adversarial proceedings. Admittedly,
these procedures are modest relative to the judicial and administrative
practices that play a role in providing authoritative interpretations in most
domestic societies. But they may prove to be well adapted to the pursuit of
"governance without government" in the decentralized setting of international society.

These are essentially top-down procedures. Yet significant as they are,
bottom-up procedures have also grown, emerging as influential elements
in the social practices that surround most successful regimes. Some of
these procedures are largely scientific in nature, as with the Scientific
Committee on Antarctic Research (SCAR) with regard to the south polar
region, and EMEP in connection with European transboundary air pollution. But as the informal community that has grown up around the Great
Lakes water quality regime makes clear, these bottom-up procedures
often extend far beyond the provision of scientific assessments and ad-
vice. In effect, they provide arenas in which alternative interpretations
of regime rules can be debated off the record and sources of pressure on
officials to take appropriate steps to resolve disagreements about the operational content of regime rules in specific situations. Regulatory arrangements that exist in a social vacuum have little chance of operating
effectively on an ongoing basis. More often than not, successful regimes
trigger the development of active communities made up of groups which
have strong interests in the operation of the relevant regulatory arrangements and which are willing to invest time and energy in making them
work. These communities perform a number of functions that are important to the operation of regimes, one of the most significant of which involves the organization of focused debates about the interpretation of regime rules and their application to specific situations.

The development of procedures to provide the authoritative interpretations needed to resolve ambiguities and adapt regulatory arrangements

60. Victor, "Montreal Protocol's Non-Compliance Procedure."
61. SIRs are discussed at length in David G. Victor, Kal Raustiala, and Eugene B. Skolnikoff,
eds., *The Implementation and Effectiveness of International Environmental Commitments* (Cambridge:
MIT Press, 1998).

to changing circumstances is a critical determinant of the success of systems of rules in every social setting. Given the decentralized character of international society, many of the familiar procedures for arriving at authoritative interpretations in domestic settings are unworkable at this level. This problem, more than that of enforcement in its ordinary sense, may well constitute the greatest challenge facing those seeking to maximize the effectiveness of international regimes. It is intriguing to observe the emergence, on a basis that is often ad hoc or case specific, of a range of procedures to meet this need in international society. The collection of procedures that have arisen is diverse. For the most part, however, they seek to deal with "behaviour that could be categorized as 'good faith noncompliance' and 'bargaining noncompliance'" in contrast to "wrongful breach[es] amounting to . . . ascertainable violation[s] of binding treaty obligation[s]."[62] Such procedures are not sufficient to track down willful violators and enforce the provisions of regimes with regard to those who know perfectly well what the rules require but are determined to cheat as a means of promoting their own interests. But they do hold out hope for coming to terms with the much larger class of situations in which there are legitimate disagreements about what the rules require of individual regime members or their subjects or uncertainties about the adaptation of regime rules to changing circumstances.

COMING BACK NOW to the concern about enforcement outlined at the beginning of this chapter, what can we conclude? Nothing I have said suggests that enforcement is irrelevant in thinking about the effectiveness of international regimes or that the enforcement mechanisms in operation in international society today are adequate to the tasks with which they are confronted. Yet the preceding analysis raises major questions about each of the propositions associated with the concern. The problem of compliance is relevant primarily to regulatory regimes as opposed to procedural, programmatic, and generative regimes. Even in the context of regulatory regimes, social conventions do not generate incentives to cheat, and violation tolerance is an important variable. Although enforcement in the sense of the threat or imposition of sanctions is by no means irrelevant as a basis of compliance, the links between actor behavior and compliance in international society are far more complex than this simple proposition would lead one to believe. This complexity results from a combination of conditions involving such things as the framing of rules, the domestication of compliance, the development of a management approach to com-

---

62. Werksman, "Designing a Compliance System," 101.

pliance, and nonutilitarian sources of actor behavior. These observations make the wave of research and writing on compliance which has emerged during the 1990s understandable. Notably, this work reflects an increasingly sophisticated appreciation of the complexity of compliance as a social phenomenon rather than a slavish insistence on the necessity of enforcement as the basis of compliance.

This account also raises questions about the need for a duly constituted public authority or a government to operate enforcement mechanisms or, more broadly, to cultivate compliant behavior. One of the more striking developments in international society is the growth of management approaches to compliance and the emergence of noncompliance procedures that can be operated on a decentralized basis. Some of the resultant procedures seem distinctly promising; none is afflicted by the negative externalities that commonly accompany the efforts of governments to enforce compliance in domestic settings. Still, the problem of producing authoritative interpretations to resolve ambiguities and to adapt rules to changing circumstances looms large at the international level. A number of the familiar judicial and administrative procedures that have grown up to handle this problem in domestic settings seem marginal or altogether unworkable at the international level. As a result, it is intriguing to observe some of the new, more decentralized procedures that are now arising to solve the problem of authoritative interpretation in connection with specific international regimes. While the magnitude of the challenge that remains is tremendous, even the limited repertoire of arrangements that are in operation at this juncture should suffice to avoid any counsel of despair in thinking about the prospects for achieving compliance in international society.

CHAPTER 5

The Effectiveness of International Regimes

A striking feature of the period from 1970 onward is the occurrence of a sharp rise both in public concern about large-scale environmental problems and in the creation of international regimes as a means of addressing these problems.[1] Many see in this development a hopeful sign regarding the prospects for solving numerous problems ranging from unsustainable uses of shared natural resources (such as boundary waters or straddling stocks of fish) through long-range transboundary pollution problems (acid rain) to the challenges associated with global environmental changes (the loss of biological diversity or the alteration of the Earth's climate system, for instance). How realistic is this hope? To ask this question is to launch an inquiry into the effectiveness of the institutional arrangements or regimes that have been established since the early 1970s to deal with a wide range of problems arising at the international level.

In this chapter, I provide a midterm report on the enterprise. In the process, I seek to (1) assess what we currently know about the effectiveness of environmental regimes, (2) determine what more we need to know about these arrangements to improve their performance in the future, (3) evaluate the relative merits of several research strategies available to those desiring to obtain this knowledge, and (4) lay the groundwork for a more general account of regime effectiveness. The picture that emerges from this survey is a mixed one. Much is already known about the determinants of regime effectiveness. Yet adding substantially to the current under-

---

1. See Oran R. Young, ed., *Global Governance: Drawing Insights from the Environmental Experience* (Cambridge: MIT Press, 1997).

standing of these matters presents major analytic challenges that will constitute cutting-edge concerns for regime theory throughout the foreseeable future.

DEFINING EFFECTIVENESS

At first glance, the meaning of *effectiveness* with regard to international environmental regimes seems intuitively obvious.[2] Regimes arise to solve problems. Accordingly, effectiveness is a measure of the extent to which these arrangements succeed in solving the problems that lead to their formation. Appealing as this approach to effectiveness is, however, it has severe limitations as a basis for analyzing the performance of international regimes. As numerous observers have pointed out, participants can and often do develop widely divergent perceptions of the nature or character of the problem to be solved, and regimes frequently come into existence in the absence of consensus in the realm of problem definition. The danger of ending up with spurious correlations is a constant threat to efforts to understand regime effectiveness construed as problem solving. The disappearance or amelioration of a problem following the formation of a regime does not constitute proof that the regime was a causal agent in the process. Conversely, the failure of a problem to disappear following regime creation does not justify the conclusion that the regime had no effect at all; the problem could well have grown more severe in the absence of the regime. More generally, the operation of a regime is typically only one of a suite of factors—both intended and unintended—that play some role in determining the course of international environmental problems. More often than not, the real challenge is not a matter of determining whether a regime matters at all but rather of finding ways to determine the proportion of the variance in the realm of problem solving that can be attributed persuasively to the operation of the regime. Yet given the limited size of the universe of cases and the amount of variance within this universe, finding ways to demonstrate the causal significance of international regimes as problem solvers is a tall order.

Faced with this somewhat daunting prospect, many analysts have sought to come up with alternative ways to think about the effectiveness of inter-

2. For an extended account of these conceptual matters, see Oran R. Young, *International Governance: Protecting the Environment in a Stateless Society* (Ithaca: Cornell University Press, 1994), chap. 6. This account draws distinctions between (1) effectiveness as problem solving, (2) effectiveness as goal attainment, (3) behavioral effectiveness, (4) process effectiveness, (5) constitutive effectiveness, and (6) evaluative effectiveness.

national regimes. An approach that is common among students of both law and politics directs attention to issues of implementation and compliance rather than to problem solving.[3] Do regime members take vigorous steps to implement regime rules or commitments within their domestic jurisdictions? Do states or subjects operating under their auspices comply with regime rules or live up to the commitments they make in creating regimes? This alternative has the virtue of being easier to operationalize; it is relatively easy to follow efforts to implement regulatory provisions or to get programmatic activities under way. But it leaves much to be desired as a way to think about effectiveness. Above all, there is no direct relationship between implementation and compliance, on the one hand, and solving pressing problems, on the other. Regimes can score high in terms of implementation or compliance without solving the problems that led to their creation. Conversely, regimes can have far-reaching consequences, even when their performance seems mediocre with respect to conventional measures of implementation and compliance, partly because some regimes are able to tolerate fairly extensive violations without becoming ineffectual, and partly because regimes may lead to substantial alterations in the behavior of key actors which have little or nothing to do with conforming to specific rules or commitments.

Given these difficulties, a growing community of analysts have directed their attention toward behavioral consequences as a measure of the effectiveness of regimes. International regimes are not actors in their own right, though they may give rise to organizations whose function is to administer their provisions.[4] Under the circumstances, the question to be answered is whether regimes or governance systems play a role in shaping or guiding the behavior of those who are actors, including both the states that are ordinarily the formal members of international regimes and the government agencies, corporations, interest groups, and even individuals whose behavior is targeted by a regime's provisions. We want to know, in other words, not only whether the United States fulfills its obligations under

3. See Abram Chayes and Antonia Handler Chayes, *The New Sovereignty: Compliance with International Regulatory Agreements* (Cambridge: Harvard University Press, 1995); Edith Brown Weiss and Harold K. Jacobson, eds., *Engaging Countries: Strengthening Compliance with International Environmental Accords* (Cambridge: MIT Press, 1998); David G. Victor, Kal Raustiala, and Eugene B. Skolnikoff, eds., *The Implementation and Effectiveness of International Environmental Commitments* (Cambridge: MIT Press, 1998); and Kenneth Hanf and Arild Underdal, eds., *The Domestic Bases of International Environmental Agreements* (Aldershot: Ashgate, forthcoming).

4. A simple way to understand this point is to say that organizations are actors, while institutions are the rules of the game that circumscribe their activities. See also Helmut Breitmeier, "International Organizations and the Creation of Environmental Regimes," and M. J. Peterson, "International Organizations and the Implementation of Environmental Regimes," both in Young, *Global Governance*, 87–114 and 115–51, respectively.

the terms of the regime dealing with ozone-depleting substances but also whether those producers and consumers of such substances which operate under the jurisdiction of the United States alter their behavior in response to the creation and operation of the regime.[5] Of course, it is important to observe that the behavioral effects of regimes include deterrence in the sense that actors are induced to refrain from taking steps they would have taken in the absence of the regime as well as compellence in the sense that the presence of the regime induces actors to take steps they would otherwise have failed to take.[6] As we shall see, moreover, both theoretical and methodological challenges are associated with efforts to demonstrate the causal connections between the operation of a regime and the behavior of affected actors. Much depends, for instance, on the extent to which actors are properly treated as unitary utility maximizers or as more complex entities that respond to a variety of nonutilitarian stimuli.[7] And regimes are almost always only one of a number of forces that operate—simultaneously or sequentially—to shape the behavior of relevant actors, a fact that makes it necessary to devise ways to sort out the relative impact of regimes from the impacts of other sources of behavior. Nonetheless, the focus on behavior lends empirical content to the study of regime effectiveness, and it has the added virtue of preserving a clear link to the underlying concern for problem solving.

These approaches to effectiveness largely map onto the distinctions students of public policy commonly draw among outputs, outcomes, and impacts.[8] Outputs are regulations, programs, and organizational arrangements that actors establish to operationalize the provisions of regimes—that is, to move them from paper to practice.[9] Outcomes encompass changes in the behavior of those subject to the provisions of regimes, whether these changes involve bringing actions into conformance with the requirements of regimes or making other adjustments that become attractive as a result of the establishment of regimes. For their part, impacts have to do with problem solving in that they involve effects measured in terms of the concerns that lead actors to create regimes in the first place. Impacts may range from marginal to decisive; there is no need to think

5. For details on this case, see Edward A. Parson and Owen Greene, "The Complex Chemistry of the International Ozone Agreements," *Environment* 37 (March 1995), 16–20, 35–43.
6. The distinction between deterrence and compellence is developed at length in Thomas C. Schelling, *Arms and Influence* (New Haven: Yale University Press, 1967).
7. For an account that emphasizes normative and cognitive sources of behavior, see W. Richard Scott, *Institutions and Organizations* (Thousand Oaks, Calif.: Sage, 1995).
8. These concepts were introduced by David Easton in *A Systems Analysis of Political Life* (New York: Wiley, 1965).
9. On the idea of a transition from paper to practice, see Ronald B. Mitchell, *Intentional Oil Pollution at Sea: Environmental Policy and Treaty Compliance* (Cambridge: MIT Press, 1994).

of them in all-or-nothing terms. Moreover, regimes may give rise to new problems, whatever their impacts in terms of the problems leading to their creation. Clearly, there is every reason to take a lively interest in all three types of regime consequences. Yet these comments also help to account for the growing tendency among regime analysts to focus particular attention on outcomes in contrast to outputs and impacts. The study of behavior allows the observer to avoid the formalism that marks many analyses of outputs, while skirting some of the analytic problems associated with efforts to demonstrate the occurrence of impacts in a convincing manner.

Three additional issues of a conceptual nature deserve comment at this juncture. *Effectiveness*, as I use the term here, is not to be confused with a variety of performance criteria such as efficiency, equity, and robustness. *Efficiency* is a measure of the extent to which problems are solved or behavior is altered with a minimum expenditure of resources; *equity* refers to the extent to which outcomes flowing from regimes conform to normative standards of fairness or justice; and *robustness* concerns the ability of institutions to sustain themselves in the face of various perturbations. Results measured by these performance criteria will not always correlate with outcomes judged according to effectiveness. Problems may be solved effectively, but in ways that leave a lot to be desired with respect to efficiency or equity. To illustrate, most observers have concluded that the shift from discharge standards to equipment standards led to a distinct improvement in the effectiveness of the regime dealing with vessel-source oil pollution. But it is difficult to defend this development in terms of efficiency. Such important concerns merit more systematic attention among those interested in regimes. But the discussion in this chapter focuses primarily on the issue of effectiveness as framed in the preceding paragraphs.

Moreover, regimes—both singly and in combination—can generate broader consequences by altering the knowledge base available to actors in international society, the relative status of international actors, or even the constitutive features of international society as a whole, quite apart from their success in solving specific problems.[10] Taken together, for example, the rise of international environmental regimes over the last several decades has surely played a part in strengthening the role of nongovernmental organizations in world affairs and in enhancing the significance of global civil society as a factor in environmental problem solving.[11] The study of these broader consequences is obviously important. In the long

10. See Marc A. Levy, Oran R. Young, and Michael Zürn, "The Study of International Regimes," *European Journal of International Relations* 1 (September 1995), 308–12.
11. Conversely, nongovernmental organizations have played increasingly important roles in shaping the character of environmental regimes. On the idea of global civil society, see Paul

run, their impact may even overshadow the performance of regimes in solving or alleviating a variety of specific environmental problems arising at the international level. But the analysis of broader consequences is separate from the study of regime effectiveness. Although much may be gained from research in this area, conflating the analysis of regime effectiveness and the study of broader consequences is a recipe for confusion.

Finally, a distinction exists between what we may call the "pure" theory of regimes and the "contextualized" theory of regimes or, for that matter, social institutions in general. The pure theory seeks to illuminate the logic of regimes on the assumptions that specific institutional arrangements are fully operational, accepted by all relevant subjects as facts of life to be complied with as a matter of course, and not subject to distortion resulting from the impact of outside forces. Analysis then focuses on the outcomes that can be expected to flow from the operation of these arrangements over time.[12] To take some concrete examples, this leads to assessments of the probable outcomes resulting from the operation of different electoral systems (for example, proportional representation versus single-member districts), different decision rules in legislative settings or committees, and different structures of property rights.[13] Contextualized theory, by contrast, focuses on issues involving the extent to which regimes actually affect the behavior of those subject to their provisions and the relationship between the character of regimes as they are intended to operate in principle and the character of institutional arrangements as they operate in practice. The central concern here is to probe whether and to what extent regimes actually do determine the flow of collective outcomes in various social settings. Pure theory is largely an analytic exercise employing deductive reasoning and, in some cases, simulations to explore the dynamics of institutions as such; the results tend to be normative rather than descriptive. Contextualized theory is mainly an empirical exercise involving the use of a battery of techniques designed to determine the proportion of the variance in the outcomes flowing from social interactions that can be explained in terms of the operation of regimes. While both

---

Wapner, "Governance in Global Civil Society," in Young, *Global Governance*, 65–84, and Ronnie D. Lipschutz, *Global Civil Society and Global Environmental Governance* (Albany: State University of New York Press, 1996).

12. For well-known examples pertaining to domestic systems, see Anthony Downs, *An Economic Theory of Democracy* (New York: Harper and Row, 1957), and James M. Buchanan and Gordon Tullock, *The Calculus of Consent* (Ann Arbor: University of Michigan Press, 1962). See also Kenneth A. Shepsle, "Studying Institutions: Some Lessons from the Rational Choice Approach," *Journal of Theoretical Politics* 1 (April 1989), 131–47.

13. See Buchanan and Tullock, *Calculus of Consent*, and Maurice Duverger, *Political Parties: Their Organization and Activity in the Modern State* (New York: Wiley, 1954).

types of analysis are worthwhile, most efforts to understand the effectiveness of international regimes take the form of contextualized theory.[14] The central questions are: do regimes matter, and what proportion of the variance in world affairs is attributable to the operation of these institutional arrangements?

VARIATIONS IN REGIME PERFORMANCE

How much do regimes vary in terms of effectiveness? How can we measure this variance under real-world conditions? Given the preceding account of the difficulties associated with the concept of effectiveness, it will come as no surprise that there is no straightforward way to operationalize the concept, much less to construct a generic index that will allow observers to chart shifts in the effectiveness of individual regimes over time or to compare and contrast different regimes with respect to levels of effectiveness. This lack is a serious problem; it limits our ability to treat effectiveness as a dependent variable whose behavior can be followed in an unambiguous and uncontroversial manner. Ideally, it would be desirable to develop an interval scale allowing us to track effectiveness in much the same way that we use temperature as a measure of the functioning of the human body or GNP as a measure of the performance of economic systems. At this stage, the development of such a scale is beyond our reach. A more realistic goal over the short run is the development of an ordinal scale that would make it possible to rank regimes from high to low in effectiveness and to monitor the performance of individual regimes over time in these terms.[15] Given the conceptual problems described in the preceding section, even the development of an ordinal scale allowing us to evaluate regime effectiveness with confidence is a tall order. Yet some such procedure is essential for those interested not only in measuring effectiveness but also in framing and testing hypotheses that can help to explain or predict variations in levels of effectiveness over time and across regimes.[16] Realistically, the aim at this stage should be to devise a relatively simple ordinal scale which differentiates among four or five levels of ef-

14. Contrast this orientation with the new institutionalism in economics as described in Malcolm Rutherford, *Institutions in Economics: The Old and the New Institutionalism* (Cambridge: Cambridge University Press, 1994).

15. For an initial effort to develop such a scale, see Edward L. Miles et al., *Explaining Regime Effectiveness: Confronting Theory with Evidence* (Cambridge: MIT Press, forthcoming).

16. Compare the discussion of such matters in Gary King, Robert O. Keohane, and Sidney Verba, *Designing Social Inquiry: Scientific Inference in Qualitative Research* (Princeton: Princeton University Press, 1994).

fectiveness and which is usable by well-informed analysts to code the effectiveness of regimes with reasonable confidence.[17]

Notwithstanding these problems of measurement, students of international regimes largely agree, at least in general terms, on the effectiveness of specific arrangements.[18] Among those regimes that are widely viewed as ranging from effective to very effective are the Antarctic Treaty System, the Great Lakes water quality regime, the arrangement covering the dumping or incineration of wastes in the North Sea, and the regime for the protection of the stratospheric ozone layer.[19] Conversely, the list of regimes that most analysts would rank as ineffective or very ineffective includes the agreement on the conservation of migratory species of wild animals, the international tropical timber regime, many of the Regional Seas arrangements operating under the auspices of the United Nations Environment Programme (UNEP), and most species-specific and area-specific arrangements dealing with marine fisheries.[20] Most would concur as well in reaching mixed conclusions regarding the effectiveness of a number of other regimes, such as arrangements dealing with long-range transboundary air pollution in Europe, international trade in endangered species of wild fauna and flora, pollutants discharged into the Rhine River, and transboundary shipments of hazardous wastes. Imprecise as they are, these widely shared rankings offer some grounds for optimism regarding efforts to assess the effectiveness of international regimes.

Most observers would also agree that there are a number of circumstances in which it is difficult to arrive at straightforward rankings regarding the effectiveness of regimes. It is common for specific arrangements to follow a kind of life cycle, typically becoming increasingly effective with the passage of time and, in some cases, outliving their usefulness in due

17. To illustrate, a 1–5 scale of effectiveness might give a 5 to a regime that decisively solves the problem at stake, a 1 to a regime that is completely ineffectual, a 2 to a regime that is marginally effective, a 3 to a regime that produces substantial effects, and a 4 to a regime that is very effective without solving the problem altogether.

18. See also the rankings in Miles et al., *Explaining Regime Effectiveness*.

19. See Olav Schram Stokke and Davor Vidas, eds., *Governing the Antarctic: The Effectiveness and Legitimacy of the Antarctic Treaty System* (Cambridge: Cambridge University Press, 1996); Lee Botts and Paul Muldoon, *The Great Lakes Water Quality Agreement: Its Past Successes and Uncertain Future* (Hanover, N.H.: Institute on International Environmental Governance, 1996); Jon Birger Skjaerseth, "Towards the End of Dumping in the North Sea: The Case of the Oslo Commission," in Miles et al., *Explaining Regime Effectiveness*; and Parson and Greene, "Complex Chemistry."

20. See Simon Lyster, *International Wildlife Law* (Cambridge: Grotius Publishers, 1985); Weiss and Jacobson, *Engaging Countries*; Miles et al., *Explaining Regime Effectiveness*; and M. J. Peterson, "International Fisheries Management," in Peter M. Haas, Robert O. Keohane, and Marc A. Levy, eds., *Institutions for the Earth: Sources of Effective International Environmental Protection* (Cambridge: MIT Press, 1993), 249–305.

course. The regime dealing with intentional oil pollution at sea, for example, clearly became more effective following a shift from discharge standards to equipment standards.[21] Many traditional conservation regimes, which focus on efforts to regulate consumptive uses of living resources, have lost effectiveness with the rise of concerns for habitat protection and ecosystems management.[22] Beyond this, serious ambiguities impede efforts to arrive at judgments about effectiveness for some regimes. Most observers agree that the regime for whales and whaling was ineffective during its early years but became more effective during the 1970s. But they differ sharply over the effectiveness of this regime in more recent years, differences that are attributable not to disagreements about the behavioral impacts of the regime but to conflicting views regarding the purpose of the regime.[23] Of course, in some instances, judgments about the effectiveness of regimes must remain tentative until these arrangements have been in place long enough to compile a track record sufficient to provide a basis for assessment. Obvious examples include the arrangements established during the 1990s to deal with such problems as climate change, the loss of biological diversity, and desertification. More generally, it is difficult to make early assessments about the effectiveness of regimes based on framework conventions that are intended to initiate a continuing process of regime formation.[24] All these issues complicate efforts to rate specific regimes in terms of effectiveness, sometimes giving rise to substantial differences of opinion. Unlike the conceptual difficulties discussed in the preceding section, however, these matters are largely empirical problems to be solved pragmatically rather than problems that point to disagreements about what we mean in speaking of the effectiveness of regimes.

Clearly, there is a long way to go in the effort to construct an empirical index to enable the systematic exploration of effectiveness as a key variable in regime analysis. But even now we know enough to lay to rest the sterile debate about whether international regimes matter or are properly understood as epiphenomena that merely reflect deeper driving forces in international society.[25] The essential point is that the effectiveness varies

21. Mitchell, *Intentional Oil Pollution*.

22. Several examples are described in some detail in Lyster, *International Wildlife Law*.

23. See Steinar Andresen, "The International Whaling Convention," in Miles et al., *Explaining Regime Effectiveness*.

24. For a study of the European Long-Range Transboundary Air Pollution (LRTAP) regime, which began in 1979 with a framework convention containing little substantive content but which has evolved steadily over the years, see Marc A. Levy, "European Acid Rain: The Power of Tote-Board Diplomacy," in Haas, Keohane, and Levy, *Institutions for the Earth*, 75–132.

25. For prominent examples of the argument that international regimes are mere epiphenomena, see Susan Strange, "*Cave! hic dragones*: A Critique of Regime Analysis," in Stephen D.

substantially both among regimes and within regimes over time. This is not to say that observers agree about the ranking of particular regimes on the scale of effectiveness. But virtually everyone concurs that some regimes have been remarkably successful, whereas others have been dismal failures. Even more common are cases in which effectiveness lies somewhere between these extremes. It follows that the appropriate course at this time is to turn our attention to a sustained examination of the sources or roots of institutional effectiveness. This exercise promises to be far more productive and interesting than a continuation of sectarian battles over whether regimes matter.

WHAT DO WE KNOW ABOUT THE SOURCES OF EFFECTIVENESS?

Research on the effectiveness of international environmental regimes is still at an early stage. Moreover, serious methodological problems stand in the way of progress in this area. Even so, research has already yielded some significant findings about the sources of institutional effectiveness in this domain, along with good leads concerning where to continue the analysis of effectiveness during the next phase of research on environmental regimes. In this section, I seek both to pinpoint what we know already about the determinants of success and to characterize what we need to know about effectiveness under five headings: problem structure, regime attributes, social practices, institutional interactions, and broader setting. I then discuss plans of attack for broadening and deepening the current understanding of these matters.

Problem Structure

Some problems are easier to solve than others. Thus, coordination problems are easier to deal with than are collaboration problems, largely because participants have no incentive to violate the rules developed to solve coordination problems.[26] Devising a successful governance system for air

---

Krasner, ed., *International Regimes* (Ithaca: Cornell University Press, 1983), 337–54, and John J. Mearsheimer, "The False Promise of International Institutions," *International Security* 19 (Winter 1994/95), 5–49, together with the responses by Robert O. Keohane, Lisa L. Martin, Charles A. Kupchan, Clifford A. Kupchan, John Gerard Ruggie, and Alexander Wendt and the rejoinder by Mearsheimer in *International Security* 20 (Summer 1995), 39–93.

26. Arthur A. Stein, "Coordination and Collaboration: Regimes in an Anarchic World," in Krasner, *International Regimes*, 115–40.

transport is less challenging than devising an effective regime to regulate transboundary air pollution. Situations featuring high levels of transparency in the sense that it is easy to tell whether those subject to regulatory rules are complying with their requirements are easier to deal with than situations in which subjects—including private actors as well as public agencies—can violate the rules clandestinely.[27] Consider the difference between equipment standards and discharge standards with regard to intentional oil pollution at sea. Other things being equal, problems involving large numbers of actors, either as parties to the agreements themselves or as subjects of the regulatory arrangements devised, are harder to deal with than small-number situations.[28] Think of the differences between the protection of the stratospheric ozone layer and the Earth's climate system in these terms. Similar remarks pertain to the length of the shadow of the future. When parties are engaged in interactions expected to last indefinitely (such as the governance system for Antarctica), incentives to cooperate will be stronger than when the relationships are short-lived (as in short-term arrangements dealing with the exploitation of a finite resource).[29]

What we lack at this stage is a comprehensive or generic index to use in ranking and comparing problems in terms of the difficulty of solving them. Several analysts have made sustained efforts to develop an index of this sort (see Chapter 3). The most influential of these efforts involve the problem-structural approach of the Tübingen group, which looks at regime formation as a means of solving conflicts and rates problems according to what is called "regime conduciveness,"[30] and the work of the Oslo/Seattle group, which focuses on interests or preferences and looks to game-theoretical constructs as a way of differentiating among problems in terms of how hard it will be to solve them.[31] Each approach has added to our understanding of problem structure. But both are fraught with analytic difficulties and problems of operationalization that limit their usefulness as procedures for rating real-world problems on a scale of hardness.

27. Ronald B. Mitchell, "Compliance Theory: An Overview," in James Cameron, Jacob Werksman, and Peter Roderick, eds., *Improving Compliance with International Environmental Law* (London: Earthscan Publications, 1996), 3–28.

28. Kenneth A. Oye, "Explaining Cooperation under Anarchy: Hypotheses and Strategies," in Oye, ed., *Cooperation under Anarchy* (Princeton: Princeton University Press, 1986), 1–24.

29. Robert Axelrod, *The Evolution of Cooperation* (New York: Basic, 1984).

30. Volker Rittberger and Michael Zürn, "Regime Theory: Findings from the Study of 'East-West' Regimes," *Cooperation and Conflict* 26 (1991), 165–83.

31. Arild Underdal, "One Question, Two Answers," in Miles et al., *Explaining Regime Effectiveness*.

Regime Attributes

Regime design matters.[32] Because regimes are not actors in their own right, it is inappropriate to think of these constructs as agents that succeed or fail in connection with assignments they receive from their creators.[33] Nevertheless, institutional arrangements do serve to channel the behavior of both their formal members and wider arrays of actors operating under the auspices of regime members. In the process, they affect the content of collective outcomes flowing from interactions among actors in international society. Here, too, some knowledge of the roots of institutional effectiveness is available. A capacity to respond flexibly and to evolve is particularly important to the success of regimes that deal with environmental issues, where understanding of the relevant biophysical systems is developing rapidly—in some instances as a consequence of the operation of the regimes themselves. Well-constructed SIRs are important in almost every case as methods of retaining the attention of policymakers and avoiding the onset of the "out of sight, out of mind" syndrome.[34] There is much to be said for institutional arrangements that treat issues of compliance with the rules and decisions of regimes as management problems rather than enforcement problems.[35] The extent to which regimes require secure sources of funding to prove successful depends on the nature of the tasks they are expected to perform. Such programmatic tasks as helping developing countries to avoid increases in the production and consumption of ozone-depleting substances, for instance, present greater funding requirements than procedural tasks like making annual decisions regarding allowable harvest levels for living resources.

As in the case of problem structure, much remains to be learned about the role of regime attributes as determinants of effectiveness. While many see the widespread use of consensus rules at the international level as a source of weakness, for example, the links between decision rules and regime effectiveness are poorly understood.[36] Similar remarks pertain to the

32. Ronald B. Mitchell, "Regime Design Matters: Intentional Oil Pollution and Treaty Compliance," *International Organization* 48 (Summer 1994), 425–58.

33. For a general discussion of agency, see Gary Miller, *Managerial Dilemmas* (Cambridge: Cambridge University Press, 1993).

34. On systems of implementation review, see Victor, Raustiala, and Skolnikoff, *International Environmental Commitments*.

35. On the distinction between management models and enforcement models of compliance, see Chayes and Chayes, *New Sovereignty*.

36. For a general account of decision rules that contrasts the transaction costs of increasing the size of the majority needed to win with the welfare losses to those in the minority arising from reductions in the number needed to win, see Buchanan and Tullock, *Calculus of Consent.*

role of what we now think of as NCPs in contrast to more formal DSPs, which are typically included in the constitutive provisions of international environmental regimes but seldom loom large in the actual operations of these regimes.[37] More generally, we need to improve our understanding of the relationships between regime attributes, on the one hand, and effectiveness construed in terms of outputs, outcomes, and impacts, on the other. Thus, regimes that look impressive at the level of outputs are not necessarily successful when it comes to solving the problems that lead to their creation in the first place. Regimes that produce striking results at the level of outcomes can generate unintended side effects that offset or even swamp the progress they bring about in terms of curbing or redirecting the behavior giving rise to the problem to be solved. Thus, it is difficult to provide a clear assessment of the effectiveness of a regime for the management of fish or marine mammals which succeeds only by shifting the attention of harvesters from one area or one species to another.[38]

Social Practices

Institutionalization enhances effectiveness. To be more specific, an important finding emerging from studies of effectiveness concerns the relationship between institutional arrangements in the narrow sense and the social practices that grow up around them. Regimes are sets of rules, decision-making procedures, and programs. But every successful regime gives rise to an encompassing social practice in which the members themselves become enmeshed in an increasingly complex web of interactive relationships and in which a variety of actors with no formal roles in the regime emerge as players. It is the growth of a vibrant social practice that typically serves to legitimize a regime in the thought processes of various actors, to flesh out the constitutive provisions of a regime with a range of important informal understandings, to transform the rules of a regime into standard operating procedures, and to give rise to an informal but attentive community of actors interested in the success of the regime and prepared to function as watchdogs to keep track of its performance.[39] At this stage, our understanding of the connections between regimes in the narrow sense and social practices is quite limited. But it is already clear that

---

37. Jacob Werksman, "Designing a Compliance System for the UN Framework Convention on Climate Change," in Cameron, Werksman, and Roderick, *Improving Compliance*, 85–112.

38. For a striking case involving pollock in the Bering Sea, consult William V. Dunlap, "Bering Sea," *International Journal of Marine and Coastal Law* 10 (February 1995), 114–35.

39. For a case study that explores this theme in depth, see Botts and Muldoon, *Great Lakes Water Quality Agreement*.

the way forward will involve a sustained effort to integrate insights drawn from the institutionalism of economics, which typically focuses on regimes in the narrow sense, and the institutionalism of sociology, which tends to direct attention to the character of social practices.[40]

During the 1990s, students of regimes have become aware that civil society exists at the international level just as it does at the domestic level.[41] Construed as a network of social connections that exists above the level of the individual (or the individual state in international society) and below the level of the state (or the assemblage of governance systems in international society), civil society provides much of the social glue that holds governance systems together and allows them to operate effectively in a wide range of social settings.[42] There are large challenges facing those who take on the task of understanding the role of civil society as a backdrop for the functioning of specific governance systems. It is difficult to find ways to pin down this concept for purposes of empirical analysis in any setting, much less to develop testable hypotheses about the role of civil society. Without doubt, these analytic challenges are even greater at the international or global level than they are at the domestic level. Yet it seems increasingly clear that the costs of ignoring the role of civil society as a determinant of the effectiveness of environmental regimes—or international institutions more generally—will be great.

Institutional Linkages

Links to other regimes can cut both ways in terms of their impact on effectiveness. Students of international regimes tend to treat these entities as stand-alone arrangements and to conduct detailed case studies focused on individual regimes. Given the relative difficulty in grasping the concept of regimes and the complexity of specific arrangements, this practice is perhaps understandable. But with the growth in the population of environmental regimes in international society, this procedure is no longer tenable. Institutional linkages are widespread, and they clearly make a difference in terms of the effectiveness of individual regimes. In coming to terms with this phenomenon, it is helpful to draw a distinction between horizontal linkages and vertical linkages. *Horizontal linkages* refer to con-

---

40. Contrast the economic perspective set forth in Rutherford, *Institutions in Economics*, with the sociological perspectives discussed in Scott, *Institutions and Organizations*.

41. See Wapner, "Governance in Global Civil Society," and Lipschutz, *Global Civil Society*.

42. For a range of perspectives on civil society, see Jean L. Cohen and Andrew Arato, *Civil Society and Political Theory* (Cambridge: MIT Press, 1992). The idea of global civil society is discussed in Jessica T. Mathews, "Power Shift," *Foreign Affairs* 76 (January/February 1997), 50–66.

nections between individual regimes and other institutional arrangements that operate at the level of international society. Some observers have been struck by the dangers of interference by individual regimes with one another's operations in ways that impair effectiveness; they have begun to speak of "institutional overlap" or "congestion" as a label for this phenomenon.[43] But the prospect of mutual reinforcement and other, more positive connections seems equally important. These observations have given rise to an examination of nested regimes, as with links between regional seas arrangements and the overarching law of the sea; clustered regimes, such as the linked but differentiable components of the Antarctic Treaty System; and embedded regimes, as in the case of free-trade arrangements embodying larger principles of the neoliberal economic order.[44] It has also led to a consideration of structures of institutional arrangements and an examination of similarities and differences in structures of environmental institutions in contrast to economic institutions.[45]

Vertical linkages refer to connections between international regimes and institutional arrangements operating at lower levels of social organization. Many students of domestic institutions have observed that arrangements devised at the national level produce better results when they are compatible with regional or local practices than when they work at cross-purposes with these practices. Studies of local arrangements centered on the use of common pool resources, for example, are replete with accounts of the disruptive consequences of national arrangements devised in ignorance of long-standing local procedures for "governing the commons."[46] These linkages are all the more important at the international level, where compatibility across several levels of social organization becomes an issue. Much of the criticism that has been leveled at the international regime for trade, currently embodied in the GATT/WTO, centers on claims pertain-

43. See R. A. Herr, ed., *Antarctica Offshore: A Cacophony of Regimes?* (Hobart: University of Tasmania, 1995), and Edith Brown Weiss, "International Environmental Law: Contemporary Issues and the Emergence of a New World Order," *Georgetown Law Journal* 81 (March 1993), 675–710.

44. An influential account of embedded regimes is John Gerard Ruggie, "International Regimes, Transactions, and Change: Embedded Liberalism in the Postwar Economic Order," in Krasner, *International Regimes* (Ithaca: Cornell University Press), 195–232.

45. Konrad von Moltke, "Institutional Interactions: The Structure of Regimes for Trade and the Environment," in Young, *Global Governance*, 247–72.

46. Elinor Ostrom, *Governing the Commons: The Evolution of Institutions for Collective Action* (Cambridge: Cambridge University Press, 1990). For a case study that highlights the disruptive consequences in question, see Narpat S. Jodha, "Property Rights and Development," in Susan S. Hanna, Carl Folke, and Karl-Göran Mäler, *Rights to Nature: Ecological, Economic, Cultural, and Political Principles of Institutions for the Environment* (Washington, D.C.: Island Press, 1996), 205–20.

ing to the destructive or exploitative impacts these global arrangements are alleged to have on long-standing resource regimes operating at regional and even local levels.[47] Knowledge of such matters remains relatively superficial at this stage; much more attention needs to be devoted to institutional linkages in future efforts to understand the sources of regime effectiveness.

Broader Setting

Regimes are highly sensitive to the larger settings within which they operate. International environmental regimes do not operate in a socio-economic or biophysical vacuum. Rather, they arise and function in settings that have obvious implications for their capacity to succeed in solving specific problems. Periods marked by economic recessions or depressions, for example, are likely to pose severe problems for efforts to solve environmental problems. The existence of political tensions among key players or the occurrence of hostilities exogenous to the problems at hand is apt to overshadow efforts to solve environmental problems. Consider, for example, the extent to which broader political problems impede efforts to devise effective regimes for international rivers in such areas as the Middle East or the Indian subcontinent.[48] At the same time, many aspects of the broader setting are not well understood. Is regime effectiveness a function of the extent to which members have similar or homogeneous domestic political systems, and does it matter whether these systems are *democratic* in some meaningful sense of that term? Do regimes work better when their members have what are known as "strong" states in terms of state-society relations?[49] Can effective regimes arise in situations in which their creators are motivated more by political concerns than by a desire to solve environmental problems as such? Are there ways to immunize regimes dealing with specific problems from fluctuations in broader political and economic relations among their members?

With regard to environmental regimes more specifically, consideration of the relationships between the institutional arrangements themselves and the character of the ecosystems to which they relate is critical. It is easy

47. See David P. Ross and Peter J. Usher, *From the Roots Up: Economic Development as if Community Mattered* (Croton-on-Hudson, N.Y.: Bootstrap Press, 1986).

48. Peter H. Gleick, "Water and Conflict: Fresh Water Resources and International Security," *International Security* 18 (Summer 1993), 79–112, and Miriam R. Lowi, *Water and Power: The Politics of a Scarce Resource in the Jordan River Basin* (Cambridge: Cambridge University Press, 1993).

49. On the distinction between "strong" and "weak" states, see Joel Migdal, *Strong Societies and Weak States: State-Society Relations and State Capabilities in the Third World* (Princeton: Princeton University Press, 1988).

to speak, in general terms, about the need for congruence between regime features and ecosystem attributes. But what does this mean in practice? Some answers to this question are beginning to emerge.[50] The more resilient an ecosystem is, for instance, the less important it is to create monitoring mechanisms that can track changes in the system quickly and sensitively. The greater the homogeneity of the ecosystem, the less need there is for tailoring the components of a regime to the specific characteristics of the various subsystems that make up the overarching biophysical system. At the same time, improving understanding of the fit between ecosystems and institutional arrangements is a growth area in which there is a strong argument for investing resources intended to upgrade our ability to explain and predict the effectiveness of international environmental regimes.[51]

Let me step back now and put these comments about the various sources of regime effectiveness into perspective. Regimes matter in the sense that they play a causal role in determining the content of collective outcomes at the international level. By itself, however, this observation is of limited interest. What makes the study of regime effectiveness both complex and challenging is that institutions constitute only one of a set of social drivers which typically interact with one another as determinants of collective outcomes at the international level and which assume different values in individual cases. This makes it difficult to separate out the role of various categories of drivers and to assess just what proportion of the variance in collective outcomes is attributable to institutional arrangements in contrast to such other factors as material conditions and ideas.[52] It greatly reduces the prospects that we can construct simple generalizations about the role of institutions couched in the form of statements that specify necessary or sufficient conditions for success in problem solving. And it raises questions about the extent to which it is helpful to treat some social drivers as underlying forces and others as intervening variables.[53] None of this means that international regimes are of only marginal significance when it comes to solving environmental problems at the international level. But

50. See the papers included in part 1 of Hanna, Folke, and Mäler, *Rights to Nature*, and Fikret Berkes and Carl Folke, eds., *Linking Social and Ecological Systems: Management Practices and Social Mechanisms for Building Resilience* (Cambridge: Cambridge University Press, 1998).

51. Oran R. Young, "Science Plan for the Project on the Institutional Dimensions of Global Environmental Change," *IHDP Report*, no. 9 (Bonn: International Human Dimensions Programme on Global Environmental Change, 1999).

52. See Oran R. Young, ed., *The Effectiveness of International Environmental Regimes: Causal Connections and Behavioral Mechanisms* (Cambridge: MIT Press, 1999), chaps. 1, 5.

53. See, for example, Stephen D. Krasner, "Structural Causes and Regime Consequences: Regimes as Intervening Variables," in Krasner, *International Regimes*, 1–21.

it does mean that future efforts to gain ground in understanding the effectiveness of international regimes must tackle multivariate relationships head-on and anticipate the prospect that the same factors, such as problem structure or regime attributes, which loom large under some conditions will produce no more than marginal effects under other conditions.

THE ROAD AHEAD

How can we go about improving our understanding of regime effectiveness? The answer to this question depends, in part, on the objectives we are seeking to achieve. The current understanding of effectiveness constitutes a good start toward illuminating this complex phenomenon. What is more, studies that pertain to this subject currently constitute a growth industry among those interested both in international institutions and in environmental governance.[54] Yet from the point of view of learning how to design environmental regimes that have a reasonable prospect of solving the problems that motivate their creation, there is a long way to go. We should not overlook matters of compliance in efforts to solve collaboration problems, nor should we ignore problems of flexibility and learning in dealing with biophysical systems whose dynamics are poorly understood. But this is hardly sufficient to support a robust and reasonably successful effort to engage in institutional design in the realm of environmental governance.[55] How should we proceed, assuming that this line of inquiry is concerned not only with understanding environmental problems as an end in itself but also with solving them?

In responding to this question, I will begin by drawing a distinction between two streams of analysis that merit sustained attention during the next phase of research on the effectiveness of international environmental regimes. One stream features an effort to consolidate and refine the existing body of ideas about effectiveness; the other calls for an effort to break new ground, thus shifting this field of study onto a higher level of understanding.[56] Much of existing knowledge about effectiveness is tentative, partly because many of the relationships in question have not been

54. See Weiss and Jacobson, *Engaging Countries*; Victor, Raustiala, and Skolnikoff, *International Environmental Commitments*; Young, *Effectiveness of International Environmental Regimes*; Miles et al., *Explaining Regime Effectiveness*; and William C. Clark, J. van Eijndoven, and Jill Jaeger, eds., *Learning to Manage Global Environmental Risks: A Comparative History of Social Responses to Climate Change, Ozone Depletion, and Acid Rain* (Cambridge: MIT Press, forthcoming).

55. For a range of approaches to institutional design, see Robert E. Goodin, ed., *The Theory of Institutional Design* (Cambridge: Cambridge University Press, 1996).

56. I am indebted to Arild Underdal for calling my attention to this distinction.

formulated with sufficient precision to allow for rigorous testing. We know that certain simple propositions about effectiveness are not valid, such as the notion that the existence of a dominant actor or a hegemon is necessary for regimes to prove successful.[57] But this hardly licenses the conclusion that power in the structural or material sense is unimportant in accounting for the effectiveness of specific regimes.[58] What we need in this connection is a definition of power that is easy to operationalize, avoids the pitfalls of circular reasoning, and can be used in efforts to test a battery of specific hypotheses about the links between power and effectiveness.[59] Similar comments pertain to the role of epistemic communities in the operation of environmental regimes.[60] Clearly, the idea of epistemic communities has struck a responsive chord with many observers of environmental regimes, and it is relatively easy to point to specific cases in which groups exhibiting some of the characteristics of epistemic communities appear to have made a difference.[61] Yet the concept of an epistemic community has proven to be illusive when it comes to systematic empirical assessments. Observers frequently find themselves disagreeing not about the roles that epistemic communities actually play but about whether we can say with certainty that an epistemic community is present. And these are not isolated examples. On the contrary, they exemplify a common problem plaguing efforts to turn interesting insights into a core of established propositions about the factors that determine the effectiveness of environmental regimes.

Where propositions have been spelled out with sufficient precision to allow for testing, moreover, researchers commonly discover the importance of contingent relationships. It is relatively easy to disprove many—perhaps most—propositions about effectiveness stated as invariant relationships, such as statements purporting to specify necessary or sufficient conditions for the achievement of effectiveness.[62] The presence of a dominant actor is not always critical to the achievement of effectiveness. The

57. Duncan Snidal, "The Limits of Hegemonic Stability Theory," *International Organization* 39 (Autumn 1985), 579–614.

58. See Arild Underdal, "Patterns of Effectiveness: Examining Evidence from Thirteen International Regimes," in Miles et al., *Explaining Regime Effectiveness*.

59. For an account that emphasizes the differences between power in the structural sense and bargaining power or leverage, see Young, *International Governance*, chap. 5.

60. Peter M. Haas, "Do Regimes Matter? Epistemic Communities and Mediterranean Pollution Control," *International Organization* 43 (Summer 1989), 377–403, and Ernst B. Haas, *When Knowledge Is Power: Three Models of Change in International Organizations* (Berkeley: University of California Press, 1990).

61. See the essays collected in Peter M. Haas, ed., *Knowledge, Power, and International Policy Coordination* (Columbia: University of South Carolina Press, 1997).

62. Young, *Effectiveness of International Environmental Regimes*, chap. 5.

use of decision rules that call for consensus or even unanimity does not always pose a problem for effectiveness. Uncertainty is not invariably a pitfall that needs to be mitigated or even eliminated altogether in the interests of achieving effectiveness. Yet none of this means that such factors as the distribution of power among regime members, the nature of decision rules, and the state of knowledge about the problem at stake can be dismissed in the effort to understand the determinants of effectiveness. What is needed is work to formulate a body of contingent propositions about such matters—that is, statements which both specify links and spell out as explicitly as possible the conditions or combinations of conditions under which these propositions can be expected to hold. Only in this way can we turn interesting speculation into usable knowledge about effectiveness.

These tasks of consolidation and refinement constitute a large and challenging research agenda for those interested in the effectiveness of international environmental regimes. With sufficient effort, this line of reasoning can yield a core of firmly established propositions that are useful to those responsible for designing or operating regimes. Impressive as it would be, however, such an accomplishment would provide only a limited ability to make constructive contributions to the design and operation of effective environmental regimes. Particularly important now are efforts to extend and even redirect the study of effectiveness which will allow us to build on our initial accomplishments in order to move to a higher level of understanding of the sources of effectiveness.

Most students of effectiveness focus on states as the formal members of regimes and proceed to construct models in which these actors are treated as unitary and self-interested utility maximizers.[63] Much can be said for this procedure as a point of departure; additional insights may well flow from further work with such models. But forward movement in this field requires relaxation of these behavioral assumptions in a controlled manner, comparing and contrasting the insights that flow from a suite of differentiable models of actor behavior rather than from a single stylized model. Three distinct steps in this realm seem particularly important— singly and in combination—to an understanding of the effectiveness of international environmental regimes. First, there is a need to explore alternatives to utility maximization as sources of the behavior of regime members. To do so involves opening up this research program to what sociologists such as Richard Scott call the "normative" and "cognitive" pillars of social institutions and supplementing the logical rigor of economic models with the empirical insights of sociological analyses of institutions

---

63. For a particularly clear example, see Miles et al., *Explaining Regime Effectiveness*.

in the process.[64] A second step turns on relaxing the unitary actor assumption embedded in many behavioral models in this field of study, thus considering what Robert Putnam and others have characterized as the logic of two-level games, a perspective that highlights bargaining over the terms of international regimes among different factions at the domestic level.[65]

The third step then features a move to extend the analysis to include roles played by various nonstate actors in determining the effectiveness of environmental regimes.[66] Because most environmental regimes involve a two-step process in which states are the formal members but it is the behavior of a variety of other actors (corporations or even individual consumers) that actually causes the problems under consideration, those interested in international environmental regimes have recently directed attention to the efforts of states to implement commitments made at the international level as they apply to the behavior of private or semiprivate actors operating under their jurisdiction.[67] But it is increasingly clear that nonstate actors, such as the DeBeers Corporation in the case of diamonds, the Chicago Board of Trade in commodities, or Lloyds of London in marine insurance, can become major players in international environmental regimes in their own right. There are even regimes of some significance in which states are not among the major players.[68] Relaxing all these assumptions at once is a recipe for theoretical confusion. Yet we cannot hope to make a successful transition to the next level of understanding regarding the sources of regime effectiveness so long as we remain unwilling to modify conventional models that assume all the important actors are states that can be treated as unitary and rational utility maximizers.

64. Scott, *Institutions and Organizations*, chap. 3. A study that pursues this line of thinking regarding international regimes is Young, *Effectiveness of International Environmental Regimes*.

65. Robert D. Putnam, "Diplomacy and Domestic Politics: The Logic of Two-Level Games," *International Organization* 42 (Summer 1988), 427–60, and Peter B. Evans, Harold K. Jacobson, and Robert D. Putnam, eds., *Double-Edged Diplomacy: International Bargaining and Domestic Politics* (Berkeley: University of California Press, 1993).

66. Thomas Princen and Matthias Finger, *Environmental NGOs in World Politics: Linking the Local and the Global* (London: Routledge, 1994); Steve Charnovitz, "Two Centuries of Participation: NGOs and International Governance," *Michigan Journal of International Law* 18 (Winter 1997), 183–286; and Mathews, "Power Shift." A case study that helps to clarify the role of nonstate actors in the operation of regimes is Lasse Ringius, "Environmental NGOs and Regime Change: The Case of Ocean Dumping of Radioactive Waste," *European Journal of International Relations* 3 (March 1997), 61–104.

67. See Weiss and Jacobson, *Engaging Countries*.

68. Studies of regimes in which some or all of the key players are nonstate actors include Debora L. Spar, *The Cooperative Edge: The Internal Politics of International Cartels* (Ithaca: Cornell University Press, 1994); Virginia Haufler, "Crossing the Boundary between Private and Public: International Regimes and Non-State Actors," in Volker Rittberger, ed., *Regime Theory and International Relations* (Oxford: Clarendon, 1993), 94–111; and Virginia Haufler, *Dangerous Commerce: Insurance and the Management of International Risk* (Ithaca: Cornell University Press, 1997).

Quite apart from the underlying theoretical concerns regarding the actors and the sources of their behavior, various analytic issues also require attention in the next wave of studies of regime effectiveness. Advancing the understanding of regime effectiveness will require an analysis of multivariate relationships. In itself, this conclusion is unremarkable and similar to those about many social phenomena. Here, however, severe limits on the use of most forms of statistical inference pose a major challenge. This is not to say that there is no place for inductive reasoning in the next phase of research on effectiveness. Several projects that apply such reasoning to good effect have been completed.[69] But this situation does indicate the need to engage in a sustained effort to understand the causal mechanisms or behavioral pathways through which regimes affect the behavior of various actors and, in the process, shape the content of collective outcomes in international society.

Like other social institutions, regimes are not actors in their own right. Accordingly, they can affect the content of collective outcomes only by influencing the behavior of regime members or other relevant actors. How do they do this? One attempt to answer this question adopts a broadly utilitarian perspective and directs attention to what have become known as the three "Cs." Thus, regimes can increase the concern of relevant actors about the issues at stake, improve the contractual environment in the issue area, and enhance the capacity of key actors to carry out the terms of constitutional contracts.[70] Another significant study seeks to expand the range of behavioral mechanisms considered, looking at regimes as utility modifiers, enhancers of cooperation, bestowers of authority, learning facilitators, role definers, and agents of internal realignment.[71] Clearly, these studies constitute no more than preliminary forays into a complex subject. But they do point the way toward an important line of inquiry for students of regime effectiveness. Given the constraints on the use of inductive procedures, one way to proceed is to focus more attention on tracing the causal chains through which institutional arrangements impact the behavior of various actors and through such impacts affect the content of collective outcomes in international society. Among other things, this line of thinking is likely to prove particularly helpful to those concerned with practical matters of institutional design.

---

69. See especially Weiss and Jacobson, *Engaging Countries*; Victor, Raustiala, and Skolnikoff, *International Environmental Commitments*; and Clark, van Eijndoven, and Jaeger, *Global Environmental Risks*.

70. The three "Cs" were introduced in Haas, Keohane, and Levy, *Institutions for the Earth*, and used again to good advantage in Robert O. Keohane and Marc A. Levy, eds., *Institutions for Environmental Aid: Pitfalls and Promise* (Cambridge: MIT Press, 1996).

71. Young, *Effectiveness of International Environmental Regimes*.

Whether the focus is on consolidation and refinement or on extension and redirection, those seeking to improve our understanding of the effectiveness of environmental regimes must come to grips with some important methodological problems. The most critical of these is undoubtedly the need to develop reliable and harmonized data sets that are easily accessible to those desiring to explore a variety of hypotheses dealing with the sources of institutional effectiveness. The current practice of relying on stand-alone case studies in which the individual regime is the unit of analysis has served us well, and room exists for more work of this kind in the pursuit of knowledge about effectiveness. Yet a critical need during the next phase will be a capacity to subject both specific hypotheses about determinants of effectiveness and alternative models of the role of regimes to systematic empirical examination based on evidence drawn from sizable numbers of cases.[72] Does the nature of the decision rules employed by environmental regimes, for instance, make a difference in terms of effectiveness? What is the connection between the establishment of noncompliance procedures and effectiveness? Is the presence of nonstate actors among a regime's members significant when it comes to the achievement of effectiveness?

The construction of a suitable database is an expensive proposition that is difficult to justify to funding agencies as an end in itself. Once in place, however, such a database could become a public good available to all members of the relevant research community on convenient terms. Starting in 1993, the International Institute for Applied Systems Analysis (IIASA) supported an effort to develop an International Regimes Database (IRD) as part of its project Implementation and Effectiveness of International Environmental Commitments.[73] At this juncture, the IRD is still under construction, having outlived the project that gave birth to it and found material support from other sources.[74] If my argument in this section is correct, the research community concerned with regime effectiveness has a compelling need for the continued development of the IRD or some reasonable facsimile thereof.

---

72. A useful, though limited, start in this direction is made in Miles et. al., *Explaining Regime Effectiveness*.

73. On the International Regimes Database, see Helmut Breitmeier, Marc A. Levy, Oran R. Young, and Michael Zürn, "International Regimes Database (IRD): Data Protocol," WP-96-154, International Institute for Applied Systems Analysis, 1996, and Helmut Breitmeier, Marc A. Levy, Oran R. Young, and Michael Zürn, "The International Regimes Database as a Tool for the Study of International Cooperation," WP-96-160, International Institute for Applied Systems Analysis, 1996.

74. Funding for the database now comes from the National Science Foundation (NSF) in the United States and the German Science Foundation (DFG).

The research strategies that I have outlined offer no guarantee of success in developing a substantial collection of established propositions about the determinants of regime effectiveness. Much like the study of global warming, the theoretical, analytic, and methodological challenges facing students of effectiveness are great. But research in this field also resembles the study of climate change in the sense that the need for improved understanding is compelling and that the problems of formulating useful answers are worthy of the attention of the best and brightest analysts interested in international environmental issues. We have already made real progress in this field. But much remains to be done to arrive at results that will prove helpful to policymakers in a general way, much less serve as a useful guide for focused efforts in the realm of institutional design. Here, as elsewhere, the prizes will go to those who succeed in finding ways to overcome barriers involving causal inferences and to relax problematic assumptions embedded in current models without incurring undue losses of analytic rigor.

BECAUSE THIS CHAPTER is itself a survey of ongoing work on regime effectiveness, I will not summarize its contents. But there is one point that deserves special attention here. What we can realistically hope for in this realm is an ability to act like physicians who develop superb diagnostic skills rather than like cooks who are very good at following recipes. Although variations are certainly possible, recipes are expected to produce satisfactory results with a high degree of predictability and under a wide range of specific circumstances. In effect, they rest on a collection of statements spelling out sufficient conditions to transform collections of ingredients into finished products. The diagnostician, on the other hand, knows that there is a long list of factors which may play a role in explaining the condition of individual patients and that diagnoses based on necessary or sufficient conditions are few and far between. It is frequently possible to frame contingent or ceteris paribus propositions regarding the impacts of various factors and to observe complex interactions among a number of factors that are in play with regard to specific cases. But the role of the diagnostician is not to follow simple recipes that will ensure the health of individual patients. Rather, he or she must build up a convincing interpretation of each case based on considering a variety of factors that taken together appear to account for the condition at hand. The prescription then follows from this interpretive account.

Applied to international environmental regimes, these comments suggest that we should never expect to be able to solve complex governance problems through applications of simple recipes. What works with marine systems may not work with atmospheric or terrestrial systems. What makes sense in dealing with both ecosystems and social systems that are highly resilient may not work with systems that are vulnerable to nonlinear changes. What proves effective in cases where the behavior of the relevant systems is well understood may not work where our understanding of this behavior is limited and subject to rapid change. I am not suggesting that analyses of the sources of institutional effectiveness have nothing to contribute to the initial design or subsequent modification of international environmental regimes. Rather, the most useful contributions of regime analysis to solving large-scale environmental problems will take the form of interpretive accounts based on efforts to join general knowledge with an in-depth understanding of individual cases in contrast to the application of simple recipes to complex problems of governance in world affairs.

CHAPTER 6

Toward a Theory of Institutional Change

Once formed, international regimes rarely become static, unchanging structures. On the contrary, they normally set in motion highly dynamic social practices that change continually—sometimes dramatically—in response to both endogenous forces and exogenous pressures. As the case of whales and whaling suggests, profound changes in ends as well as means can follow shifts in the composition of a regime's membership. The regimes related to Antarctica and long-range transboundary air pollution, by contrast, feature a broadening of functional scope resulting from the addition of new institutional components that enlarge the range of substantive issues which they address. For its part, the case of stratospheric ozone illustrates how institutional changes can flow from new understandings of the nature of the problem to be solved. Yet another perspective on change emerges from the experience with oil pollution at sea, where the failure of an initial set of policy instruments led to a radical shift from discharge standards to equipment standards as mechanisms for bringing this form of marine pollution under control. And these examples are merely indicative of the wide array of institutional changes that occur in connection with many—perhaps most—international regimes on a regular basis.

Institutional change is intimately related as well to the resilience of international regimes, that is, their capacity to survive disturbances or to adapt to changing circumstances without losing their essential or constitutive characteristics.[1] Regime change and resilience are not simply oppo-

1. Resilience encompasses two distinct dimensions: robustness and brittleness. *Robustness* is the capacity of a regime to endure chronic stresses. *Brittleness*, by contrast, is a measure of vulnerability to acute stresses of short duration—that is, crises. For a discussion of the idea of resilience in connection with ecosystems, see C. S. Holling, "Resilience of Ecosystems: Local Sur-

site sides of the same coin. Many institutional changes have no significant consequences for the resilience of regimes. Others actually increase the resilience of institutional arrangements by improving the fit between regimes and the biophysical or social settings in which they operate. But at some point, institutional changes will call into question the resilience of even the most durable regimes. In the extreme, change can lead to the decay and eventual collapse of regimes. Short of that, change may prove more or less destabilizing and pose serious challenges to the capacity of regimes to remain effective. It follows that those desiring to maintain or increase the resilience of regimes will join those seeking to alter or reform regimes in exhibiting a lively interest in studies aimed at improving our understanding of regime dynamics.

Yet the burgeoning literature on international institutions contains surprisingly few sustained efforts to describe and explain regime change or to account for the dynamics of regimes in the period following their initial establishment. This is not to say that there is no intellectual capital on which to draw. At an early stage in the development of regime analysis, Robert Keohane and Joseph Nye directed attention to the sources of regime change.[2] Their fourfold distinction among economic process models, overall structure models, issue structure models, and international organization models as tools for understanding institutional change remains helpful today. Thomas Gehring's more recent work on dynamic regimes is another notable exception. His emphasis on negotiations that concern the content of social norms deserves consideration in any study of regime change.[3] Some of the ideas developed by students of regime formation are also worthy of consideration in efforts to understand regime change. The distinction between processes featuring self-generation, negotiation, and imposition, for example, is surely relevant in thinking about how institutions change following their initial establishment.[4] Given that international institutions, like all other social institutions, are constantly in flux, however, it is remarkable that regime analysis has had so little to say over

---

prise and Global Change," in W. C. Clark and R. E. Munn, eds., *Sustainable Development of the Biosphere* (Cambridge: Cambridge University Press, 1986), 292–317. A variety of perspectives on resilience in connection with linked social and ecological systems appear in Fikret Berkes and Carl Folke, eds., *Linking Social and Ecological Systems: Management Practices and Social Mechanisms for Building Resilience* (Cambridge: Cambridge University Press, 1998).

2. Robert O. Keohane and Joseph S. Nye, Power and Interdependence, 2d ed. (Glenview, Ill.: Scott, Foresman, 1989), chap. 3.

3. Thomas Gehring, *Dynamic International Regimes: Institutions for International Environmental Governance* (Frankfurt: Peter Lang, 1992).

4. Oran R. Young, *International Cooperation: Building Regimes for Natural Resources and the Environment* (Ithaca: Cornell University Press, 1989), chap. 4.

the last twenty years about the patterns, processes, sources, and consequences of institutional change.

In this chapter, I take some initial steps toward rectifying this situation, providing a general account of regime change as a focus for analysis, and endeavoring to elevate the study of institutional change to a level equivalent to that occupied by regime formation and regime effectiveness among contributors to the new institutionalism in international relations.[5] My treatment of this subject proceeds in three principal stages. In the first, largely descriptive stage, I ask what kinds of institutional changes we should expect to encounter and how we can best organize our thinking about the range of institutional change. I then turn to the sources of institutional change, seeking to evaluate the significance of a variety of driving forces that play a role in causing changes to occur in international institutions. Finally, I take up the question of consequences, addressing the implications of institutional change for the ability of regimes to operate effectively within their own issue areas as well as for the operation of international society more generally. Although I frequently use examples drawn from the experience of regimes for whales and whaling, Antarctica, long-range transboundary air pollution, stratospheric ozone, and oil pollution at sea, the issues are generic, arising in every field of international governance.

THE RANGE OF CHANGE

Change is a pervasive feature of the world of social institutions. There is no aspect of institutional arrangements that is immune to change, whether we are considering international society or any other social setting. Yet there is no established vocabulary—much less accepted classificatory system—in terms of which to identify and describe the domain of institutional change. The purpose of this section is to initiate the development of such a system of classification and to convey, in the process, a sense of the range of phenomena of interest to those concerned with regime dynamics. To this end, I differentiate between types of change, forms of change, patterns of change, and processes of change.

Types of Change

In the nature of things, classification systems are neither right nor wrong, neither correct nor incorrect. They are merely more or less useful for the

5. Oran R. Young, *International Governance: Protecting the Environment in a Stateless Society* (Ithaca: Cornell University Press, 1994), introduction.

analytic tasks that their creators have in mind. Even so, there is no escaping the need to make clear-cut choices in this realm; the alternative is an analytic effort lacking in structure and thus condemned to incoherence. Here, my goal is to broaden and deepen knowledge of the effectiveness of regimes and of the fate of these institutional arrangements during the period following their initial formation. In this connection, I have found it helpful to distinguish between changes in the constitutive attributes of regimes and changes in their operational elements. To this I would add a concern for changes in the character of the problems regimes address and in the broader biophysical and social settings in which they operate. Although problem structure and setting are not, strictly speaking, features of regimes themselves, they are so closely bound up with institutional arrangements that any account of regime dynamics will be incomplete without some consideration of these issues.

The constitutive attributes of a regime are those features which define its essential character. In the first instance, these attributes have to do with the framing of the problems that regimes address and the basic strategies they adopt for solving or at least managing those problems. The shift from conservation to preservation during the 1970s as the objective of the regime for whales and whaling, for example, constitutes a change of this kind. So also does the restructuring of the oil pollution regime during the 1970s, involving both the incorporation of this regime into the larger regulatory structure of the International Convention for the Prevention of Pollution from Ships (MARPOL) 1973/78 and the shift from the use of discharge standards to equipment standards as a means of controlling intentional oil pollution at sea.

Beyond this, changes in constitutive attributes commonly involve alterations in membership, functional scope, and geographic domain. Both the addition and the subtraction of members, as well as alterations in the level or degree of role differentiation among members, belong to this category. Thus, the addition of new members was largely responsible for the reframing of the problem in the regime for whales and whaling; the admission of new members to the status of Consultative Party played a key role in defusing conflicts surrounding the regime for Antarctica during the 1980s. Shifts in functional scope can take the form of changes in the mix of regulatory, procedural, programmatic, and generative tasks that a regime performs as well as additions to or subtractions from the range of issues for which a regime is responsible. The movement from the 1985 Vienna Convention to the 1987 Montreal Protocol, for example, represents a major step toward the adoption of regulatory responsibilities in the case of stratospheric ozone. The addition of the arrangements covering living resources and environmental protection in the case of Antarctica, by contrast, exemplifies functional change in the form of an expansion in the range of issues covered. Changes in geographic domain are typically linked to alterations in other constitutive elements. The move to add living resources to the issues covered by the Antarctic Treaty System, for instance, necessitated a considerable expansion in the area covered by the regime. The adoption of the ecosystem approach in the case of the Great Lakes Water Quality Agreement made it essential to expand the coverage of the regime from the lakes themselves to a much larger area encompassing the watersheds surrounding the lakes.

Changes in operational elements may take a much wider range of forms. Yet they are less fundamental than changes in constitutive attributes because they do not call into question the survival of regimes and because many—perhaps most—do not even lead to watersheds. Changes of this sort may affect the regulatory provisions, procedural mechanisms, or programmatic activities of regimes. The development of new or revised management procedures for whales and whaling, the designation of specially protected areas in Antarctica, and the acceleration of phaseout schedules for CFCs and related chemicals in the ozone regime are all examples of this sort of change. Similarly, changes in operational attributes may involve compliance mechanisms, funding sources, dispute resolution procedures, implementation review mechanisms, or the development of organizations needed to administer regimes. The debate over the need for a permanent secretariat for the Antarctic regime, the creation of the Multilateral Fund to help developing countries phase out CFCs and related chemicals, and the development of procedures to allow classification societies to monitor compliance with equipment standards for new tankers are instances of such changes. The range of potential changes in operational attributes is very wide, and most regimes undergo numerous changes on a continual basis through both formal and informal processes. When taken individually, these changes are less significant than those involving constitutive elements, yet the cumulative impact of changes in operational attributes can produce profound effects. Thus regimes that have been in operation for some time are often hard to recognize on the basis of a reading of the formal agreements on which they rest.

The framing or characterization of the problem to be addressed is a constitutive attribute of any specific regime. But major changes can also occur in the nature of the problem itself, whether or not they are reflected in a reframing of the problem by a regime's members. Sometimes, these changes arise from technological advances, such as the development of far more efficient methods of killing whales—and other marine organisms—

and the development of new chemicals likely to affect the atmosphere. In other cases, changes in the problem stem from large-scale economic developments or from political developments that affect the capacity of regime members to participate effectively. Vessel-source oil pollution became a serious concern with the advent of a global economy and the dramatic rise in dependence on fossil fuels as a source of energy in the postwar decades. Regimes involving the former Soviet Union had to be reformulated—in some cases drastically—as a consequence of the collapse of the Soviet Union and the emergence of Russia and a sizable number of other successor states. Often, major economic swings affect the ability and willingness of member states to respond energetically to the regulatory requirements or programmatic demands of regimes. What seems eminently doable during a period of vigorous growth may seem particularly onerous during a period of recession or even depression.

Moreover, in a study of regime dynamics, it is important to pay attention to the broader biophysical and social settings within which regimes operate. The last several decades, for example, have provided a setting that is generally conducive to the growth and development of environmental regimes. The demand for environmental governance is demonstrably growing owing both to the effects of a rapidly increasing human population and to expanded capabilities arising from technological advances and economic growth. At the same time, there has been a rapid diffusion both of the realization of the need for governance in world affairs and of awareness of the limitations of the United Nations as a vehicle for the supply of governance, resulting in a period of institutional innovation in the field of environmental affairs, with many new regimes coming into existence and many of those already in existence experiencing rapid development. But this favorable setting must not be regarded as a fact of life—that is, a condition that will last forever. More or less severe crises affecting both the biophysical setting and the social setting within which regimes operate are perfectly possible. Today, an acute awareness exists of the significance of discontinuous or nonlinear changes as they affect both natural and social systems, and processes of this sort are likely to have major consequences for the development of environmental regimes.[6] Whether the results are positive or negative from the perspective of particular regimes, it would be a serious mistake to ignore changes in the biophysical and social settings in an effort to come to grips with regime dynamics.

6. For an example relating to fisheries, see James A. Wilson, James M. Acheson, Mark Metcalfe, and Peter Kleban, "Chaos, Complexity, and Community Management of Fisheries," *Marine Policy* 18 (July 1994), 291–305.

Forms of Change

The discussion of types of change seeks to identify the range of regime attributes and elements that need to be considered in a study of regime dynamics. A consideration of form, by contrast, directs attention to how or in what manner institutional changes come about, leading to a series of useful distinctions between intended and unintended change, formal and informal change, rule-governed and ad hoc change, discrete and linked change, slow and rapid change, and linear and nonlinear change.

Although it is natural to think about intended changes in an examination of regime dynamics, many changes in existing institutions come about as unintended—and often unforeseen—by-products or side effects of actions taken for other purposes. There is an important difference, for example, between unplanned or de facto changes in the regime for whales and whaling attributable to the growth of the animal rights movement in a variety of settings, and changes in the regime for marine pollution arising from the conclusion that discharge standards were not working and the resultant shift to equipment standards as a means of remedying the defects in the prior system. Perhaps even more important is the distinction between formal and informal changes in institutional arrangements. Many students of regimes—especially lawyers and political scientists—show a marked propensity to focus on formal changes that take such forms as the addition of substantive protocols to framework conventions, the acceptance of amendments to preexisting conventions or treaties, and the formal actions of such bodies as the Antarctic Treaty Consultative Meetings (ATCMs) and the Meeting/Conference of the Parties (M/COP) of the ozone regime. Important as these changes are, however, much of the action in the realm of regime dynamics would be missed by an approach limited to formal changes. As sociologists often remind us, rights, rules, programs, and decision-making procedures experience continuous change as a result of interpretive processes and de facto responses to experience derived from operating regimes.[7] And as Elinor Ostrom has argued persuasively, rules in use can and generally do differ quite significantly from the rules specified in constitutive documents.[8] Although this can become a source of confusion and even disagreement in some circumstances, regime members generally understand rules in use perfectly well, despite the

---

7. Walter W. Powell and Paul J. DiMaggio, eds., *The New Institutionalism in Organizational Analysis* (Chicago: University of Chicago Press, 1991).

8. Elinor Ostrom, *Governing the Commons: The Evolution of Institutions for Collective Action* (Cambridge: Cambridge University Press, 1990).

fact that they are apt to reflect a variety of informal changes that have come about through custom or practice rather than formal agreement.[9]

Equally important is the distinction between rule-governed and ad hoc change. Rule-governed changes are alterations brought about through procedures prescribed by the regime itself. Most constitutive agreements contain provisions for amending the documents themselves. Many regimes also establish decision-making procedures that can handle a variety of changes that do not require alterations in the constitutive agreements. One of the primary tasks of the ATCMs, for example, is to adopt agreed measures concerning a wide range of matters pertaining to human activities in Antarctica; the M/COP of the ozone regime regularly makes decisions involving changes that can go into effect without ratification as well as changes requiring ratification on the part of the members. The rules governing change vary significantly from one regime to another in terms of their stringency or, in other words, the height of the hurdles they pose for those advocating the adoption of specific changes. Thus the frequency of ad hoc changes tends to vary with the stringency of the rules that regimes adopt regarding rule-governed change. Several complications arise, however, in efforts to apply the distinction between rule-governed and ad hoc change to specific situations. As the case of whales and whaling suggests, parties may seek to present what are ultimately ad hoc changes in a form implying they are rule-governed changes. Thus, the move to prohibit harvesting of great whales has been implemented in formal terms by setting harvest quotas to zero in what is known as the "Schedule." Conversely, those who succeed in initiating ad hoc changes in regimes commonly make efforts to get the changes accepted after the fact through rule-governed procedures. The collapse of the Convention on the Regulation of Antarctic Mineral Resource Activities surely deserves to be treated as an ad hoc change. One of the motives for negotiating the Protocol on Environmental Protection on a fast track was undoubtedly to bring about a return to rule-governed change following the dramatic departure from normal practice reflected in the demise of CRAMRA.

The next three distinctions regarding forms of change can be treated as a package. The first involves the scope of change. Although there is obviously a continuum here, it is helpful to differentiate cases involving discrete changes in the sense of changes pertaining to a single component or a small part of an institutional arrangement from cases encompassing linked changes or changes affecting many components of a regime at the same time. Changing the phaseout schedule for a particular chemical un-

9. Such phenomena lie at the heart of what lawyers know as "common law" in municipal systems and "customary law" in international society. For an eloquent example, see Guido Calabresi, *A Common Law for the Age of Statutes* (Cambridge: Harvard University Press, 1982).

der the terms of the ozone regime is one thing, but moving from the very limited framework provisions of the Vienna Convention to the substantial provisions of the Montreal Protocol is another. Much the same can be said about the rate of change or the distinction between slow changes and fast changes. Many observers argue that institutional change at the international level is inordinately slow, especially by comparison with analogous processes at the domestic level. Although this is a subject that requires more systematic study, the evidence does not appear to bear out this view. International regimes can and do experience rapid change—consider the experience of the ozone regime during the period from 1985 to 1992. And domestic institutions can prove highly resistant to change, regardless of their fit with changing biophysical or social settings. Think of the regime for hard-rock mining on public lands in the United States as a striking example. The distinction between linear and nonlinear or chaotic change is also relevant at this juncture. Without consciously considering the matter, many observers assume that institutional change is a slow and steady process, one that is continuous rather than discontinuous. But the evidence from actual cases raises profound questions about the accuracy of this assumption. Whereas some changes (such as the expansion of the ozone regime to cover additional chemicals) do involve more or less continuous developments, big institutional changes (for instance the imposition of a moratorium on harvesting in the case of whales or the addition of the environmental protocol in the Antarctica regime) tend to take the form of discontinuous jumps.

Patterns of Change

Given the diversity of types and forms of change, it is only natural that students of international regimes will be drawn to a search for patterns of institutional change. Are there any recurrent patterns of change that will allow us to make sense out of the complexities described in the preceding paragraphs? Perhaps the most tempting response to this question is to turn to the concept of a life cycle as a means of coming to terms with the subject of regime dynamics. In essence, this would mean approaching institutional change via a model featuring birth, development, maturation, decay, and eventual death or termination.[10] This approach is not altogether implausible. It is relatively easy to identify a point of birth or creation for

---

10. In this connection, the evolution of regime analysis from an initial interest in regime formation to a growing focus on institutional effectiveness and an incipient interest in regime change is perfectly understandable. For a collection of essays that exemplifies this progression, see Oran R. Young, ed., *The International Political Economy and International Institutions*, 2 vols. (Cheltenham: Edward Elgar, 1996).

international regimes, as with the signing of the International Convention on the Regulation of Whaling in 1946 and of the Antarctic Treaty in 1959. Moreover, it is possible to discern a point of termination or death for some institutional arrangements, as with the collapse of the regime for northern fur seals in 1985. And many regimes experience developmental processes that might be treated according to the concept of a life cycle. Some will undoubtedly think in these terms in evaluating the dynamics of the ozone regime, an arrangement that has certainly experienced a pattern of growth over the years since its inception and could well come to an end following the final phaseout of all chemicals likely to cause harm to ozone resident in the stratosphere.

Yet the use of the concept of a life cycle to bring order to thinking about regime dynamics seems fraught with problems. Many regimes are expected to operate on a long-term basis and therefore to have indefinite life spans. No one expects the need for a governance system to deal with human activities in Antarctica, for instance, to disappear any time soon. Even more important, the ideas of growth and decay associated with the concept of a life cycle seem difficult to apply to institutional change in a sensible manner. Regimes typically do develop over time. But there is little reason to interpret such changes as genetically programmed developmental sequences, and changes in specific cases may dramatically redirect regimes in ways that seem to have nothing to do with a life cycle. The shift in the regime for whales and whaling from a conservation arrangement to a preservation arrangement, for example, is understandable in terms of the changing composition of the membership but is difficult to interpret as a life cycle process. Nor is it easy to identify processes of aging or decay in many institutional arrangements. Some regimes do become increasingly rigid or begin to break down as the coalitions on which they are based shift or unravel.[11] But this is not equivalent to decay in life cycle terms. As the cases of whales and whaling and marine pollution suggest, regimes can pass through times of troubles but reemerge later on some new or restructured footing. While the temptation to adopt the concept of a life cycle in the search for patterns of change is understandable, therefore, I would argue that this dangerous practice should be avoided or pursued with great care.

Yet there is much to be said for the proposition that regime dynamics frequently do give rise to a pattern of progressive development. What this means is that specific regimes often begin as relatively limited or modest arrangements and take on added scope and complexity as a response to is-

11. On the concept of "institutional arthritis," see Mancur Olson Jr., *The Rise and Decline of Nations* (New Haven: Yale University Press, 1982).

sues arising during the course of their operation. This process may take a variety of forms, such as drawing in additional members to cope with the problem of ozone depletion, adding new functional components to deal with an expanding range of human activities in Antarctica or a broader range of transboundary pollutants, devising new management procedures to impose more effective constraints on the harvesting of whales, or introducing new funding arrangements to facilitate a shift away from the use of ozone-depleting substances on the part of developing countries. These developments are not genetically programmed but typically result from bargaining processes among regime members, and many possible paths involving progressive development are not taken.[12] In addition, there is no basis for assuming that progressive development is a gradual or steady process. More often, it proceeds by fits and starts, with notable achievements emerging occasionally from protracted bargaining processes. In some ways, it is reasonable to think of progressive development as a goal that those involved in the operation of regimes may adopt to guide their efforts rather than as a description of what actually happens in the typical case. In effect, progressive development may arise from the efforts of those who support regimes but is by no means guaranteed to occur as a natural process.

Many instances of institutional change follow a pattern best described in terms of the concept of punctuated equilibrium.[13] Of course, small— often informal—changes occur in international institutions all the time. With respect to more far-reaching developments, however, a tendency exists for regimes to resist change over relatively long periods of time and then to shift to some new configuration rather quickly. The shifts in the regime for whales and whaling from conservation to preservation and in the marine pollution regime from discharge standards to equipment standards appear to reflect such a process. This pattern parallels similar observations that many analysts have made about changes in economic and political arrangements at the domestic level. To the extent that punctuated equilibrium is important in the dynamics of social institutions, it is desirable to focus analytic attention on the conditions giving rise to nonlinear processes and on the trigger mechanisms that lead to discontinuities or

12. Seminal works on bargaining include Thomas C. Schelling, *The Strategy of Conflict* (Cambridge: Harvard University Press, 1960), and Richard E. Walton and Robert B. McKersie, *A Behavioral Theory of Labor Negotiations: An Analysis of a Social Interaction System* (New York: McGraw-Hill, 1965). For an account of institutional bargaining at the international level, see Young, *International Governance*, chaps. 4, 5.

13. For a well-known expression of the idea of punctuated equilibrium in biology, see Niles Eldredge and Stephen Jay Gould, "Punctuated Equilibria: An Alternative to Phyletic Gradualism," in T. J. Schopf, ed., *Models in Paleobiology* (San Francisco: Freeman, Cooper and Company, 1972), 82–115.

what a number of students of international regimes have called "watershed changes."[14] With regard to policymaking, these observations also make clear why there are good reasons to focus attention on the relative merits of possible alterations even in cases of regimes that appear to be highly resilient. The timing of nonlinear changes is hard to predict. But when they come, windows of opportunity to restructure many features of constitutive contracts arise. There is much to be said for being prepared to seize these opportunities to introduce changes that have been thought through carefully in advance.

Processes of Change

To complete this survey of change in international regimes, it is important to consider processes of change. Regardless of the types, forms, and patterns discernible in the domain of change, can we differentiate among the principal processes through which changes in institutional arrangements occur? The fundamental proposition I wish to advance in this connection is that the processes involved in changing existing regimes belong to the same broad categories as the processes that dominate regime formation. In other words, it is helpful in analyzing regime dynamics to think in terms of spontaneous or self-generating change, negotiated change, and imposed change.[15]

Spontaneous processes of change feature outcomes that arise from the self-interested activities of many actors but are not specifically sought by anyone.[16] These are the processes that lawyers have in mind when they speak about the development of common law in domestic systems and customary law at the international level. But similar processes occur in many other social settings, ranging from the emergence of new patterns of speech in language communities to the development of new paradigms for framing issues and thinking about problems in scientific communities and in policy communities. Many informal changes are spontaneous in nature, though it is not uncommon for them to be codified in more explicit or formal terms after they have emerged as de facto elements of social practices. The opening up of the meetings of the International Whaling Commission (IWC) and of the ATCMs in the Antarctic Treaty System to active participation on the part of nonstate actors constitutes an im-

14. On the idea of watershed changes, see Helmut Breitmeier, Marc A. Levy, Oran R. Young, and Michael Zürn, " International Regimes Database (IRD): Data Protocol," WP-9-154, International Institute for Applied Systems Analysis, 1996.

15. For an account of these types of change, see Young, *International Cooperation*, chap. 4.

16. A seminal account of such processes appears in Friedrich A. Hayek, *Rules and Order*, vol. 1 of *Law, Legislation, and Liberty* (Chicago: University of Chicago Press, 1973).

portant example of such processes. No synoptic or even conscious decisions were made to bring about this change; the shift occurred as a consequence of a variety of informal initiatives on the part of many actors. Somewhat similar comments pertain to the expansion of the Antarctic regime to cover a wide range of environmental concerns, a development that was largely unforeseen in the drafting of the 1959 treaty.[17] Some analysts divide institutions into those in which spontaneous processes are of central importance (common law systems) and those in which such processes are of more marginal importance (civil law systems). But spontaneous change appears to be a significant feature of virtually all international regimes, a condition that may have something to do with the relatively underdeveloped character of legislative and judicial systems in international society.

Negotiated changes, by contrast, are outcomes of processes in which a variety of self-interested actors bargain vigorously over the terms of proposed alterations in institutional arrangements. The process of negotiating changes in existing regimes differs somewhat from the process of negotiating the formation of new regimes because it exhibits elements of legislative bargaining in contrast to institutional bargaining.[18] Whereas those negotiating the terms of the 1946 convention on whaling sought to devise provisions that all the participants could accept, those who engineered the adoption of the 1982 moratorium on whaling sought to construct a coalition capable of meeting the rule requiring a three-fourths majority for making decisions of this kind. But it is easy to exaggerate this distinction. A sizable fraction of international regimes—the Antarctic Treaty System is one example—have decision rules requiring unanimity or at least some relatively strong form of consensus to arrive at collective choices involving institutional changes. Some decisions about institutional changes (such as the inclusion of additional chemicals in phaseout schedules in contrast to changes in phaseout schedules for chemicals already included in the ozone regime) require ratification on the part of individual members after they have been approved by the conference of the parties. In other cases, individual members can opt out of institutional changes, at least with regard to their own participation in the regime, by entering objections or reservations to decisions adopted by the majority. The result is a form of negotiation that lies somewhere between institutional bargain-

17. The sole expression of interest in environmental issues in the 1959 Antarctic Treaty is the reference in article 9(1)(f) to "preservation and conservation of living resources in Antarctica." For an account of the evolution of the Antarctic Treaty System, see M. J. Peterson, *Managing the Frozen South: The Creation and Evolution of the Antarctic Treaty System* (Berkeley: University of California Press, 1988).

18. On the idea of institutional bargaining, see Young, *International Governance*, chaps. 4, 5.

ing and legislative bargaining and often involves a complex mix of the two. Because processes of negotiation loom large in connection with efforts to alter international institutions, especially when changes are intended, formal, and rule governed, there is much to be said for investing considerable time and energy in improving the understanding of this hybrid form of bargaining.

Nothing in the preceding paragraphs should be taken to suggest that processes marked by imposed changes are unimportant in the realm of regime dynamics.[19] Self-interested actors regularly seek to bring pressure to bear to promote or to resist institutional changes, especially where the changes in question deal with constitutive elements and seem likely to bring about fundamental shifts in the outcomes flowing from the operation of regimes. That said, it is important to note that the process of imposed change is not simply a matter of the great powers calling the shots or dictating the terms of institutional change to lesser powers.[20] The United States, for example, resisted the addition of the Multilateral Fund to the ozone regime but eventually gave in to the pressure of others on this fundamental question. Japan has found itself relatively powerless to hold off changes in the regime for whales and whaling which it regards as inimical to Japanese interests. And the Antarctic club, which has long included the world's major powers, found itself under irresistible pressure to grant Consultative Party status to a variety of outsiders, whose credentials were dubious in objective terms, as a means of staving off a move on the part of several developing countries to bring the Antarctic regime into some sort of formal relationship with the United Nations. None of this is to deny the role of power in the material sense as a factor in processes of institutional change. The capacity of the United States, for example, to wield unilateral sanctions has played a role in promoting changes in the regime for whales and whaling, and the central role of the United States in the world oil market certainly provided it a strong position in the development of equipment standards applicable to oil tankers. Accordingly, the analysis of imposition as a process of institutional change requires a careful consideration of the political dynamics of individual cases.

These processes of change are not mutually exclusive in the sense that the presence of one excludes the operation of the others. On the contrary, many—perhaps most—institutional changes feature a complex mix of

19. For a well-known expression of the view that international institutions are properly understood as surface manifestations or reflections of underlying power relations, see Susan Strange, "*Cave! hic dragones*: A Critique of Regime Analysis," in Stephen D. Krasner, ed., *International Regimes* (Ithaca: Cornell University Press, 1983), 337–54.

20. For an account that stresses the difference between bargaining leverage and structural power in this context, see Young, *International Governance*, chap. 5.

the three processes. For analysts, then, the task is not to look for smoking guns that tell whether particular changes are spontaneous, negotiated, or imposed in nature. Rather, we should seek to develop causal narratives that both separate out the roles of self-generation, negotiation, and imposition and show how these distinct processes interact with one another to produce the outcomes that occur in specific cases.[21] This, of course, carries us well beyond the realm of description and into an examination of the sources or causes of institutional change. As such, it constitutes a natural point of transition from this initial stage of delineating the range of change to the stage of looking systematically at the sources of change.

SOURCES OF CHANGE

The range of change to be considered in a general account of regime dynamics is broad. Thus the construction of a simple, unified theory of institutional change during the foreseeable future seems unlikely. Nonetheless, it is essential to move on from a largely descriptive consideration of the range of change to tackle the key analytic issues associated with regime dynamics. The first of these centers on the sources of institutional change or the causal mechanisms that produce changes in international regimes during the period following their initial formation. In this section, I start with some observations on the contributions of others to this topic and then proceed to develop a more general framework for use by those seeking to develop a systematic account of regime dynamics in the future.

Earlier Contributions

An early and still important contribution is the work of Robert Keohane and Joseph Nye on "explaining international regime change."[22] Keohane and Nye propose to account for institutional change in terms of four distinct models that focus respectively on economic processes, overall power structure in the world, power structure within issue areas, and power capabilities as affected by international organization. Helpful as these models are as a first cut at explaining the source of institutional change, they have several serious drawbacks that limit their attractions for those endeavoring to devise a general account of regime dynamics. To begin with, they direct attention not only to what I have called the "social setting"

---

21. This is a matter of what David Dessler calls "causal analysis." See Dessler, "The Architecture of Causal Analysis," paper presented at the Harvard Center for International Affairs, Cambridge, 1992.
22. This is the title of chapter 3 in Keohane and Nye, *Power and Interdependence.*

within which regimes operate but also and more specifically to material conditions that shape the social setting. Thus, the first three models deal exclusively with developments relating to the material environment. Even the international organization model is tied to material conditions in that it looks to the role of institutions as modifiers of arguments focused on power in the structural sense rather than as an independent force in the system. In effect, the momentum associated with sets of "networks, norms, and institutions" can play a role in accounting for lags between shifts in power structure or capabilities and subsequent adjustments in international regimes, but these organizational considerations do not play an independent role in processes of institutional change.[23] As we shall see, these largely material factors must be included in any general account of the sources of change in international institutions. But they need to be seen in context as only one among a number of types or categories of forces producing change.

A very different approach to regime dynamics is reflected in the more recent work of Thomas Gehring. Stressing the importance of norms, expectations, and bounded rationality, Gehring directs attention to processes of negotiation in which regime members interact directly with each other regarding proposed changes in existing arrangements and seek to arrive at "cooperative agreements."[24] A moment's reflection suggests both that such processes do play a role in many cases of institutional change and that this perspective, like the one developed by Keohane and Nye, focuses on only one element of what would need to be included in a more general theory of institutional change. Here the emphasis is largely on endogenous processes in which various forms of negotiation predominate, not the exogenous forces affecting the social setting or environment that interest Keohane and Nye. In some ways, this account provides a particularly useful counterpoint to the approach that Keohane and Nye espouse. It also serves to remind us that a variety of partial approaches to regime dynamics are possible and that we need to devise a system of analysis that can subsume all these approaches in developing a more general theory of institutional change.

How, then, should we proceed in the search for a broader account of regime dynamics? In this section, I sketch such an approach to the sources or causes of institutional change, an approach based on a central distinction between endogenous and exogenous forces of change.

---

23. Ibid., 54–58. This phenomenon subsequently became a major theme in Keohane's research. See Robert O. Keohane, *After Hegemony: Cooperation and Discord in the World Political Economy* (Princeton: Princeton University Press, 1984).

24. Gehring, *Dynamic International Regimes*, chap. 11.

Endogenous Forces

Endogenous forces encompass those arising from the operation of re-gimes themselves. That is, they represent internal forces associated with the functioning of institutions in contrast to outside forces that impact the operation of regimes. To start with some extreme cases, regimes can undergo change as a consequence of their own success or failure. Although many international regimes deal with ongoing activities of indefinite duration, the very success of a regime can lead to the disappearance of the problem it is designed to solve. Something of this sort may occur in the case of ozone-depleting substances if the use of CFCs and all other chemicals likely to disturb stratospheric ozone is phased out completely. Perhaps more common are situations in which serious shortcomings with regard to performance become driving forces in efforts to alter institutional arrangements. The dramatic failure of the regime for whales and whaling to halt declines in stocks of several species of great whales during the first several decades of its operation and the equally striking failure of discharge standards to solve the problem of oil pollution at sea certainly played a critical role in energizing the forces for change in these regimes. The results were the elimination of the blue whale unit and the eventual imposition of a moratorium on the harvesting of great whales, and the shift from discharge standards to equipment standards in the case of marine pollution.

Numerous other endogenous forces can give rise to institutional change. Sometimes these forces are reflections of institutional contradictions, as when regimes dealing with marine living resources (such as marine fisheries) seek to encourage, at one and the same time, the conservation of stocks and the growth of fishing industries. In other instances, the force for change is gridlock in the sense of institutional arrangements that become paralyzed by the presence of blocking coalitions which make it impossible to arrive at collective decisions regarding the issues over which the regime has jurisdiction. Many observers worry about problems of this kind in conjunction with the arrangements covering marine living resources within the Antarctic Treating System. Yet another endogenous force involves social learning in that experience derived from the operation of a regime gives rise to a better understanding of the problem to be solved or to new ideas regarding mechanisms for coming to terms with the problem.[25] A striking example of this process at work is visible in the efforts of the regime dealing with long-range transboundary air pollution (LRTAP) and

25. For a study of social learning as a mechanism for institutional change at the international level, see Ernst B. Haas, *When Knowledge Is Power: Three Models of Change in International Organizations* (Berkeley: University of California Press, 1990).

especially in the operation of EMEP, a program that constitutes an important element of the LRTAP arrangement.[26] Shifts in member interests resulting from the operation of a regime or the addition or subtraction of members through prescribed institutional procedures also deserve consideration in this account of endogenous forces. The acceptance of additional Consultative Parties in the case of Antarctica and the accession of new members in the regime for whales and whaling occurred as normal processes associated with the operation of the regimes themselves. But in both instances, the dynamics of these regimes changed substantially as a consequence of these adjustments in membership.

Some observers will see broader or deeper mechanisms at work in the operation of these specific endogenous forces. It is possible, for example, to look for the operation of a dialectical process, whether it be material or ideational. Some will see the emergence of preservationist ideas as an antithesis to the dominance of ideas centered on consumptive use within the regime for whales and whaling, asking whether we are presently searching for and possibly moving toward a new synthesis that will somehow incorporate elements of both conservationism and preservationism. Others may look for evidence of progressive development or some sort of unilinear movement toward greater and greater success in problem solving in seeking to understand the meaning of institutional change in specific cases. Such progression may be unfolding in the cases of ozone and LRTAP. Still others will seek to impose a cyclic model—in contrast to a model of progressive development—on the record of institutional change in specific cases, looking, for instance, for evidence of the development of new chemicals that pose threats to stratospheric ozone and are likely to touch off additional rounds in the battle to protect the ozone layer. These mechanisms are, of course, familiar to students of history or social processes more generally; they serve as frameworks for those seeking to provide interpretive order in thinking about complex realities.[27] Clearly, none of them is correct in any objective sense. But they may prove useful as devices for helping us to organize our thinking about endogenous sources of institutional change.

Exogenous Forces

Juxtaposed to these endogenous forces are exogenous forces that impact regimes in a variety of ways. Familiar to political scientists who focus

---

26. See Juan Carlos di Primio, "Monitoring and Verification in the European Air Pollution Regime," WP-96-47, International Institute for Applied Systems Analysis, 1996.
27. Consider, for example, the linear theories of history developed by Hegel and Marx and the cyclical theories of Spengler and Toynbee.

on the distribution of power among the members of international society and tend to treat institutions as reflections of underlying power relations or as outgrowths of bargaining dominated by applications of power, these forces involve developments occurring in the biophysical setting as well as the social setting within which regimes operate.[28] In thinking about these exogenous forces, we must first distinguish between proximate causes and social drivers. *Proximate causes* are surface-level forces that are relatively easy to identify and play some role in accounting for changes in institutional arrangements. The defection of Australia and France from the coalition that crafted the 1988 Convention on the Regulation of Antarctic Mineral Resource Activities, for instance, constitutes an important factor in any account of the collapse of the minerals convention. Similar observations pertain to the decision of the United States to accept the London Amendments to the Montreal Protocol and thus to become a reluctant supporter of the move to create what has become known as the Multilateral Fund in the ozone regime. But these proximate causes are reflections of deeper developments taking place in the biophysical and social settings within which regimes operate. These deeper developments—that is, *social drivers*—are the main focus of interest for those seeking to understand exogenous forces that give rise to changes in international regimes. In the following paragraphs, I employ a common distinction among material conditions, institutions, and ideas in seeking to characterize how these social drivers generate changes in specific regimes.[29]

Material conditions encompass developments relating to technology, population, and the distribution of structural power in international society. Dramatic advances in the technology used to harvest marine mammals and fish, for instance, have caused the collapse of a number of regimes that were able to regulate harvesting relatively successfully under preexisting conditions. To be more specific, the advent of the high-endurance stern trawler effectively destroyed numerous regimes dealing with these resources.[30] The need to add new provisions concerning environmental protection to the Antarctic Treaty System became evident with the growth in human capacity to launch large-scale and sustained activities on and around the continent. Pressure to devise new approaches to the control of vessel-source oil pollution has been fueled by the dramatic growth in

---

28. See, for example, Susan Strange, *States and Markets: An Introduction to International Political Economy* (New York: Basil Blackwell, 1988), and Joseph M. Grieco, *Cooperation among Nations: Europe, America, and Non-Tariff Barriers to Trade* (Ithaca: Cornell University Press, 1990).

29. See, for example, Robert W. Cox, "Social Forces, States, and World Orders: Beyond International Relations Theory," in Robert O. Keohane, ed., *Neorealism and Its Critics* (New York: Columbia University Press, 1986), 204–54.

30. For a striking account, see William W. Warner, *Distant Water: The Fate of the North Atlantic Fisherman* (Boston: Little, Brown, 1983).

the number and size of tankers carrying crude oil over long distances during the postwar decades. The decline in the dominant position occupied by the United States has led participants in many international regimes to initiate efforts to adjust institutions to the new configuration of power in international society that Robert Keohane has described as "after hegemony."[31] The collapse of the Soviet Union has raised questions about the ability of Russia—as the successor to the Soviet Union in most international regimes—to participate effectively in a variety of specific arrangements, such as those dealing with Antarctica or with long-range transboundary air pollution. But at the same time, this material change has opened up prospects for developing regimes dealing with Arctic issues, which were off-limits during the era of the cold war.[32] And these are merely illustrations of a large class of social drivers that belong to the category of material conditions.

Although regimes are social institutions in their own right, institutional forces can also operate as exogenous drivers with regard to the dynamics of specific regimes. Essentially, what occurs is that developments take place either in other regimes with which a particular institutional arrangement interacts or in the overarching character of international society.[33] As the density of regimes operating in international society rises, interactions among specific regimes as well as functional relationships among them inevitably increase.[34] The formation of a regime for Antarctic marine living resources in 1980 and the more recent creation of a regime for marine mammals in the North Atlantic, for example, have obvious implications for the operation of the regime for whales and whaling. The expansion of the regime for marine pollution to cover a variety of other vessel-source pollutants and the incorporation of the arrangement for oil pollution into these larger arrangements through the development of MARPOL 1973/78 has clearly affected the operation of the oil pollution regime. With respect to overarching arrangements, it is hard to overlook the establishment of the United Nations Environment Programme in 1973, which now provides secretariat services for a number of regimes, including CITES, ozone, and biological diversity and which plays an important role in generating and disseminating information that is important to those responsible for op-

31. Keohane, *After Hegemony.*

32. Donald R. Rothwell, *The Polar Regions and the Development of International Law* (Cambridge: Cambridge University Press, 1996).

33. For a seminal account of the idea of international society, see Hedley Bull, *The Anarchical Society: A Study of Order in World Politics* (New York: Columbia University Press, 1977).

34. Oran R. Young, "Institutional Linkages in International Society: Polar Perspectives," *Global Governance* 2 (January–April 1996), 1–24.

erating many regimes.[35] It is too early to predict with confidence whether the United Nations Commission on Sustainable Development (CSD), set up as a programmatic element of the United Nations Economic and Social Council (ECOSOC) in response to a recommendation of the 1992 United Nations Conference on Environment and Development (UNCED), will prove to have significant consequences for the operation of specific regimes such as those dealing with ozone and marine pollution. Nonetheless, individual regimes are embedded in broader institutional environments that can play a role as drivers of regime dynamics in specific cases.

Just as interest in institutions has risen in recent years, so also is awareness growing that ideas or, more generally, cognitive forces can emerge as important social drivers in connection with institutional change.[36] In some instances, the role of ideas can be addressed under the rubric of endogenous forces of change, such as when social learning occurs as a result of experience with the operation of regimes themselves (for example, the development of knowledge concerning the performance of various policy instruments in regulating emissions of airborne and waterborne pollutants). But cognitive forces often involve much broader developments that are not precipitated by the operation of specific regimes but have far-reaching consequences for regime operation.[37] The erosion of the idea of maximum sustainable yield and its replacement first by the concepts of multispecies management and ecosystems management and more recently by a growing awareness of the importance of chaotic or nonlinear processes, for instance, have played a major role in the evolution of regimes originally constructed on an MSY base, such as the arrangement for whales and whaling. Among other things, this development has given rise to ideas like the precautionary principle and to the normative precept that the burden of proof should fall on those advocating consumptive uses to demonstrate that such uses will not prove disruptive rather than on those advocating the termination of consumptive uses. Similar observations pertain to shifts in values such as those associated with the development of preservationism as an alternative to conservationism. The preservationist

35. M. J. Peterson, "International Organizations and the Implementation of Environmental Regimes," in Oran R. Young, ed., *Global Governance: Drawing Insights from the Environmental Experience* (Cambridge: MIT Press, 1997), 115–51.

36. For a variety of perspectives on the role of ideas in the development of international regimes, see Peter M. Haas, ed., *Knowledge, Power, and International Policy Coordination* (Columbia: University of South Carolina Press, 1997). Broader accounts of the role of ideas in international affairs appear in Judith Goldstein and Robert O. Keohane, eds., *Ideas and Foreign Policy: Beliefs, Institutions, and Political Change* (Ithaca: Cornell University Press, 1993).

37. For a discussion of the stratospheric ozone case in these terms, see Karen T. Litfin, *Ozone Discourses: Science and Politics in Global Environmental Cooperation* (New York: Columbia University Press, 1994).

movement is not a product of the effort to protect whales but the result of a far broader shift in ideas regarding human/environment relations. But there can be no doubt that the rise of this movement has played a crucial role in the campaign to change the regime for whales and whaling by putting a stop to the harvesting of great whales, except in certain special cases such as aboriginal whaling.

Causal Mixes

The separation between endogenous forces and exogenous forces is helpful in thinking about the sources of change in international institutions. The dynamics associated with these forces are distinct and call for different types of analysis. Yet endogenous and exogenous forces not only operate simultaneously but can also interact with one another in complex ways. Some of these linkages are relatively straightforward. Changes in policy direction within key member states that have nothing to do with specific regimes may lead either to gridlock in the operation of regimes or conversely to the breaking of logjams that were blocking progress within regimes. Shifts in the world economy can ease or intensify fights within specific regimes about sources of revenue for funding mechanisms (consider the ozone regime's Multilateral Fund) or the conditions to be attached to transfers of technology from developed members to less developed members. At the same time, ideas emerging from endogenous processes associated with particular regimes (for instance, developments in models of population dynamics which arise from the effort to understand whale stocks) can quickly diffuse to become part of the overall supply of intellectual capital and to play a role in the operation of other regimes. The same is true of experience with innovative arrangements relating to such matters as implementation review mechanisms and noncompliance procedures.[38] The effort to draw lessons that are applicable to other cases (such as the climate regime) from the experience with noncompliance procedures in the ozone regime is striking in this regard. There is no need to enter into an argument about the relative weight of one set of forces or another in seeking to understand such interactions. The purpose of differentiating among a variety of sources of institutional change is to understand the range of forces at work, thus providing a basis for examining the ways in which combinations of forces interact with each other to explain the changes that actually take place in specific circumstances.

---

38. James Cameron, Jacob Werksman, and Peter Roderick, eds., *Improving Compliance with International Environmental Law* (London: Earthscan Publications, 1996).

This observation has important implications for our efforts to understand regime dynamics. Many—perhaps most—changes in international regimes are products of a number of forces that operate simultaneously. Moreover, equifinality is a prominent feature of institutional change in the sense that different combinations of forces can lead to similar outcomes. Thus simple generalizations stating necessary or sufficient conditions for the occurrence of specified institutional outcomes are not likely to stand up well to empirical testing. In fact, what David Dessler has described as "variation finding analysis" seems likely to be of limited value in the development of a theory of institutional change. Instead, we will often find ourselves constructing causal narratives or developing genetic explanations in which complex combinations of forces—often interacting with one another—account for the institutional changes we observe. This approach to explanation, which Dessler describes as "tendency finding or causal analysis," has obvious drawbacks both from a scientific perspective and from the point of view of policy applications.[39] It does not allow for simple predictions stating that the occurrence of a particular condition will be followed by a specified type of institutional change or that such changes will not occur in the absence of a particular condition. Nonetheless, the products of this type of analysis are by no means insignificant or uninteresting. They not only allow for an understanding of the forces at work in accounting for institutional changes that have occurred in the past but also offer guidance that can help us to avoid facile interpretations of current situations and therefore to head off tendencies to jump to prescriptive conclusions that will lead to additional difficulties rather than solving current problems.

CONSEQUENCES OF CHANGE

Although it is essential to identify the sources of institutional change, this does not exhaust the analytic concerns that require consideration in a comprehensive theory of regime dynamics. The other major component of this analytic agenda centers on the consequences of institutional change. In this section I address this topic, starting with a relatively narrow consideration of the impact of institutional change on the performance of regimes and then proceeding to a broader account of the influence of change on the institutional character of the regimes themselves. Finally, I discuss the consequences of changes in specific regimes for developments in other issue areas and in international society as a whole. The result,

39. Dessler, "Architecture of Causal Analysis."

again, is an analysis that emphasizes the wide range of concerns to be addressed in any satisfactory theory of institutional change.

Effects on Regime Performance

Although there is some tendency to assume that the results of institutional change will be positive in the sense of increasing regime capacity to perform various tasks, institutional change may produce negative as well as positive results in these terms. This is especially true of unintended changes such as the institutional responses to new technologies that have increased the harvesting capacity of fishers and consumers of marine mammals so greatly and so quickly that the regulatory arrangements embedded in existing regimes are simply swamped.[40] But negative effects can follow from conscious or deliberate changes in regimes as well. Adding to areas declared off-limits to harvesters of living resources can intensify pressures on stocks of fish or animals located elsewhere. Strengthening regulations dealing with the disposal of wastes in certain media (say, at sea) or in certain places (Antarctica) can increase the impacts of waste disposal in other areas. Imposing new limits on trade in endangered species can lead to the emergence of black markets that are much more difficult to control than legal markets. None of this is to imply that negative effects are pervasive or that they outweigh positive effects when they do occur. But any analysis of the consequences of institutional change that does not recognize the occurrence of both positive and negative effects will miss an important piece of the puzzle.

Perhaps the most critical issue regarding the impact of institutional change on performance involves the capacity of regimes to solve the problems that prompt their creation or to perform the tasks (whether regulatory, procedural, or programmatic) their founders set for them. Regime change does enhance problem-solving capacity in some cases. The shift from discharge standards to equipment standards led to improvements in the problem-solving capacity of the regime for vessel-source pollution. The creation of the Multilateral Fund was essential to persuading such key developing countries as China and India to join the ozone regime and therefore to ensuring that the phaseout of production and consumption of CFCs and related chemicals would make a difference. The addition of the Protocol on Environmental Protection has served to rationalize the growing focus on environmental protection within the Antarctic Treaty

40. For a general account, see James R. McGoodwin, *Crisis in the World's Fisheries: People, Problems, and Policies* (Stanford: Stanford University Press, 1990).

System. Of course, some institutional changes improve performance only at the margin; they do not bring about wholesale shifts from failure to success. Additionally, the continuation over time of improvements that do occur cannot be taken for granted. Whenever actors stand to profit from behavior that violates the letter or the spirit of an institutional arrangement, there will be a need to monitor performance continuously and to make appropriate adjustments to meet new challenges on a regular basis.

Important as it is, improving the capacity of regimes to solve problems is not the only measure of performance that requires consideration in thinking about the consequences of institutional change. Changes may also lead to developments that are significant in terms of efficiency, equity, and endurance or institutional resilience. Critics have pointed out, for example, that equipment standards leave much to be desired from the point of view of efficiency because they do not allow the actors affected to respond to regulatory requirements in a manner that minimizes costs.[41] On the other hand, advocates of the use of joint implementation in conjunction with arrangements concerning ozone depletion or climate change regularly argue that a contribution to minimizing costs is one of the attractions of this policy instrument. Similar observations are in order about the implications of institutional change for the achievement of equity. A powerful argument in favor of the creation of the Multilateral Fund was that some such arrangement was essential to meet the requirements of fairness, regardless of its significance with respect to problem solving. But the changes in the regime for whales and whaling, in which a newly emerging majority has insisted on imposing its preference for a termination of harvesting on an unhappy minority, clearly show that institutional changes do not always improve the performance of regimes with respect to the criterion of equity. Moreover, consider the implications of change for the robustness of institutional arrangements. Whereas judgments about efficiency require cost-benefit calculations that are difficult to make even after the fact, the impacts of institutional change on resilience are often relatively easy to observe. Analysts may debate whether the approach adopted in the environment protocol to the Antarctic Treaty could have been improved in terms of efficiency, for instance, but it seems quite clear that the development of this comprehensive arrangement for the environmental issues now arising in Antarctica has added to the resilience of the Antarctic Treaty System as a whole.

41. For a more general account of the reasoning behind the increasingly popular movement toward incentive systems in contrast to regulation, see William C. Mitchell and Randy T. Simmons, *Beyond Politics: Markets, Welfare, and the Failure of Bureaucracy* (Boulder, Colo.: Westview, 1994).

Effects on Institutional Character

Quite apart from their effects on performance, changes can have significant consequences for the institutional character of regimes. In some cases, it is appropriate to treat these changes as developmental or adaptive in nature. Developmental effects occur where changes reflect a progression that seems inherent within a regime or that reflects a logical pattern of growth from one stage to another. In the ozone regime, for example, a framework agreement (the 1985 Vienna Convention) was followed by a substantive protocol (the 1987 Montreal Protocol), which in turn has spawned a series of amendments (the 1990 London Amendments and the 1992 Copenhagen Amendments) that are easy to interpret as a developmental sequence. Somewhat similar observations pertain to the development of regimes that deal with a growing range of related concerns (such as the addition of protocols on SO_2, NOx, VOCs, and POPs in the case of the LRTAP regime) or a range of newly emerging activities within the same issue area (the use of living resources in the Antarctic Treaty area, for instance). Adaptive changes, by contrast, typically take the form of adjustments to meet developments occurring in the biophysical or social settings rather than changes that involve a realization of potential inherent within the regime itself. An interesting example can be seen in the regime for whales and whaling. Whereas developments begun in the early 1980s in this regime require treatment as more fundamental changes in the character of the whole arrangement, the changes of the 1970s centered on the introduction of the New Management Procedure (NMP) are properly treated as an effort to adapt the regime to growing evidence of continued decline in stocks of most species of great whales. In an important sense, both developmental and adaptive changes generally enhance the resilience of international regimes. Developmental changes do so by fleshing out arrangements to realize their full potential. Adaptive changes, by contrast, take the form of adjustments that improve the fit between institutions and the biophysical and social settings within which they operate.

Many institutional changes go beyond what we can reasonably treat as development or adaptation. Dissatisfied actors both within regimes and outside their ambit regularly strive to reform institutional arrangements in more significant ways. Reform may involve relatively simple changes in means or somewhat more ambitious efforts to restructure strategies used to pursue the basic objectives of regimes, but it generally stops short of redefining the problem or changing the content of the basic principles or norms on which specific regimes rest. Thus, the shift from discharge standards to equipment standards in the regime for marine pollution constitutes a major reform of the approach to pollution control employed by this regime. Still, it is a case of reform in the sense that it does not involve a major expansion of the functional scope of the regime (the addition of other forms of pollution) or a redefinition of the problem (recasting the issue to include land-based as well as vessel-source pollutants). There is a sense, too, in which the creation of the Protocol on Environmental Protection is properly understood as a process of reforming the Antarctic Treaty System. The protocol does not change the overarching goal of the regime; the objective is still to avoid jurisdictional problems in the area and to protect the integrity of the region's ecosystems. Yet the failed minerals convention, which would have added a regulatory arrangement for non-renewable resource development to the existing arrangement for living resources, constituted the logical developmental sequence in this case. Accordingly, it is fair to regard the collapse of the minerals convention and the substitution of the environmental protocol as a significant case of institutional reform. A similar issue of reform is being hotly contested at the present time in the case of the regime for whales and whaling. The debate over what is known as the Revised Management Procedure (RMP) has come to symbolize this case of institutional change. For conservationists, the refinement and adoption of the RMP is a matter of reform because the essential concern is to allow for consumptive uses of whales in a fashion that is demonstrably sustainable. For preservationists, by contrast, the issue goes beyond reform; their objective is to defeat the RMP or to frame it in such a way that it effectively ends all consumptive uses of whales.

As this last example suggests, there comes a point at which institutional reform gives way to the transformation of regimes. The concept of transformation is a notoriously difficult one to operationalize in thinking about social institutions. It clearly has something to do with the defining or constitutive characteristics of institutional arrangements, such as the nature of the problem to be solved, the basic principles on which a regime is founded, and the composition of a regime's membership. But it is hard to devise a simple test that will tell us when transformation occurs in specific cases. Even so, it is often relatively easy to distinguish between reform and transformation. The advocates of moving from discharge standards to equipment standards in the case of marine pollution were reformers. Those who now say that land-based and vessel-source pollution should be treated together, on the other hand, are calling for institutional transformation. Those who champion a complete cessation of the consumptive use of whales, as opposed to those who see the RMP as an effective measure to regulate consumptive uses, are transformers rather than reformers. Similarly, those who believe that it would be desirable to integrate the ozone regime, the climate regime, and LRTAP into a single "law of the atmosphere" are clearly thinking in terms of transformation.[42] It is not always easy to control processes of change which affect international regimes. Efforts to reform existing arrangements can touch off sequences of events that lead over time to transformation, which helps explains why not one of the Consultative Parties has called for the review conference permitted under the provisions of the Antarctic Treaty at any time since 1991. At the same time, advocates of transformation are often forced to settle for reform. In this connection, it will be interesting to see whether some sort of balance between preservation and consumptive use emerges from the current travail of the regime for whales and whaling.

Broader Consequences

Changes in specific regimes can also lead to changes outside the particular issue areas in which these arrangements operate. Sometimes this is simply a matter of impacts in other distinct issue areas, including demonstration effects, ripple effects, and allocational effects. Changes occurring in one regime are often taken by those concerned with other issues as potential models to be adopted or adapted to their own needs. Yet the results of such emulation are not always constructive. Efforts to model rules of procedure for the Arctic Council formed in 1996 on those which have long been in use in the Antarctic Treaty System, for instance, ignored a variety of important differences between the two polar regions. As a number of observers have pointed out, however, analogic reasoning is a powerful force in thinking about governance at the international level.[43] Ripple effects, by contrast, are more a matter of momentum than of analogic reasoning. Efforts to reform specific regimes that bear fruit can energize those seeking to bring about changes in other arrangements. This is particularly true, of course, in cases where there are linkages between regimes, so that changes in one may generate a growing demand for changes in the other(s). But momentum for change can build up even in cases where no such linkages exist. It is not surprising, therefore, that periods of institutional change and institutional stasis seem to alternate in many social settings. Conversely, a preoccupation with change in a particular regime can produce allocational effects in that the investment of time and energy in the case at hand can lead to a period in which other arrangements are set

42. For a comprehensive account of the growth of international regimes dealing with atmospheric issues, see Marvin S. Soroos, *The Endangered Atmosphere: Preserving a Global Commons* (Columbia: University of South Carolina Press, 1997).

43. See, for example, M. J. Peterson, "The Use of Analogies in Developing Outer Space Law," *International Organization* 51 (Spring 1997), 245–74.

aside or ignored. This is especially true when the same agencies—whether domestic or international—are charged with the operation of each of the regimes in question. It is no cause for surprise, therefore, when the competition for scarce resources results in placing other arrangements on the back burner during periods when change in a regime becomes the focus of attention. Ripple effects and allocational effects are apt to operate simultaneously, and it is often unclear which of these effects will prove more influential in any one situation.

Finally, broader consequences may take the form of developments that have significant implications for the nature of international society as a whole. Partly, this involves changes in the role of nonstate actors in a system that has long been treated as a society of states. The opening up of the regime for whales and whaling and the regime for Antarctica to the participation of nonstate actors (such as Greenpeace and the Antarctic and Southern Ocean Coalition), for example, has unquestionably played a role in increasing the overall prominence of nonstate actors in the conduct of world affairs. A less visible but arguably equally important development is the enhanced role of classification societies and insurance companies in the operation of the marine pollution regime since the shift from discharge standards to equipment standards. In part, these broader effects involve the role of regime dynamics in recasting, if not decisively altering, some of the constitutive principles of international society. It is difficult to avoid the conclusion, for example, that specific regimes are developing in ways that necessitate reformulations in the conventional understanding of sovereignty.[44] This conclusion pertains especially to regimes, such as the ozone regime and LRTAP, that lead to the development of ever more complex social practices in which states become enmeshed regardless of their declaratory policies or preferences. Here, the actual ability of individual states to exercise the prerogatives of sovereignty is increasingly circumscribed, whether or not they are prepared to acknowledge this development in formal terms. In effect, what is happening is a process that involves the development of customary law and, through it, significant changes in the character of international society which are likely to prove cumulative over time.[45]

---

44. For a range of perspectives on the changing nature of sovereignty, see Gene M. Lyons and Michael Mastanduno, eds., *Beyond Westphalia: State Sovereignty and International Intervention* (Baltimore: Johns Hopkins University Press, 1995); Thomas J. Biersteker and Cynthia Weber, eds., *State Sovereignty as Social Construct* (Cambridge: Cambridge University Press, 1996); and Karin T. Litfin, ed., *The Greening of Sovereignty in World Politics* (Cambridge: MIT Press, 1998).

45. See Barry Buzan, "From International System to International Society: Structural Realism and Regime Theory Meet the English School," *International Organization* 47 (Summer 1993), 327–52.

INSTITUTIONAL CHANGE, I have argued in this chapter, is pervasive but not well understood by students of international regimes. Just as the initial focus on regime formation has been supplemented by a growing concern for regime effectiveness, it makes sense to expect that the next addition to the agenda of regime analysis will be a growing concern with regime dynamics. Such a development would not only add a significant component to the new institutionalism in international relations but also be an unambiguous indicator of the robustness of regime analysis as a productive field of study. When students of international institutions do turn their attention to regime dynamics in a sustained manner, they will find a large research agenda awaiting their consideration. While the pioneering contributions of such analysts as Keohane, Nye, and Gehring will remain noteworthy in this connection, their efforts deal only with isolated pieces of a much larger agenda of concerns belonging to the study of regime dynamics. In this chapter, I have sought to map out the contours of this agenda and to provide some intellectual road signs that may prove useful to those who pick up this challenge. In essence, I have suggested a classificatory scheme that should help analysts to identify the range of institutional changes that need to be accounted for, and proposed that special attention be directed to understanding the sources of change and the consequences of change. If others are inspired to pick up this challenge and add to the overall understanding of regime dynamics, I shall consider my effort successful.

CHAPTER 7

Institutional Interplay in International Society

Most students of international regimes treat the arrangements as self-contained or stand-alone entities that can be analyzed in isolation from one another. As a means of grasping the essential nature of international institutions as well as enhancing analytic tractability in ongoing efforts to understand these complex phenomena, this strategy undoubtedly has much to recommend it.[1] But more-recent studies of international regimes have made it clear that this approach has serious limitations when it comes to the pursuit of knowledge about the success of institutional arrangements—specifically, their ability to (re)direct the behavior of those actors whose behavior gives rise to collective-action problems in international society.[2]

Typically, issue-specific regimes exhibit complex linkages to other institutional arrangements, and the resultant institutional interplay has significant consequences for the outcomes flowing from the operation of each of the affected regimes. Moreover, this sort of institutional interplay is destined to loom larger in the future, as interdependencies among functionally distinct activities rise in international society and the density of inter-

1. Stephen D. Krasner, ed., *International Regimes* (Ithaca: Cornell University Press, 1983), and Volker Rittberger, ed., *Regime Theory and International Relations* (Oxford: Clarendon Press, 1993).

2. Oran R. Young, "The Effectiveness of International Institutions: Hard Cases and Critical Variables," in James N. Rosenau and Ernst-Otto Czempiel, eds., *Governance without Government: Order and Change in World Politics* (Cambridge: Cambridge University Press, 1992), 160–94; Peter M. Haas, Robert O. Keohane, and Marc A. Levy, eds., *Institutions for the Earth: Sources of Effective International Environmental Protection* (Cambridge: MIT Press, 1993); and Marc A. Levy, Oran R. Young, and Michael Zürn, "The Study of International Regimes," *European Journal of International Relations* 1 (September 1995), 267–330.

national regimes increases. Just as we have learned to acknowledge the importance of thinking systematically about issue linkages in the effort to comprehend the dynamics of collective action at the international level,[3] therefore, we must now add a sustained effort to understand institutional linkages in order to take additional steps toward broadening and deepening our knowledge of international institutions.

In this chapter, I first propose a set of analytic distinctions among types of institutional linkages as a means of sorting out different phenomena. I focus on *horizontal interplay* in the sense of linkages among arrangements operative at the same level of social organization—international society— rather than *vertical interplay*, or interactions among institutions operative at different levels of social organization.[4] I then turn to the dynamics of institutional interplay, exploring in the process the forces likely to give rise to the several types of linkages identified in the preceding section. Finally, I adopt a strategic perspective, looking to the calculations of policymakers faced with opportunities to use institutional linkages instrumentally or the necessity of reacting to such linkages resulting from the actions of others. This account relies on several plausible premises regarding the consequences of institutional interplay; a sustained treatment of these consequences must await another occasion. But if I am right about the significance of these linkages, this topic should become a prominent item on the agenda of regime theory in the future.

At this early stage, the analysis centers on classic regimes—that is, interstate arrangements articulated in explicit, albeit not necessarily legally binding, agreements.[5] To lend substance to the analysis, I draw frequently on experience with institutional arrangements operating in the polar lregions—the Arctic and the Antarctic—as a source of illustrations of the phenomena under consideration.[6] But institutional interplay oc-

3. James K. Sebenius, "Negotiation Arithmetic: Adding and Subtracting Issues and Parties," *International Organization* 37 (Spring 1983), 281–316.

4. For an account that differentiates clearly between horizontal and vertical linkages, see Oran R. Young, "Science Plan for the Project on the Institutional Dimensions of Global Change," *IHDP Report*, no. 9 (Bonn: International Human Dimensions Programme on Global Environmental Change, 1999).

5. Institutional arrangements in which some of the key players are nonstate actors (such as commodities regimes) or supranational actors (the European Union) may differ somewhat from classic regimes with regard to institutional linkages. In this introductory account, I have deliberately set these cases aside in the interests of making progress on the core issue.

6. I have chosen to illustrate the analysis that follows with polar examples not only because I have followed developments in this realm closely over the last twenty years but also because I have become a player on several occasions in the development and operation of such arrangements. In the process, I have gained numerous insights on the significance of institutional linkages in these regions.

curs in all issue areas, and the ideas I set forth here are intended to constitute a first cut at understanding phenomena that arise throughout international society.

TYPES OF INSTITUTIONAL LINKAGES

All institutional linkages involve politically significant connections between institutional arrangements that are differentiable in the sense that they have distinct creation stories and ongoing lives of their own. But not all linkages are alike. This section draws distinctions among four types of linkages that give rise to what I call embedded regimes, nested regimes, clustered regimes, and overlapping regimes. I hasten to add that these distinctions are analytic in nature and therefore not intended to describe phenomena that are mutually exclusive in real-world situations. Also, I do not claim that they constitute an exhaustive typology; others may discern additional types of linkages among international institutions that are worthy of consideration. Yet the distinctions I lay out do point to a number of differentiable phenomena and thus enable movement toward understanding the nature and significance of institutional linkages in international society.

Embedded Regimes

For the most part, issue-specific regimes are deeply embedded in overarching institutional arrangements in the sense that they assume—ordinarily without saying so explicitly—the operation of a whole suite of broader principles and practices that constitute the deep structure of international society as a whole.[7] The regime for Svalbard articulated in the 1920 Treaty of Spitsbergen, the 1973 Agreement on Conservation of Polar Bears, the various components of the Antarctic Treaty System (ATS), and the emerging environmental protection regime for the Arctic, for example, are all predicated on an understanding of international society as made up of territorial states possessing exclusive authority over their own

---

7. John Gerard Ruggie, "International Regimes, Transactions, and Change: Embedded Liberalism in the Postwar Economic Order," in Stephen D. Krasner, ed., *International Regimes* (Ithaca: Cornell University Press, 1983), 195–231, and John Gerard Ruggie, "Embedded Liberalism Revisited: Institutions and Progress in International Economic Relations," in Emanuel Adler and Beverly Crawford, eds., *Progress in Postwar International Relations* (New York: Columbia University Press, 1991), 201–34.

domestic affairs, enjoying sovereign equality in their dealings with one another, and refusing to be bound by rules of the game to which they have not consented explicitly. This helps explain why such regimes are rarely open to the inclusion of nonstate actors as members in any formal sense, are normally articulated in explicit (although not necessarily legally binding) agreements, are not considered binding on states that have not acceded to them, and are rarely endowed with dependable sources of revenue subject to their own control.

Although we often take them for granted, however, the broader principles and practices of international society are not immutable. Those who speak of the decline of the nation-state and the rise of global civil society, for instance, have gathered evidence to suggest that international society is even now showing signs of evolving into a new form of social order or, perhaps, into some form of dualism in which the society of states coexists with a global civil society based on alternative premises.[8] The presence of a stable social order is hardly sufficient to ensure that regimes dealing with specific Arctic or Antarctic issues will arise, much less prove effective once they are in place. The record of recent efforts to come to terms with the issues of mining in Antarctica[9] and the form of pollution known as Arctic haze—a type of long-range transboundary air pollution—in the far north[10] offers clear evidence of the problems that can arise even in a stable social order. Yet much can be said for the proposition that the presence of such an order is necessary for the establishment of effective regimes to deal with complex problems, such as the management of multiple-use conflicts in large marine ecosystems (the Bering Sea), or even more specific problems, like the management of high-seas fishing in a geographically limited area (the Jan Mayen/Iceland capelin fishery). In fact, it seems unlikely that issue-specific arrangements dealing with such matters could succeed in guiding behavior in a broader institutional environment marked by uncertainty or open disagreement about the charac-

8. James N. Rosenau, *Turbulence in World Politics: A Theory of Change and Continuity* (Princeton: Princeton University Press, 1990); Ronnie D. Lipschutz, "Restructuring World Politics: The Emergence of Global Civic Society," *Millennium* 21 (Winter 1992), 389–420; Paul Wapner, *Environmental Activism and World Civic Politics* (Albany: State University of New York Press, 1996); Jessica T. Mathews, "Power Shift," *Foreign Affairs* 76 (January/February 1997), 50–66; and Paul Wapner, "Governance in Global Civil Society," in Oran R. Young, ed., *Global Governance: Drawing Insights from the Environmental Experience* (Cambridge: MIT Press, 1997), 65–84.
9. Arnfinn Jorgensen-Dahl and Willy Østreng, eds., *The Antarctic Treaty System in World Politics* (New York: St. Martin's, 1991).
10. Marvin S. Soroos, "Arctic Haze and Transboundary Air Pollution: Conditions Governing Success and Failure," in Oran R. Young and Gail Osherenko, eds., *Polar Politics: Creating International Environmental Regimes* (Ithaca: Cornell University Press, 1993), 186–222.

ter of regime members, much less the deep structure of relationships among them.[11]

Nested Regimes

Institutional nesting, by contrast, is a matter of linkages in which specific arrangements that are restricted with regard to functional scope, geographic domain, or some other relevant criterion are folded into broader institutional frameworks that concern the same general issue area but are less detailed in their application to specific problems. In effect, the nested components bring the premises of a broader regime—rather than the constitutive principles or rules of international society as a whole—to bear on specific topics. Perhaps the most familiar examples today arise in connection with the nesting of substantive protocols into arrangements set forth in framework conventions (such as the integration of the sulfur dioxide, nitrogen oxide, and volatile organic compounds protocols into the framework established in 1979 by LRTAP).

Institutional nesting occurs with some frequency in the polar regions. A striking example involves the bilateral Norwegian/Russian regime governing fishing in the Barents Sea, on the one hand, and the evolving law of the sea, on the other.[12] It is no accident that the Norwegian/Russian regime came into being in conjunction with the emergence of the broader arrangements developed during the 1970s and articulated formally in the 1982 United Nations Convention on the Law of the Sea (UNCLOS). It is doubtful, for example, if these Arctic partners could have succeeded in excluding third-party operators from the lucrative commercial fisheries of the Barents Sea in the absence of the opportunity to nest their bilateral arrangement into the provisions of the new law of the sea pertaining to fishery conservation zones and exclusive economic zones (EEZs), codified in part 5 of the 1982 convention but already a de facto reality by the late 1970s. Moreover, both the declining emphasis in the overall law of the sea on precise principles for delimiting the maritime boundaries of adjacent states and the growing interest in the value of regional cooperation among users of living resources located in well-defined marine ecosystems—see

11. Timothy Dunne, "International Society: Theoretical Promises Fulfilled?" *Cooperation and Conflict* 20 (1995), 125–54.

12. Olav Schram Stokke and Alf Håkon Hoel, "Splitting the Gains: Political Economy of the Barents Sea Fishery," *Cooperation and Conflict* 24 (1991), 49–65, and Olav Schram Stokke, Lee G. Anderson, and Natalia S. Mirovitskaya, "The Barents Sea Fisheries," in Oran R. Young, ed., *The Effectiveness of International Environmental Regimes: Causal Connections and Behavioral Mechanisms* (Cambridge: MIT Press, 1999), 91–154.

especially UNCLOS article 63—served to support establishment of a bilateral Norwegian/Russian regime for the fisheries of the Barents Sea.[13]

Similar cases of institutional nesting in the polar regions arise in connection with the ice-covered areas provision of UNCLOS article 234 and the special areas provision of MARPOL 1973/78, the regime that deals with several categories of vessel-source pollution. Given the tension between Canada and the United States over the legal status of the Northwest Passage, not to mention Soviet/American frictions engendered by the cold war, the authority granted to Arctic states under the terms of article 234 to promulgate special regulatory arrangements to protect ice-covered areas produced little institutional development in the years immediately following the conclusion of the 1982 law of the sea convention.[14] Today, however, the emergence of new opportunities for cooperation after the end of the cold war and the growth of interest in transforming the Northern Sea Route running along the coast of the Eurasian Arctic into an international commercial waterway have produced a serious interest in development of a regime for ice-covered areas to be nested into UNCLOS.[15] In the south polar region, Antarctica has been recognized since 1992 as a MARPOL special area, a designation that makes it possible to nest special restrictions regarding vessel-source pollution in this region into the general provisions of the marine pollution regime. Although no similar action has been taken so far in the north polar region, a number of actors have suggested using the MARPOL special areas provision as a means of regulating environmental impacts that result from the development of offshore oil and gas reserves located both in the North American Arctic (the Beaufort Sea) and in the Eurasian Arctic (the Barents Sea).[16]

Clustered Regimes

Institutional clustering occurs when those engaged in the formation or operation of governance systems for specific issues find it attractive to knit several of these arrangements together into institutional packages, even when there is no compelling functional need to nest the individual com-

13. This point is particularly striking in light of the general reluctance of Norway during that period to enter into bilateral agreements with the Soviet Union.

14. Franklyn Griffiths, ed., *Politics of the Northwest Passage* (Kingston: McGill-Queen's University Press, 1987).

15. Willy Østreng, "The Northern Sea Route and the Barents Region," in Olav Schram Stokke and Ola Tunander, eds., *The Barents Region: Cooperation in Arctic Europe* (London: Sage, 1994), 159–72.

16. James M. Broadus and Raphael V. Vartanov, eds., *The Oceans and Environmental Security: Shared U.S. and Russian Perspectives* (Washington, D.C.: Island Press, 1994), chap. 6.

ponents into a common and more generic framework. The system of arrangements included in the 1982 convention on the law of the sea, with its
functionally differentiated provisions for navigation, fishing, deep seabed
mining, marine pollution, scientific research, and so forth, constitutes a
classic example. What holds these elements together and makes it meaningful to treat them collectively as the law of the sea is a common concern
for issues relating to marine areas rather than the presence of an overarching institutional framework into which the individual components are
nested.[17] Much the same can be said about proposals for the development
of a law of the atmosphere, which have surfaced from time to time—so far
with little effect—in connection with the development of specific regimes
for transboundary air pollution, ozone depletion, and climate change.[18]

Recent developments in the polar regions suggest that several possible
rationales exist for creating clustered regimes. Joining together analytically differentiable issues, such as fishing, offshore hydrocarbon development, navigation, and marine pollution in the Bering Sea, may prove attractive as a means of achieving success in institutional bargaining.[19] In
effect, the prospect of being able to work out package deals covering several distinct issues can facilitate efforts to devise constitutive contracts that
offer net benefits to all participants.[20] In other cases, institutional clustering may seem attractive as a means of achieving economies of scale in the
operation of regimes once they are in place. Such reasoning appears to
have played a role in the thinking of at least some supporters of the Canadian initiative that led to creation in 1996 of the Arctic Council, whose coverage extends to a wide range of functional concerns related to the high
latitudes of the Northern Hemisphere. Beyond this, clustered regimes will
appeal to those seeking to foster consciousness raising and ultimately the
emergence of a shared vision of a given region or cluster of issues as a politically potent construct. Reasoning of this sort appears to have influenced
the thinking of those who developed and promoted the idea of the Bar-

17. Robert L. Friedheim, *Negotiating the New Ocean Regime* (Columbia: University of South
Carolina Press, 1993). This feature of the UNCLOS package has also made it feasible to split off
the regime for deep seabed mining for restructuring without jeopardizing the viability of the
other elements in the package. See also "Law of the Sea Forum: The 1994 Agreement on Implementation of the Seabed Provisions of the Convention on the Law of the Sea," *American Journal of International Law* 88 (October 1994), 687–714.

18. For a helpful comparison of marine and atmospheric issues, see James K. Sebenius, "The
Law of the Sea Conference: Lessons for Negotiations to Control Global Warming," in Gunnar
Sjösted, ed., *International Environmental Negotiation* (Newbury Park: Sage, 1993), 189–216.

19. For an extended discussion of this case, see Oran R. Young, "Governing the Bering Sea
Region," paper presented at the Jesup Centenary Conference "Constructing Cultures Then
and Now," New York, 13–17 November 1997.

20. Sebenius, "Negotiation Arithmetic."

ents Euro-Arctic Region in 1992–93.[21] Here, a significant effect of clustering was propagation of the image of a politically appealing grouping of actors and issues where none had previously existed.[22]

Overlapping Regimes

Overlapping regimes are a separate category of linkages in which individual regimes formed for different purposes and largely without reference to one another intersect on a de facto basis, producing substantial impacts on one another in the process. Well-known to those responsible for creating and operating institutional arrangements in domestic social settings, these institutional intersections—commonly unforeseen and unintended by the creators of individual regimes—are fast becoming an object of attention among students of international institutions.[23] The burgeoning literature on intersections between trade and environmental arrangements is perhaps the most prominent expression of this trend.[24] But recent developments affecting large marine ecosystems in the polar regions, such as the Bering Sea or the Barents Sea, also suggest that institutional overlaps will become progressively more important as determinants of the effectiveness of functionally restricted regimes as human activities that extend beyond the jurisdictional reach of individual states continue to grow during the foreseeable future.

Consider the complications now arising as Russia and the United States (and to a lesser extent Canada, China, Japan, Korea, and Poland) seek to develop separate arrangements concerning commercial fishing, the protection of marine mammals, offshore hydrocarbon development, transit passage, pollution control, the creation of protected natural areas, and the activities of indigenous peoples in the Bering Sea region.[25] Again and

21. Sverre Jervell, "A Report from Europe's Northern Periphery," in Mare Kukk, Sverre Jervell, and Pertti Joenniemi, eds., *The Baltic Sea Area: A Region in the Making* (Oslo: Europaprogrammet, 1992), 13–25.

22. Stokke and Tunander, *Barents Region*, and Jan Åke Dellenbrant and Mats-Olov Olsson, eds., *The Barents Region: Security and Economic Development in the European North* (Umeå: Umeå University, 1994).

23. R. A. Herr, *Antarctica Offshore: A Cacophony of Regimes* (Hobart: Antarctic Cooperative Research Center, 1995), and Edith Brown Weiss, "International Environmental Law: Contemporary Issues and the Emergence of a New World Order," *Georgetown Law Review* 81 (March 1993), 675–710.

24. Steve Charnovitz, "GATT and the Environment: Examining the Issues," *International Environmental Affairs* 4 (Summer 1992), 203–33, and Konrad von Moltke, "Institutional Interactions: The Structure of Regimes for Trade and the Environment," in Oran R. Young, ed., *Global Governance*, 247–72.

25. Oran R. Young, *Resource Management at the International Level* (London: Pinter Publishers, 1977); David A. Shakespeare, "Recent U.S.-U.S.S.R. Agreements Relating to the Bering Sea Region," *Arctic Research of the United States* 5 (Fall 1991), 37–47; Richard Townsend, ed., *Proceedings*

again, those pursuing goals defined in terms of one or another of these functional areas are finding it difficult to achieve success without taking into account the development of rules relating to one or more of the other functional areas. This is one reason why many of the analytic tools developed in the 1950s and 1960s to manage individual fisheries are now being discarded or drastically restructured.[26] With regard to the Bering Sea, there is a growing prospect that efforts to create regimes addressing these linked issues on a piecemeal basis will give way to a meaningful commitment to devise a clustered regime for this area treated as a large marine ecosystem.[27]

Similar observations are in order regarding the growing concern for harmonizing the various components of the Antarctic Treaty System. Much of the increasing interest in the creation of a general-purpose organization to operate or manage this regime is attributable to such a concern. Yet such institutional mergers are often hard to effect owing to the increasing number of distinct and sometimes conflicting interests that must be accommodated as the functional scope or geographic domain of a regime expands. Experience with comparable issues at the domestic level, moreover, suggests that initiatives designed to broaden institutional arrangements to cope with overlaps often result in regimes that harbor internal inconsistencies or even outright contradictions.

Drawing on an insight associated with the literature on externalities, I pause here to note that institutional overlaps may have positive as well as negative implications—or some combination of the two—for the effectiveness of international institutions. Clearly, overlapping institutions may involve incompatible arrangements that pose problems for those seeking to achieve the goals of each of the affected regimes. Witness the problems that arise in trying to sort out the overlapping provisions of the functionally delimited international regime covering whales and whaling and the geographically delimited arrangements for the Southern Ocean articulated in the 1980 Convention on the Conservation of Antarctic Marine

---

of the Conference on Shared Living Resources of the Bering Sea Region (Washington, D.C.: Council on Environmental Quality, 1991); Natalia S. Mirovitskaya and J. Christopher Haney, "Fisheries Exploitation as a Threat to Environmental Security: The North Pacific Ocean," *Marine Policy* 14 (July 1992), 243–59; William T. Burke, "Fishing in the Bering Sea Donut: Straddling Stocks and the New International Law of Fisheries," *Ecology Law Quarterly* 16 (1989), 285–310; and Broadus and Vartanov, *Oceans and Environmental Security*, chap. 3.

26. P. A. Larkin, "An Epitaph for the Concept of Maximum Sustainable Yield," *Transactions of the American Fisheries Society* 106 (1977), 1–11.

27. Kenneth Sherman, "Large Marine Ecosystems," in *Encyclopedia of Earth System Science* (New York: Academic Press, 1992), 2:653–73, and Young, "Governing the Bering Sea Region."

Living Resources (CCAMLR).[28] Yet institutional intersections can lead to the development of unusually effective international regimes by stimulating efforts to think in terms of whole ecosystems and to devise integrated management practices. A striking example is the initiative spearheaded by Norway to create cooperative arrangements for the Barents Euro-Arctic Region treated as an integrated system and codified in a ministerial declaration signed at Kirkenes in January 1993.[29] Another is the emerging interest in developing a comprehensive regime for the Bering Sea Region.[30]

Related distinctions involve the degree to which institutional overlaps are unidirectional, reciprocal, and symmetrical. Whereas the flow of impacts is largely unidirectional in some cases (such as the impact of the global ozone regime on the various elements of the Antarctic Treaty System), in many situations institutional impacts are reciprocal in nature (the mutual impacts of CCAMLR and the whaling regime). This consideration is likely to have important consequences for the politics of overlapping regimes. Where impacts are not only reciprocal but also roughly symmetrical in nature, there will typically be greater incentives to work toward mutual adjustment and possibly the creation of clustered regimes than in cases that are highly asymmetrical. An understanding of these matters will prove helpful to participants in the processes of institutional bargaining that give rise to specific regimes in the first place.

THE DYNAMICS OF INSTITUTIONAL LINKAGES

How can we explain or account for patterns of institutional linkages that emerge among individual regimes in international society? To what extent are linkages products of conscious efforts on the part of individual actors to pursue their own interests as opposed to de facto consequences of interactive behavior? This large topic calls for extensive analysis on the part of those interested in institutional arrangements operative in a variety of issue areas. Yet it is possible to initiate an analysis of this subject on the basis of current observations. In this section I draw on the distinctions among types of linkages to launch an inquiry into the dynamics of institutional linkages in international society.

28. At its 1994 annual meeting, the International Whaling Commission voted to designate the Southern Ocean as a whale sanctuary. This may serve to alleviate intersections between the whaling regime and CCAMLR, although the boundaries of the Southern Ocean whale sanctuary do not coincide with the boundaries of CCAMLR's domain.

29. Stokke and Tunander, *Barents Region*, and Oran R. Young, *Creating Regimes: Arctic Accords and International Governance* (Ithaca: Cornell University Press, 1998).

30. Young, "Governing the Bering Sea Region."

In one sense embeddedness is a fact of life from the point of view of those seeking to create issue-specific regimes. In effect, these links reflect and represent the deep structure of international society. Most people engaged in processes of regime formation simply take it for granted that the general rules governing activities in this social setting will apply to any specific institutional arrangements they may create; it is hard to get those who have been thoroughly socialized into this way of pursuing their goals to think otherwise. The negotiators who produced the 1973 Agreement on Conservation of Polar Bears, for example, had no hesitancy about treating this effort as a matter of creating a regime among the five range states—Canada, Denmark/Greenland, Norway, Russia, and the United States—each of which would have full authority over the implementation of the agreement's provisions within its own jurisdiction. They deliberately finessed a number of broader jurisdictional issues relating to the conservation of polar bears in order to avoid having to tackle problems that would be hard to resolve within the framework established by the general rules of international society.[31] For their part, even those who pushed hard to scuttle the Antarctic minerals convention and to seize the resultant opportunity to negotiate what became the 1991 Protocol to the Antarctic Treaty on Environmental Protection—actors that included influential environmental advocacy groups with no great interest in perpetuating the dominance of the nation-state—consented to the creation of an institutional arrangement that is entirely compatible with the basic rules of international society.[32]

Yet this is not the whole story with regard to the dynamics of embedded institutions. Because it is difficult to reform—much less to transform—the institutional substructure of international society through direct actions, those desiring to change the basic rules of this social system frequently concentrate on the establishment of issue-specific regimes in the hope that they can start trends that will spread from one issue area to another and eventually lead to perceptible changes in the deep structure of the system as a whole. Important pressure points in this connection involve such matters as the roles to be played by nonstate actors in international regimes, the decision rules governing efforts to arrive at social choices regarding the issues covered by institutional arrangements, and the sources

31. The most striking case in point is the absence of any language in the agreement about the protection of polar bears located beyond the boundaries of national jurisdiction. See, in general, Anne Fikkan, Gail Osherenko, and Alexander Arikainen, "Polar Bears: The Importance of Simplicity," in Young and Osherenko, *Polar Politics*, 96–151.

32. Christopher Joyner, *Governing the Frozen Commons: The Antarctic Regime and Environmental Protection* (Columbia: University of South Carolina Press, 1998).

of revenue available to finance the activities of those responsible for administering individual regimes.

Here, again, recent polar experience offers interesting examples. The creation and development of the Arctic Environmental Protection Strategy (AEPS)—a regionwide action plan adopted in a 1991 ministerial declaration signed in Rovaniemi, Finland[33]—has become a vehicle for indigenous peoples to push their claims to representation at the international level beyond participation as members of national delegations.[34] The organizational arrangements emerging in connection with the Barents Euro-Arctic Region (BEAR) include not only a Barents Euro-Arctic Council composed of representatives of the national governments of the states involved but also a Regional Council comprised of representatives of the eight counties or subnational units of government that make up the region; indigenous peoples constitute a ninth constituency represented in the council.[35] The arrangement set forth in the failed 1988 Convention on the Regulation of Antarctic Mineral Resource Activities would have provided for decisions to be made by a two-thirds majority vote in the regulatory committees established to manage individual mining sites, and for funds to be raised through a system of levies on companies operating under the auspices of the regime.[36]

Suggestive as these polar cases are, they also indicate how difficult it is in practice to change entrenched features of international society. Whatever the fate of the Barents Euro-Arctic Region, it is clear that one of the major snags that held up progress for some years on the Canadian initiative to establish an Arctic Council encompassing the Arctic Eight—Canada, Denmark/Greenland, Finland, Iceland, Norway, Russia, Sweden, and the United States—was the opposition of several governments to the vision of those who initially called for a council featuring a multilevel system of representation that would allow the voices of indigenous peoples, environmental groups, and subnational units of government, among others, to be heard.[37] Representatives of the foreign ministries of several of the Arctic states found it difficult even to grasp the meaning of early Ca-

33. See Young, *Creating Regimes.*
34. Monica Tennberg, *The Arctic Council: A Study in Governability* (Rovaniemi: University of Lapland, 1998).
35. Jervell, "Report."
36. Jorgensen-Dahl and Østreng, *Antarctic Treaty System.*
37. Arctic Council Panel, *To Establish an International Arctic Council: A Framework Report* (Ottawa: Canadian Arctic Resources Committee, 1991). Meeting in Ottawa during February 1995, President Clinton and Prime Minister Chretien issued a joint statement endorsing the idea of creating an Arctic Council. This effectively broke the logjam surrounding the proposal and led to the signing of the Declaration on the Establishment of the Arctic Council in Ottawa on 19 September 1996.

nadian ideas regarding the composition of the Arctic Council. As far as CRAMRA is concerned, the institutional innovations incorporated in this convention disappeared for all practical purposes with the political collapse of the proposed minerals regime as a whole. Whatever its merits in other respects, the Environmental Protocol that came into being in the wake of CRAMRA's demise is considerably less innovative in institutional terms than the minerals regime would have been. Those who pushed for the adoption of the protocol obviously opted for the substantive provisions of this arrangement over the institutional innovations of the minerals convention.[38]

Consideration of nested regimes brings into focus additional observations about the dynamics of institutional linkages. Several distinct motives can lead the creators of specific arrangements to nest them into broader institutional frameworks. One obvious motive is to avoid raising larger and more fundamental issues by placing new, functionally specific regimes into familiar categories represented by existing regulatory structures. This process is well illustrated by the care with which new arrangements for marine living resources and environmental protection have been tied into the overarching Antarctic Treaty System as a means of deflecting the efforts of several developing countries—led by Malaysia—to move the consideration of Antarctic issues into the forum of the United Nations rather than the arena of the Antarctic Treaty Consultative Meetings.[39] A striking feature of this case is the extent to which those involved in the ATS have proven willing to set aside their own differences (for example, clashes between environmental groups and national Antarctic science programs) to present a united front against the challenge of the developing states, a challenge energized in considerable part by a desire to share in any economic benefits that might flow from the exploitation of Antarctic resources treated as the common heritage of humankind.

Those engaged in regime formation may also find nesting appealing as a means of legitimizing issue-specific arrangements or simply making it easier for affected parties to accept new initiatives by incorporating them into existing arrangements whose implementation in domestic arenas has become a routine matter for the participants. Important as this motive for nesting is in some situations, regime-building efforts in the polar regions have often proven resistant to this type of linkage. Unlike the Scientific

38. Joyner, *Governing the Frozen Commons.*
39. D. Edmar, "The Antarctic Treaty System and the United Nations," in R. A. Herr, H. R. Hall, and M. G. Howard, eds., *Antarctica's Future: Continuity or Change?* (Hobart: Tasmanian Government Printing Office, 1990), 189–92, and Peter Beck, "The United Nations and Antarctica: Still Searching for the Elusive Convergence of View," *Polar Record* 29 (October 1993), 313–20.

Committee on Antarctic Research, for example, the International Arctic Science Committee (IASC) has features (such as the Regional Board composed of individuals expected to represent the interests of the Arctic Eight governments) that make it difficult to incorporate this arrangement into the International Council of Scientific Unions (ICSU) family.[40] Those who have taken the lead in efforts to make progress toward managing the Bering Sea Region and even the whole Arctic Ocean as large marine ecosystems have generally resisted the idea of nesting such arrangements into the Regional Seas Programme of the United Nations Environment Programme.[41] So far, the idea of creating special areas for various parts of the Arctic under MARPOL has not borne fruit. But these cases should not allow us to lose sight of other situations in which the legitimizing role of nesting has proven or will prove attractive in the polar regions. As I have suggested, nesting the Norwegian/Russian regime for the fisheries of the Barents Sea into the broader structure of the emerging law of the sea became a means of legitimizing the phasing out of third-party fishers. Similarly, there is every reason to expect that those now striving to come to terms with nuclear contamination in Arctic waters will see much to be gained from nesting any agreements they reach regarding this problem into the overarching structure provided by the 1972 London Convention on the dumping of wastes at sea.[42]

In other cases, nesting is simply an artifact of the limits of the process of institutional bargaining leading to the creation of international regimes.[43] Those endeavoring to create regimes often find themselves faced with a choice between holding out for preferred substantive provisions that may prove elusive or settling for mutually acceptable framework agreements in the hope that the launching of a regime will trigger a dynamic which serves to increase the probability that more substantive provisions will follow. When such hopes are realized, it is perfectly natural to nest ensuing

40. E. F. Roots, "Co-operation in Arctic Science: Background and Requirements," in Franklyn Griffiths, ed., *Arctic Alternatives: Civility or Militarism in the Circumpolar North* (Toronto: Science for Peace/Samuel Stevens, 1992), 136–55. At this writing, IASC is exploring the idea of seeking associate membership in ICSU in contrast to SCAR's status as a scientific committee of ICSU.

41. Erik Franckx, *Maritime Claims in the Arctic: Canadian and Russian Perspectives* (Dordrecht: Martinus Nijhoff, 1993).

42. A 1993 protocol to the London Convention extends the coverage of this regime to the disposal of low-level radioactive waste at sea. Although Russia did not sign the protocol, the Russian government has promised to make an effort to comply with the spirit of this new provision. See Lasse Ringius, "Environmental NGOs and Regime Change: The Case of Ocean Dumping of Radioactive Waste," *European Journal of International Relations* 3 (March 1997), 61–104.

43. Oran R. Young, *International Governance: Protecting the Environment in a Stateless Society* (Ithaca: Cornell University Press, 1994), chaps. 4, 5.

substantive provisions into the framework arrangement established in the first phase of the process of regime formation. A striking and familiar example that has major implications for the polar regions is the ozone regime, in which the nesting of the Montreal Protocol of 1987 followed by the London Amendments of 1990 and the Copenhagen Amendments of 1992 into the relatively weak framework provisions of the 1985 Vienna Convention for the Protection of the Ozone Layer has produced an arrangement that shows every sign of succeeding in phasing out the production and consumption of CFCs and related chemicals thought to be harmful to stratospheric ozone.[44]

Another interesting case involves the effort to build an environmental protection regime for the Arctic under the terms of the Arctic Environmental Protection Strategy. This effort owes much to experience with the LRTAP regime in Europe, in which the establishment of an effective monitoring system (EMEP) catalyzed movement toward the adoption of a succession of substantive protocols that concern specific pollutants.[45] The AEPS combines a relatively weak framework arrangement with the initiation of several programmatic efforts such as the Arctic Monitoring and Assessment Programme (AMAP). As the Arctic Council becomes operational, the AEPS itself is being nested into the broader framework of the council. It will be a matter of considerable interest to see whether the parties are able to nest a series of substantive provisions into this overarching framework over the next few years.[46]

As to clustered regimes, there is no mystery in the emergence of interest in such arrangements in the context of institutional bargaining. As we know from domestic experience, the dynamics of bargaining tend to favor clustering even when the linkages are largely matters of political convenience. Yet an examination of polar cases also suggests that individual participants may well discover strong incentives to oppose clustering either to avoid pressures to compromise on priority issues or to minimize the chances of getting drawn into regional arrangements that could produce negative consequences for their interests in other regions or in interna-

44. Edward A. Parson, "Protecting the Ozone Layer," in Haas, Keohane, and Levy, *Institutions for the Earth*, 27–73. For an interesting discussion of some of the issues that have arisen in the process of implementing the ozone regime, see Edward A. Parson and Owen Greene, "The Complex Chemistry of the International Ozone Agreements," *Environment* 37 (March 1995), 16–20, 35–43.

45. See Marc A. Levy, "European Acid Rain: The Power of Tote-Board Diplomacy," in Haas, Keohane, and Levy, *Institutions for the Earth*, 75–132.

46. See Donald R. Rothwell, *The Polar Regions and the Development of International Law* (Cambridge: Cambridge University Press, 1996), and Sanjay Chaturvedi, *The Polar Regions: A Political Geography* (Chichester, Eng.: Wiley, 1996).

tional society as a whole. This interpretation may help to explain the reluctance of the United States to join in creating the AEPS and the initial lack of American enthusiasm for the Canadian initiative to establish the Arctic Council.[47] Regarding itself as a superpower with global interests, the United States is sensitive to developments (such as the growth of a strong, multidimensional Arctic regional regime) that could lead others to conclude that the United States is shifting its attention away from other regions of the world (the Middle East or East Asia) or from issues that are global in character (human rights, climate change).

Aggregation of institutional bits and pieces into clustered regimes is apt to prove increasingly difficult after the fact. Once distinct arrangements are established, they take on lives of their own. That they do so partly reflects the norms and principles or the cognitive visions on which regimes are founded. It is not easy, for example, to marry regimes established to deal with a few species over a broad geographic range (the whaling regime) with regimes covering broader functional concerns over a narrower range (the emerging Bering Sea regime). Moreover, individual regimes acquire administrative arrangements of their own and loyal constituents or supporters who have personal stakes in the survival of regimes as they know them. The result is a kind of institutional inertia that can effectively preclude efforts to create clustered regimes through mergers of existing arrangements, even when the case for doing so on functional grounds is persuasive. Although it is important during the course of institutional bargaining to avoid clustering for purely tactical reasons, it is equally important to recognize that successful clustering normally requires decisive action at the outset.

In some respects, overlapping regimes present a distinctive picture of the dynamics of linkages. Whereas nesting and clustering are almost always products of conscious choices, institutional intersections typically take the form of unintended by-products of separate initiatives undertaken by different groups of actors pursuing their own objectives, with little concern for possible institutional linkages. This situation commonly occurs in cases that feature the coexistence of regimes which are functionally narrow but geographically broad and regimes that cover a number of functions within a more restricted geographic area. The intersection between the worldwide arrangement for whales and whaling and the regime dealing with

---

47. Oran R. Young, *Arctic Politics: Conflict and Cooperation in the Circumpolar North* (Hanover, N.H.: University Press of New England, 1992). Interestingly, the revised Arctic policy statement released by the United States in September 1994 expresses strong support for the AEPS; it also led to a more favorable attitude on the part of the United States toward the Canadian proposal to establish a council.

marine living resources in the waters adjacent to Antarctica exemplifies this type of situation. Overlaps also arise from uncoordinated efforts to deal with a number of problems which are functionally distinct but which pertain to the same geographic area. Independent efforts to solve problems involving high-seas fishing, offshore oil and gas development, marine pollution, and protected natural areas in the Bering Sea Region, for example, are bound to intersect at numerous points.[48] Not surprisingly, this concern has become a prominent argument advanced by advocates of the creation of a comprehensive international regime to manage human activities affecting the Bering Sea Region treated as a large marine ecosystem.

Nevertheless, institutional overlaps can result from deliberate actions. Some of these linkages are consequences of efforts on the part of disaffected parties to solve problems associated with the operation of existing regimes by creating new institutions that they believe will foster reform in existing regimes or, alternatively, produce more favorable results under new auspices. An example is the creation of the North Atlantic Marine Mammals Commission (NAMMCO), an arrangement established formally in 1992 by Iceland and Norway, together with the residents of the Faeroe Islands and Greenland, to manage consumptive uses of marine mammals, including whales, in the North Atlantic area in the wake of the refusal of the International Whaling Commission to sanction the resumption of whaling on the part of anyone other than aboriginal subsistence whalers.[49]

There are, as well, cases in which institutional intersections have more positive origins. Those involved in building new regimes, for example, may deliberately encourage the growth of intersections with existing institutions to promote the proposition that economies of scale may be realized from establishing a single set of organizations to administer the provisions of two or more distinct regimes. Common practice in domestic settings— especially with regard to organizational arrangements designed to deal with matters of authoritative interpretation, compliance, and dispute resolution—this mode of operation is just beginning to achieve prominence at the international level. But if, as most observers expect, the demand for governance continues to grow in international society, intersections aris-

48. Young, *Resource Management.*

49. Alf Håkon Hoel, "Regionalization of International Whale Management: The Case of the North Atlantic Marine Mammals Commission," *Arctic* 46 (June 1993), 116–23; David D. Caron, "The International Whaling Commission and the North Atlantic Marine Mammals Commission: The Institutional Risks of Coercion in Consensual Structures," *American Journal of International Law* 89 (1995), 154–74; and Gudrun Petursdottir, ed., *Whaling in the North Atlantic* (Reykjavik: Fisheries Research Institute, 1997). Canada, Japan, and Russia have participated in NAMMCO activities as observers.

ing from processes of this sort will become increasingly common. In effect, the prospect of institutional congestion will drive parties to think seriously about building substantive links among arrangements that began life as unrelated regimes.

IMPLICATIONS FOR POLICY AND POLICYMAKERS

How can policymakers who recognize the growing importance of institutional linkages use their knowledge of such matters to make progress toward achieving their own ends in designing international regimes? Conversely, what can those who are responsible for managing specific regimes learn from the analysis of institutional linkages that will maximize the probability that these institutional arrangements will prove effective in achieving their stated—or unstated—goals? Drawing on the preceding analysis, I now turn to a preliminary exploration of these strategic questions to show how the study of institutional linkages can illuminate matters of immediate interest to the policy community. In the process, I suggest that these linkages are often subject to conscious manipulation on the part of actors seeking to promote their own ends.

Attitudes toward institutional embeddedness typically break down along ideological lines. Conservatives—those deeply committed to the status quo with regard to the defining features of international society—generally see embeddedness as a good thing. Basing issue-specific regimes squarely on the fundamental principles of international society not only serves to reaffirm these basic precepts but also minimizes the likelihood that issue-specific regimes will get out of hand, precipitating institutional changes capable of triggering a dynamic that ultimately undermines important tenets of international society as a whole (the rule restricting membership to states, for instance). Thus the act of embedding regimes constitutes a barrier against piecemeal developments leading to broader, more systemic changes.

Contrast this perspective with two others on embeddedness. Technocrats—those who focus on the success of individual regimes on their own terms while remaining neutral on the character of international society as a whole—approach the issue of embeddedness in a purely instrumental fashion. They will embrace embeddedness when it seems useful as a means of promoting the effectiveness of the regimes they care about but otherwise de-emphasize or even ignore embeddedness. Negotiators representing the twelve signatories to the 1959 Antarctic Treaty, for example, devised a set of provisions generally supportive of the basic tenets of international society; at the same time, they ignored or set aside some of the usual rules pertaining to jurisdiction in order to craft the crucial compromise needed to alleviate the problem of overlapping and contested jurisdictional claims as an obstacle to mutually beneficial cooperation in the region.[50] A similar instrumental perspective appears to underlie current efforts to provide larger and more autonomous roles for nonstate actors in emerging Arctic arrangements, such as the Arctic Council and the Barents Euro-Arctic Region, without calling into question the proposition that international society is fundamentally a society of states.

Those desiring to use the creation of issue-specific regimes as a vehicle for promoting larger changes in international society must engage in a continuous balancing act with regard to embeddedness.[51] Pushing too hard runs the risk of blighting the prospects for success with respect to the regime at hand as well as provoking a backlash on the part of defenders of the faith when it comes to the central tenets of international society. Yet undue caution runs the risk of failing to take advantage of opportunities to use specific regimes as vehicles for reforming international society. Choices concerning the proper balance between these risks will normally vary as a function of both the modus operandi of different actors and strategic or contextual factors. It is no accident, for example, that Greenpeace has adopted a more radical posture than has the World Conservation Union—formerly the International Union for the Conservation of Nature and Natural Resources—in seeking to use Antarctica as a vehicle for promoting larger agendas of nonstate actors, or that indigenous peoples organizations (such as the Inuit Circumpolar Conference) have been particularly active in treating the newly emerging multilateral regimes in the Arctic as opportunities to attack the underlying norm limiting membership in international regimes to states. With regard to context, it is interesting to observe that the Antarctic and Southern Ocean Coalition accepted an environmental regime for Antarctica that is relatively conventional in its orientation toward the basic tenets of international society. In effect, the 1991 Protocol on Environmental Protection represented such a dramatic substantive improvement over CRAMRA that the environmental advocacy groups were willing to embrace it without quibbling over its embeddedness in the existing structure of international society.

What about the policy relevance of nesting? Since the 1970s, the virtues

50. H. Robert Hall, "International Regime Formation and Leadership: The Origins of the Antarctic Treaty," Ph.D. diss., University of Tasmania, 1994.

51. Paul Wapner, "Politics beyond the State: Environmental Activism and World Civic Politics, *World Politics* 47 (April 1995), 311–40.

of nesting—largely in the form of the framework convention/protocol model of regime formation—have achieved the status of conventional wisdom owing primarily to the relative success of LRTAP and the ozone regime.[52] The fact that efforts to create regimes to deal with climate change and the loss of biological diversity have followed the same path strengthens this conclusion. A desire to avoid the problems that have plagued the development of a comprehensive law of the sea has undoubtedly reinforced this trend. The impact of this development is clearly apparent in the polar regions, not only in the obvious attempt to follow the example of LRTAP in the development of the Arctic Environmental Protection Strategy but also in the tendency to reconceptualize the Antarctic Treaty System, which antedates the current interest in the framework convention/protocol model, as an arrangement resembling the nested structure of LRTAP and the ozone regime.

Still, this model, with its central focus on nesting of a particular type, may not be the preferred approach to the full range of international issues.[53] To facilitate thinking about this issue, consider the distinction among regulatory regimes, procedural regimes, and programmatic regimes. Regulatory regimes feature sets of behavioral rules or prescriptions that each of the members agrees to implement and comply with within the bounds of its own jurisdiction. The Antarctic Treaty and the polar bear regime are arrangements of this type. To a large extent the MARPOL rules relating to vessel-source pollution also exhibit this pattern. Procedural regimes emphasize the establishment of mechanisms designed to allow the members to make collective decisions in a regular and orderly fashion. The provisions of the Icelandic/Norwegian regime for the zone around Jan Mayen Island, which establish procedures for setting annual quotas for the harvest of fish and for making decisions about the development of hydrocarbons, exemplify this sort of arrangement, as does the whaling regime, with its procedures for making annual decisions about quotas and periodic decisions about the establishment of whale sanctuaries and the like. Programmatic regimes feature the initiation of collectively supported activities designed to stimulate learning about relevant problems as well as collaborative projects needed to solve them. The Arctic Environmental Protection Strategy, like LRTAP on which it is modeled, illustrates this type of arrangement. Of course, these are analytic distinctions; actual regimes can and often do include features belonging to two or even all three types.

52. Lawrence Susskind, *Environmental Diplomacy: Negotiating More Effective Global Agreements* (New York: Oxford University Press, 1994).

53. James K. Sebenius, "Designing Negotiations toward a New Regime: The Case of Global Warming," *International Security* 15 (Spring 1991), 110–48.

But these distinctions are useful for various purposes, including thinking through the virtues of nested regimes.

The advantages of nesting are indisputable in the case of evolving programmatic regimes. The point of such arrangements is to set in motion activities intended to lead to a broadening and deepening of the regimes in question. This is the genius of LRTAP, in which the operation of EMEP and related programmatic mechanisms have led to "tote-board diplomacy" involving the negotiation of a series of protocols dealing with specific types of airborne pollutants.[54] There are signs that a similar dynamic may emerge from the activities of the AMAP and the Working Group on the Conservation of Arctic Flora and Fauna (CAFF) in the case of the AEPS.[55] But the success of such evolutionary processes is hardly automatic with regard to specific regimes. Efforts to nest new elements into the regime for the Mediterranean Basin established initially under the 1976 Barcelona Convention have proved disappointing to many, a situation which eventuated in the renegotiation of the convention itself in 1995. Similarly, the addition of the 1991 Environmental Protocol may turn out to be a unique event in the evolution of the Antarctic Treaty System rather than an indication that this arrangement is now taking on the character of a programmatic regime.

The argument for nesting is far less persuasive in the cases of regulatory regimes and procedural regimes. Some regimes are based on sets of rules that are essentially complete and self-contained in their original form. This is probably a fair characterization of the regime for the conservation of North Pacific fur seals, which lasted through much of this century,[56] and of the regime for the Svalbard Archipelago, which was established in the 1920s and remains effective today.[57] In other cases, the initial set of rules may grow as a result of experience with a social practice, but in a manner that does not involve nesting of the sort under consideration here. The recommendations or agreed measures adopted over the years by the Antarctic Treaty Consultative Meetings, for instance, are properly construed as prescriptions—albeit ones that individual members are free to implement with regard to their nationals according to their own domestic

54. Levy, "European Acid Rain."

55. For information on the evolution of the Arctic Environmental Protection Strategy, see the *WWF Arctic Bulletin*, a publication of the Arctic Programme of the World Wildlife Fund (WWF).

56. Natalia S. Mirovitskaya, Margaret Clark, and Ronald G. Purver, "North Pacific Fur Seals: Regime Formation as a Means of Resolving Conflict," in Young and Osherenko, *Polar Politics*, 22–55.

57. Elen Singh and Artemy Saguirian, "The Svalbard Archipelago: The Role of Surrogate Negotiators," in Young and Osherenko, *Polar Politics*, 56–95.

procedures—that taken together have broadened and deepened this social practice. But it does not seem appropriate to describe these new elements as being nested into the original arrangement in the sense that the 1987 Montreal Protocol and the London Amendments are nested into the ozone regime or the 1994 sulfur protocol is nested into LRTAP.

As to procedural regimes, the situation is even more straightforward. Once established, procedures for arriving at collective choices can be used repeatedly. This is obviously true for decisions involving the same subject, such as setting annual quotas for specific fisheries, establishing annual harvest levels for individual species of whales, or listing individual species under the appendixes of the regime governing trade in endangered species of animals and plants. Established procedures for making collective choices may also be extended to new subjects without any need to restructure the procedures themselves. This certainly seems to be true of the ATCMs of the Antarctic regime and sessions of the M/COP operating under the terms of the Montreal Protocol on ozone-depleting substances. Of course, this does not rule out the possibility of nesting in connection with procedural regimes. New issues may require the establishment of specialized procedures for arriving at collective choices. The failed regime for mineral activities in Antarctica, for example, included several different decision systems to cover separate types of issues. If it had survived, this regime might well have acquired additional decision systems over the course of time. But nesting is much less central under these conditions than it is in the case of programmatic regimes.

As I have suggested, the negative experience with clustering in connection with the law of the sea, especially when juxtaposed to the positive experience with nesting in the cases of LRTAP and ozone, has given clustering a bad reputation. Yet it seems premature to generalize from these experiences to the conclusion that clustering in the development of institutions is a strategy to be avoided, either in the polar regions or in international society more generally. As the Mediterranean Sea case suggests, nesting may turn out to have severe limits, even in connection with the development of relatively simple programmatic regimes. Nor is there any basis for assuming that more complex problems, such as climate change, will yield to a strategy that has worked well in simpler cases, like LRTAP or ozone.[58] Under the circumstances, it is important to avoid being swept away by current fashions and to retain the option of clustering as one of a

58. David G. Victor and Julian E. Salt, "From Rio to Berlin: Managing Climate Change," *Environment* 36 (December 1994), 6–15, 25–32, and D. G. Victor and J. E. Salt, "Keeping the Climate Treaty Relevant," *Nature*, 26 January 1995, 280–82.

set of tools available for use in dealing with a range of collective-action problems at the international level.

Today, clustering may be especially attractive to those desiring to foster new perspectives on regions (the Arctic treated as a single region) or sub-regions (the Barents Euro-Arctic Region). Approaching problems on an issue-by-issue basis may prove successful in functional terms, but it is un-likely to give rise to new images or shared visions regarding larger trends in international society. This is why many actors—in both domestic and international arenas—correctly perceived the proposal for establishing the Barents Euro-Arctic Region as a realigning initiative to be supported or opposed on grounds extending well beyond the specific provisions set forth in the 1993 ministerial declaration itself. The same is true on an even larger scale of proposals to create an encompassing, treaty-based Arctic regime similar in character to the Antarctic Treaty System in its current form; even the relatively modest Arctic Council could become a vehicle for the promotion of a clustered regime for the Circumpolar North as a whole. Contrast these cases with the process of creating the Arctic Environmental Protection Strategy as an arrangement limited to environmental issues, and even then only to a circumscribed set of environmental concerns. Under the circumstances, it would be a mistake to try to understand debates over the pros and cons of clustered regimes as narrow functional issues to be resolved on technical grounds. Implicitly at least, far more than that is at stake in efforts to establish clustered regimes covering a wide range of functional matters in a well-defined region such as the Arctic.

If anything, the policy implications of my account in this chapter of over-lapping institutions are more far-reaching than those of the other types of institutional linkages. In many instances, intersections have reached—or soon will reach—the point where they not only demand a new outlook on the creation and operation of regimes but also call for the development of new bodies of knowledge to underpin these departures. Consider the case of managing fisheries in large marine ecosystems, such as the Barents Sea and the Bering Sea. The traditional models that rest on calculations of MSYs from individual stocks have broken down as bases for setting allow-able harvest levels (AHLs) on an annual basis and dealing with a suite of related issues.[59] Some have sought to replace these outmoded constructs with management models that emphasize interactions among multiple species.[60] But this approach is almost certain to prove fruitless owing to its

59. James R. McGoodwin, *Crisis in the World's Fisheries: People, Problems, and Policies* (Stanford: Stanford University Press, 1990).

60. Per Ove Eikeland, "Multispecies Management of the Barents Sea Large Marine Ecosys-tem: A Framework for Discussing Future Challenges," Fridtjof Nansen Institute Report, 1992.

failure to include a wide range of intersecting issues that have come into focus in recent years, such as offshore hydrocarbon development, vessel-source pollution, runoffs from land-based activities, and ecotourism.

One response to this development is to embrace the idea of large marine ecosystems, or LMEs.[61] But this move raises a new set of issues. As those who think in terms of marine biological diversity have pointed out, most analyses of LMEs are subject to criticism because they make arbitrary assumptions about the delimitation of marine ecosystems and because they retain the assumption that maximizing the consumptive use of renewable resources is the primary criterion for making policy choices about the management of marine ecosystems.[62] What conservation biology has taught us is that inappropriate delimitations of management units can have disastrous consequences on maintenance of biological diversity from the genetic to the landscape level. Moreover, we now face increasingly difficult questions about the goals of ecosystems management. How should we think about trade-offs between the harvesting of fish and the production of hydrocarbons in such an area as the Barents Sea? How should we incorporate the claims of subsistence harvesters in contrast to commercial harvesters in managing the fisheries of the eastern Bering Sea? How should we weigh the claims of ecotourists who want to experience a completely pristine Antarctic wilderness against the needs of scientists to build landing strips for aircraft or to deal with the inevitable flow of wastes that will result from their presence? None of these questions has a straightforward answer, much less one that is correct.

Assuming that we can develop the knowledge base needed to understand institutional intersections, how can we design regimes to cope with them? There are at least three—not necessarily mutually exclusive—responses to this question. For purposes of discussion, it may help to call them side agreements, mergers, and procedural devices. Side agreements involve efforts on the part of those concerned with a specific regime to add provisions designed to mitigate its unintended, ordinarily negative, impacts on other institutional arrangements. Perhaps the most well-known recent case involves the side agreement on environmental issues which was negotiated in connection with the North American Free Trade Agreement. When overlaps start to affect core interests, however, it seems unlikely that the negotiation of side agreements will be sufficient to solve the resultant problems. Thus it may be necessary to merge the regimes in question, creating a single, more comprehensive regime to cover two or

61. Sherman, "Large Marine Ecosystems."
62. Elliott A. Norse, ed., *Global Marine Biological Diversity: A Strategy for Building Conservation into Decision Making* (Washington, D.C.: Island Press, 1993).

more intersecting issue areas. A number of observers have proposed something of this sort for the Bering Sea Region—that is, a single regime to deal in an integrated manner with some combination of fish, marine mammals, oil and gas, marine pollution, transportation, protected natural areas, and indigenous rights. Some have begun to talk in similar terms about a comprehensive regime for the entire Circumpolar North.

Attractive as this approach may be in some areas, integrated regimes that cover numerous issue areas can become so complex that it is difficult to reach agreement on their terms, much less to administer or operate them successfully once they are established. Thus a third approach, one that features the development of procedural arrangements designed to resolve conflicts that result from institutional overlaps, becomes attractive. Of course, this approach is used in most domestic settings where conflicts of laws are everyday occurrences and both traditional judicial procedures and administrative law procedures loom large as mechanisms for sorting out day-to-day problems arising from institutional overlaps. A notable feature of this approach is that the relevant procedures often rest on some authority which is independent of the laws or institutional arrangements they are called on to interpret, a feature that is part of what is meant by those who speak of an "independent judiciary." Is it possible to imagine a similar development in international society giving rise to an independent mechanism authorized to resolve conflicts among the provisions of overlapping regimes? This possibility might seem improbable under the conditions prevailing today at the international level. But if, as I suggest, the significance of institutional intersections grows rapidly during the near future, interest in devising effective means for coming to terms with the resultant conflicts is sure to increase.

WHATEVER THE ATTRACTIONS of examining individual regimes as self-contained entities, the subject of institutional interplay arising from linkages among differentiable social practices is destined to loom larger and larger in our thinking about governance in international society. Partly, this results from the growing density of issue-specific regimes in this social space, a development that makes it increasingly likely that individual regimes will impinge on each other in significant ways, leading to what some have called "institutional congestion." In part, increasing linkages will result from the rising interdependencies among the members of international society, a more general trend that makes it more difficult to disentangle regimes created for different purposes. In this chapter, I have sought to initiate a dialogue regarding several distinct types of institutional linkages under the headings of embedded regimes, nested regimes, clustered regimes, and overlapping regimes. If I am right in my assessment of the growing importance of institutional linkages in international society, these preliminary observations should prove sufficient to trigger an increasingly sophisticated stream of work on both the causes and the consequences of such linkages, along with their implications for policymakers during the next stage in the development of regime analysis.

CHAPTER 8

Regime Theory: Past, Present, and Future

Regime theory arose in the 1970s and gained momentum during the 1980s partly as a response to the intellectual challenge posed by the study of social dilemmas or collective-action problems[1] and in part as a response to the political challenge associated with an apparent decline in the ability of the United States to function as a dominant actor in international society.[2] The theory is appealing, in large measure, because it proposes a solution to a critical puzzle: how is it possible for utility-maximizing actors to cooperate effectively under conditions of interactive decision making where there are incentives to cheat but no central political authority of the sort we would think of as a government? What emerges is a vision of "governance without government" in which the failure to create a world government to take up the slack left by the erosion of American dominance need not be regarded as a cause for serious concern among those who think about issues of governance in international society.[3] Small wonder, then, that regime theory has enjoyed remarkable popularity over the last two decades among many students of world affairs.[4]

1. For an overview of research on these issues, see Elinor Ostrom, "A Behavioral Approach to the Rational Choice Theory of Collective Action," *American Political Science Review* 92 (March 1998), 1–22.
2. See Robert O. Keohane, *After Hegemony: Cooperation and Discord in the World Political Economy* (Princeton: Princeton University Press, 1984).
3. James N. Rosenau and Ernst-Otto Czempiel, eds., *Governance without Government: Order and Change in World Politics* (Cambridge: Cambridge University Press, 1992).
4. For surveys of the evolution of regime theory in the 1980s and 1990s, see Stephen D. Krasner, ed., *International Regimes* (Ithaca: Cornell University Press, 1983), and Volker Rittberger, ed., *Regime Theory and International Relations* (Oxford: Clarendon, 1993).

What does the future hold for regime theory? Is this mode of thinking destined to become yet another of those passing fancies, like (neo)functionalism or systems theory, that litter the history of international relations as a field of study? Or will it evolve into a stream of analysis that occupies an important place in the field on a long-term basis? In this concluding chapter, I argue that four sets of considerations are likely to determine the answers to these questions. First, there is the issue of whether regime theory can transcend its initial preoccupation with a somewhat stylized approach to regime formation under conditions of interactive decision making, developing in the process a fuller and more robust research program. A second issue concerns the capacity of regime theory to forge links between the study of specific regimes and larger or broader issues pertaining to the evolution of international society and—more generally—the new institutionalism in the social sciences. Third is the ability of regime theory to come to terms with a variety of analytic and epistemological crosscurrents—and especially the challenge of constructivism—without losing its coherence as a research program. Finally, there is the question of whether regime theory can produce payoffs that will prove relevant to the concerns of those responsible for making and implementing policies at the international level. In the sections that follow, I take up these four sets of issues in turn. Although I recognize the significance and seriousness of the challenges I address here, my overall conclusion regarding the future of regime theory is cautiously optimistic.

TRANSCENDING THE CORE

Regime theory has enjoyed the distinct advantages that go with having a well-defined and relatively tractable research puzzle as a point of departure. The central issue can be stated simply: states, treated as unitary utility maximizers, engage in interactive decision making in which there are mutual benefits to be derived from cooperation but in which there are also incentives for individual participants to defect—that is, to choose non-cooperative strategies.[5] In the most severe cases—exemplified by the famous problem known as prisoner's dilemma—defection is a dominant strategy for each of the players, although mutual cooperation would yield better payoffs for all participants. Under real-world conditions, however, states—like individuals who participate in laboratory experiments involv-

5. See, inter alia, Kenneth A. Oye, ed., *Cooperation under Anarchy* (Princeton: Princeton University Press, 1986).

ing collective-action problems—succeed in arriving at cooperative outcomes some of the time, even though they also fail to cooperate with considerable frequency. The research puzzle, then, centers on a search for factors that explain this variance or—to put it another way—the determinants of cooperation under conditions of strategic interaction.

Regime theory suggests that states succeed in cooperating when and to the extent that they are able to form institutional arrangements or sets of roles, rules, and relationships of the sort we have come to think of as international regimes.[6] But this proposition does not solve the puzzle; it simply leads to a second-order question: How can we explain successes and failures on the part of groups of states that seek to solve collective-action problems through the formation of international regimes? The core of regime theory consists of an effort to answer this question in a convincing manner. The most influential answers are often grouped, for shorthand purposes, into three broad categories labeled power, interests, and knowledge.[7] A fourth—albeit somewhat different—answer highlights what has come to be known as the evolution of cooperation.

In brief, those who emphasize the role of power argue that regimes form when a dominant actor—known in this line of analysis as a hegemon—chooses to exert its influence to induce others to agree to the provisions of a constitutive contract setting forth the basic features of a regime.[8] Analysts whose thinking features interests, by contrast, see regime formation as a bargaining process and expect regimes to form whenever a contract zone exists and the benefits likely to flow from striking a bargain exceed the transaction costs associated with the bargaining process.[9] For their part, commentators who see knowledge as a key determinant of success generally stress the role of discourses in guiding the process of regime formation; some go a step further, highlighting the contributions of epistemic communities or groups of experts who share both a diagnosis of the problem to be solved and a proposed solution and who act as influential advocates of specific responses to collective-action problems.[10] Finally, some take their cue from the earlier work of Friedrich

6. For a discussion of the analytic issues surrounding the concept of a regime, see Marc A. Levy, Oran R. Young, and Michael Zürn, "The Study of International Regimes," *European Journal of International Relations* 1 (September 1995), 267–330.

7. Andreas Hasenclever, Peter Mayer, and Volker Rittberger, *Theories of International Regimes* (Cambridge: Cambridge University Press, 1997).

8. Some analysts have suggested that a small group can also perform this function. See Thomas C. Schelling, *Micromotives and Macrobehavior* (New York: W. W. Norton, 1978).

9. Hasenclever, Mayer, and Rittberger, *Theories of International Regimes*.

10. Compare Karen T. Litfin, *Ozone Discourses: Science and Politics in Global Environmental Cooperation* (New York: Columbia University Press, 1994), and Peter M. Haas, ed., *Knowledge, Power, and International Policy Coordination* (Columbia: University of South Carolina Press, 1997).

Hayek on self-generating arrangements.[11] They argue that regimes can arise spontaneously in ongoing relationships when the shadow of the future is substantial.[12]

Each of these answers sheds light on the process of regime formation, at least in some cases. Whether considered on their individual merits or taken as an interconnected set of propositions, however, they do not add up to a satisfactory theory of regime formation. The resultant propositions are often set forth in forms that are untestable, and specific propositions frequently conflict with one another. Many arguments about the role of power, for example, offer no procedure for determining in advance whether any of the parties qualifies as a hegemon. Much the same can be said about efforts to document the existence of epistemic communities in a clear and unambiguous fashion. Those who believe self-interested actors can be counted on to strike bargains without any outside pressure are apt to see no need for the efforts of a dominant power or an epistemic community to ensure that negotiations reach successful outcomes. By definition, spontaneous processes do not depend on active efforts on the part of hegemons or epistemic communities, though individual actors in such situations may follow institutional leaders much like individual citizens follow opinion leaders in deciding how to vote.

Equally important, these efforts to account for successes and failures in efforts to form regimes do not fare well when tested against evidence drawn from real-world cases. It is easy to find regimes that have formed in the absence of a dominant actor; in some instances, the most powerful member of the group emerged as a laggard that has had to be cajoled, harassed, or coerced into accepting the regime. Regimes commonly form in the absence of consensual knowledge or an epistemic community promoting a coherent solution to a well-defined problem. Although it may come back to haunt those responsible for administering regimes, some differences in thinking about the nature of the problem may even facilitate the process of regime formation.[13] Many cases of regime formation are difficult to explain in terms of mainstream approaches to bargaining, even though activities that are easily interpretable as negotiations are

11. Friedrich A. Hayek, *Rules and Order*, vol. 1 of *Law, Legislation, and Liberty* (Chicago: University of Chicago Press, 1973).

12. The most influential contribution to this line of thought is Robert Axelrod, *The Evolution of Cooperation* (New York: Basic, 1984). For more-recent developments, see Robert Axelrod, *The Complexity of Cooperation: Agent-Based Models of Competition and Collaboration* (Princeton: Princeton University Press, 1997).

13. Oran R. Young, *International Governance: Protecting the Environment in a Stateless Society* (Ithaca: Cornell University Press, 1994), chap. 4.

commonplace. While spontaneous processes in such forms as tacit bargaining are widespread, most cases of regime formation in international society are characterized by self-conscious interactions eventuating in explicit agreements that take such forms as conventions, treaties, and ministerial declarations.

Thus it is not surprising that students of international regimes have sought to expand their research agenda, first asking questions about new ways to approach regimes and regime formation and then redefining the basic research puzzle that animates regime theory so as to transcend its initial preoccupation with regime formation. With respect to efforts to redirect the study of regime formation, four sets of concerns seem especially prominent: the nature of the actors, institutional bargaining, problem structure, and stages of regime formation.

By concentrating on states treated as unitary actors that seek to maximize absolute gains, the core of regime theory has limited itself to a restricted and rather stylized set of cases. In reality, many of the most interesting insights about the creation of regimes come into focus as a result of the relaxation of one or another of these assumptions about the actors involved. Thus, states engaged in processes of regime formation typically find themselves forced to make decisions under uncertainty, a fact that stretches standard ideas about utility-maximizing behavior and makes it interesting to think about such phenomena as exploratory bargaining and social learning. Issues pertaining to international regimes also play into policy debates within states, so that what have become known as two-level games loom large in efforts to understand the processes through which many international regimes are formed.[14] What is more, nonstate actors can and often do become important players in connection with the formation of individual regimes. As those who have studied commodity chains, international cartels, and informal arrangements covering services such as insurance have pointed out, there are even regimes in which states are not the principal players.[15]

Whatever the character of the actors, efforts to form international regimes regularly feature negotiations aimed at reaching agreement on the provisions of constitutive contracts. Yet the resultant process of institutional bargaining differs in striking ways from the processes envisioned in

14. Robert D. Putnam, "Diplomacy and Domestic Politics: The Logic of Two-Level Games," *International Organization* 42 (Summer 1988), 427–60.

15. G. Gereffi and M. Korzeniewicz, *Commodity Chains and Global Capitalism* (New York: Praeger, 1994); Debora L. Spar, *The Cooperative Edge: The Internal Politics of International Cartels* (Ithaca: Cornell University Press, 1994); and Virginia Haufler, *Dangerous Commerce: Insurance and the Management of International Risk* (Ithaca: Cornell University Press, 1997).

most formal models of bargaining.[16] Participants in institutional bargaining seldom know the locus of the contract curve or the negotiation set, a fact that typically leads to a lively interest in integrative (or productive) bargaining rather than to distributive (or positional) bargaining and to the use of negotiating texts as vehicles for forging agreement on the provisions of ongoing institutional arrangements. When bargaining of this type involves n-person interactions—as it often does—the participants are more apt to strive to form coalitions of the whole than the minimum winning coalitions that game-theoretic analyses often single out for special attention.[17] In effect, institutional bargaining, as opposed to legislative bargaining, places a premium on persuading all members of the relevant group to accept the provisions of a constitutive contract. Under these conditions, crises or exogenous shocks can make a difference in energizing processes of regime formation. Similarly, leadership on the part of key individuals frequently emerges as an important determinant of success in efforts to induce all the major players or negotiating blocs to accept international agreements setting forth the terms of regimes and to take the steps necessary to transform them from paper to practice.

Although regime formation is nearly always interpretable as an exercise in problem solving, not all problems that stimulate efforts to create regimes are alike. Simply put, some collective-action problems are more difficult to solve than others. An implicit awareness of this fact underlies early contributions to regime theory which differentiated between coordination problems, which have stable—though often asymmetrical—equilibria, and collaboration problems, which leave individual participants with incentives to cheat.[18] Yet subsequent efforts to devise a generic index that would allow us to rate individual problems on a continuum from easy to solve to difficult to solve have yielded rather meager results so far (see Chapter 3). A problem such as climate change, for example, is a good deal more difficult to solve than a problem like the depletion of stratospheric ozone; such differences may play a role of considerable importance when it comes to the prospects for successful regime formation. But how can such qualitative insights be turned into a theoretical argument capable of shedding light on the process of regime formation? The challenge is to find a way to incorporate problem structure into the analysis of regime formation in a way that complements accounts that highlight pro-

16. Young, *International Governance*, chaps. 4, 5.

17. For a game-theoretic perspective, see William H. Riker, *The Theory of Political Coalitions* (New Haven: Yale University Press, 1962).

18. Arthur A. Stein, "Coordination and Collaboration: Regimes in an Anarchic World," *International Organization* 36 (Spring 1982), 299–334.

cess considerations, rather than simply replacing one line of thinking with another—equally partial—analytic perspective.[19]

Yet another important observation arising from empirical studies of regime formation concerns the division of the overall process into stages that differ from one another in important ways.[20] More often than not, the central phase of the process features organized negotiations. But this phase is ordinarily bracketed by stages that center on activities involving agenda formation, on the one hand, and operationalization, on the other. International agendas—like their domestic counterparts—are perennially congested, so that we must understand why and how particular problems make their way onto these agendas, take shape as policy issues, and rise to high enough levels on the relevant agendas to justify the expenditure of resources required to mount a successful effort to form a new regime. Similarly, the fact that many agreements degenerate into dead letters or develop into practices that differ more or less dramatically from the arrangements described in founding documents makes it important to examine the factors that govern efforts to operationalize the provisions of regimes as set forth in the agreements worked out during the negotiation stage. For those seeking to understand successes and failures in efforts to form international regimes, the significance of dividing the overall process into stages is that the individual stages have political dynamics of their own which cannot be captured in a single model of regime formation.

More generally, it is now apparent that regime formation is not an end in itself. Here, too, the research puzzle that has guided work on international regimes has proven somewhat misleading. In a highly structured situation, like prisoner's dilemma, it is reasonable to suppose that when all the participants choose the cooperative strategy, the problem will be solved and the mutual gains will accrue to the players without further action on their part. In real-world situations, by contrast, a clear distinction exists between forming regimes and solving problems. Agreements codified in formal documents may reflect an inappropriate understanding of the problem, degenerate into dead letters, get implemented in a fashion that distorts some of their key provisions, or be swamped by pressure arising from other concerns crowding international agendas. Not surprisingly, therefore, students of international regimes have become increasingly interested in what happens to regimes following their initial establishment.

19. Olav Schram Stokke, "Regimes as Governance Systems," in Oran R. Young, ed., *Global Governance: Drawing Insights from the Environmental Experience* (Cambridge: MIT Press, 1997), 27–63.

20. Oran R. Young, *Creating Regimes: Arctic Accords and International Governance* (Ithaca: Cornell University Press, 1998).

Among the themes that have emerged from this shift in perspective, four seem particularly important to the future of regime theory: effectiveness, institutional change, institutional interplay, and links to international society.

In the final analysis, effectiveness is a matter of the extent to which the operation of a regime serves to solve the problem that led to its formation originally. Because problem solving turns out to be a difficult concept to operationalize, students of international regimes often supplement this concern with a sustained effort to trace the influence of regimes on the behavior of their members and—through the efforts of members—of those whose actions are responsible for the problem to be solved. In either case, it is apparent that effectiveness is a variable. One regime may be more effective than another; the effectiveness of a single regime may vary over time, and the same regime may affect the behavior of some actors more than others. Arguments that approach the issue of effectiveness in dichotomous or all-or-nothing terms are therefore of little interest. The central problem in analyses of effectiveness involves demonstrating the causal links between regimes, on the one hand, and problem solving or behavioral change, on the other. How is it possible to avoid exaggerating the effectiveness of regimes as a result of spurious correlations or underestimating the effectiveness of regimes in cases involving masked or lagged impacts? There are no simple solutions to these analytic difficulties. But one of the keys to understanding effectiveness lies in studies of the mechanisms or pathways through which regimes influence the behavior of those actors who are subject to their rules, are involved in their decision-making procedures, or are beneficiaries of their programs. The center of gravity of regime theory has shifted from the study of regime formation as such to an effort to explain why some regimes are more successful than others in coping with the problems that lead to their establishment.[21]

The recasting of the research puzzle to differentiate between regime formation and regime effectiveness and to highlight the search for determinants of effectiveness has also drawn attention to the fact that regimes are dynamic arrangements that change continuously in response to both endogenous and exogenous forces. Despite the obvious temptation to do so, relying on some form of life cycle analysis as a way to structure thinking about institutional change does not seem like a good idea. Regimes of-

---

21. Oran R. Young, ed., *The Effectiveness of International Environmental Regimes: Causal Connections and Behavioral Mechanisms* (Cambridge: MIT Press, 1999), and Edward L. Miles et al., *Explaining Regime Effectiveness: Confronting Theory with Evidence* (Cambridge: MIT Press, forthcoming).

ten do evolve into increasingly complex structures. Yet no basis exists for equating complexity with maturity, and many regimes remain in place on an indefinite basis. The study of regime change can be approached from several distinct angles (see Chapter 6). There are, to begin with, questions about patterns of change and the forces that energize different types of change. By borrowing a concept developed by ecologists, we can approach this subject as a matter of resilience, questioning the factors that determine the capacity of regimes to withstand various types of change without breaking down or undergoing a radical shift from one state to another. At present, the study of regime change is just coming into focus as an analytic priority among those engaged in research on international institutions. Yet it is clear already that a comprehensive theory of international regimes must be concerned with the fact that regimes are highly dynamic arrangements and provide tools for thinking about what happens to individual regimes following their creation.

Another issue that surfaces once the initial preoccupation with regime formation is set aside involves what analysts have begun to describe as "institutional interplay."[22] Although those who are knowledgeable about specific regimes have often viewed them as self-contained or stand-alone arrangements, most regimes interact extensively with a variety of other institutions. Here it is helpful to distinguish between horizontal interplay and vertical interplay. Horizontal interplay occurs in situations where individual regimes interact with other institutional arrangements in international society. There is a rapidly growing stream of analysis, for instance, that examines issues involving interplay between environmental regimes containing provisions pertaining to trade (the ozone protection regime, the regime governing transboundary movements of hazardous wastes, the regime regulating trade in endangered species) and the overarching GATT/WTO system that covers international trade in goods and services.[23] Vertical interplay, by contrast, involves interactions between international regimes and domestic arrangements that deal with similar concerns within individual member states. Interest is growing, for example, in the compatibility of such international arrangements as LRTAP and the regulatory arrangements that individual countries have created to deal with problems of acid rain at the domestic level. Concerns of this sort underlie the rapid growth of interest among students of international re-

22. Oran R. Young, "Science Plan for the Project on the Institutional Dimensions of Global Change," *IHDP Report*, no. 9 (Bonn: International Human Dimensions Programme on Global Environmental Change, 1999).

23. Konrad von Moltke, "Institutional Interactions: The Structure of Regimes for Trade and the Environment," in Young, *Global Governance*, 247–72.

gimes in a broad range of questions concerning efforts to implement the provisions of specific arrangements.[24]

The realization that individual regimes coexist and typically interact with a range of institutional arrangements operating in other issue areas has added an important new dimension to the research program of regime theory (see Chapter 7). This development has not dispelled altogether the impression that these arrangements operate in a kind of social vacuum. Nonetheless, individual regimes operate within the larger setting provided by international society, which has far-reaching consequences both for the effectiveness of regimes in solving specific problems and for the broader consequences flowing from activities undertaken in connection with individual regimes. Recognized early on in such ideas as John Gerard Ruggie's concept of "embedded liberalism,"[25] these concerns fell by the wayside in efforts to formulate specific propositions about the determinants of regime formation. The time has come to think more systematically about the links between regimes and the broader social setting within which they operate.

FORGING BROADER LINKS

What is international society, and how should we think about the links between issue-specific regimes and the overarching social context in which they operate? As members of the English school of writers on international affairs have emphasized repeatedly, the fact that international society is anarchical in the sense that it has no centralized political authority does not mean that it is lacking in standards setting forth requirements for membership, in rules governing the interactions of individual members with one another, and in mechanisms for dealing with problems of governance.[26] In effect, international society constitutes the deep structure within which issue-specific regimes operate, and efforts to understand the creation, performance, and evolution of individual regimes that ignore this broader social context are doomed to failure.[27]

24. Edith Brown Weiss and Harold K. Jacobson, eds., *Engaging Countries: Strengthening Compliance with International Environmental Accords* (Cambridge: MIT Press, 1998), and David G. Victor, Kal Raustiala, and Eugene B. Skolnikoff, eds., *The Implementation and Effectiveness of International Environmental Commitments* (Cambridge: MIT Press, 1998).

25. John Gerard Ruggie, "International Regimes, Transactions, and Change: Embedded Liberalism in the Postwar Economic Order," *International Organization* 36 (Spring 1982), 379–415.

26. For a seminal formulation, see Hedley Bull, *The Anarchical Society: A Study of Order in World Politics* (New York: Columbia University Press, 1977).

27. Tony Evans and Peter Wilson, "Regime Theory and the English School of International Relations: A Comparison," *Millennium* 21 (Winter 1992), 329–51, and Barry Buzan, "From

Looked at from the perspective of individual regimes, the connection to international society is both enabling and confining. Regimes can and do draw on established principles and procedures in international society to deal with an array of issues that range from the authority of states to make decisions about the treatment of ecosystems lying within their own jurisdictions through the obligations of states to refrain from actions likely to harm ecosystems located within the jurisdictions of others, to the proper procedures to be used in settling international disputes over the use or abuse of ecosystems. In effect, the existence of these arrangements can be taken for granted by those responsible for creating and administering issue-specific regimes; there is no need to start from scratch in each case or to expend time and energy revisiting such matters, except in situations where specific regimes call for departures from the prevailing social order. As Ruggie's concept of embedded liberalism suggests, moreover, specific regimes often draw on and gain strength from the influence of modes of thought or discourses that have become common currency within international society as a whole.[28] Just as each new trade agreement can build on the basic principles of neoclassical economics, it is now safe for those engaged in devising new environmental regimes to assume that the basic principles of ecosystem science are acceptable to the members of specific regimes without going through a process of restating these principles with particular reference to the problems at hand.

This link to international society is clearly a source of strength for many efforts to build regimes and to administer them effectively. Yet the deep structure of international society can emerge as a significant constraint for those trying to solve specific problems. Consider, for example, the situation confronting those concerned with the problem of avoiding or minimizing the environmental impacts of international trade systems. Were they allowed to start with a clean slate, the designers of governance systems intended to solve such problems would almost certainly favor mixed arrangements in which transnational corporations (TNCs) and NGOs as well as states would be accorded the status of members. But the existing structure of international society, which limits membership to actors that qualify as states, makes it difficult and often impossible to adopt such strategies. Similar comments pertain to the role of state sovereignty—one of the cardinal principles of the states system—as an obstacle to equipping regimes with flexible decision rules and providing them with significant revenue

International System to International Society: Structural Realism and Regime Theory Meet the English School," *International Organization* 47 (Summer 1993), 327–52.

28. Ruggie, "International Regimes."

sources of their own. It is not surprising, therefore, that ambitious initiatives, such as the funding mechanisms envisioned for the International Seabed Authority under the terms of part 11 of the 1982 United Nations Convention on the Law of the Sea or for the Antarctic Mineral Resource Commission under the terms of the 1988 Convention on the Regulation of Antarctic Mineral Resource Activities, never became operational.

The deep structure of international society is not fixed, thus regime dynamics do not play out against an unchanging societal backdrop. It is not necessary to endorse proclamations concerning the decline or obsolescence of the nation-state or to embrace the idea of "power shift" in international society to recognize that the deep structure of international society has experienced important changes in the postwar era.[29] Changes in the number, variety, and internal political arrangements of the members as well as in the distribution of influence within the system—what political scientists know as *polarity*—are obviously important. So also are developments often lumped together under the rubric of "economic globalization," along with technological advances centered on the electronic transmission of information. On balance, these changes have enhanced the demand for governance systems that are capable of handling a wide range of problems associated with rising levels of interdependence within the international system.[30] Yet, while the demand for governance is rising steadily in this social setting, the probability that a central political authority—a "government"—will be established is low. Thus the establishment of a growing collection of regimes that offer some hope of fulfilling the promise of governance without government at the level of international society is a trend that holds considerable appeal for scholars and practitioners alike.

Conversely, the operation of issue-specific regimes seems an attractive vehicle for those desiring to bring about conscious or intentional changes in the deep structure of international society. Given the absence of a central political authority or any recognized procedures for altering the constitutive features of international society as such, advocates of change are apt to find themselves in the frustrating situation of lacking an accepted method for pursuing their goals at the systemic level. One way of proceeding in such a situation is to introduce changes at the level of issue-specific regimes and then to make a concerted effort to spread the resultant institutional innovations from one issue area to another until they come to dominate the larger society. Something like this appears to have

29. Jessica T. Mathews, "Power Shift," *Foreign Affairs* 76 (January/February 1997), 50–66.
30. Robert O. Keohane and Joseph S. Nye Jr., *Power and Interdependence: World Politics in Transition* (Boston: Little, Brown, 1977).

happened with regard to the growing role of NGOs in international society.[31] Even more far-reaching changes may emerge from moves to include various nonstate actors as members of regimes and ultimately to create regimes whose membership is made up primarily of nonstate actors. Among other things, this is one plausible way to envision the growth of global civil society, a development which could evolve from a flow of issue-specific initiatives but which is hard to imagine occurring as a consequence of initiatives aimed at creating such a society in some holistic sense.[32] Unlike the process of regime formation, which often involves conscious exercises in institutional design, few opportunities exist to bring design principles to bear on international society as a whole. As a result, those whose ultimate goal is to reconfigure institutional arrangements at the societal level often find it expedient to focus on the design of issue-specific regimes as a means of making progress toward their overarching goal.

It follows from this discussion that a robust and productive research program for regime theory must direct attention to the links between regimes and international society as a whole rather than limiting attention to the search for testable propositions pertaining to the formation and effectiveness of regimes treated as a self-contained universe of cases. Beyond this, regime theory as it has developed among students of international relations belongs to a much larger intellectual development known as the "new institutionalism" in the social sciences. For the most part, the leaders of regime theory have adopted the rational choice perspective on institutions, which has it roots in economics, game theory, and public choice.[33] But there is an alternative perspective on institutions—associated more with the work of sociologists and anthropologists—that takes a different tack on the role of social institutions and can provide additional intellectual capital for students of international relations who are seeking to understand how regimes work at the international level.[34] In essence, the two approaches, which I have called the collective-action perspective and the social-practice perspective, highlight distinct processes through which regimes affect the behavior of subjects and thus the content of collective outcomes in international society.

31. Thomas Princen and Matthias Finger, *Environmental NGOs in World Politics: Linking the Local and the Global* (London: Routledge, 1994).

32. Ronnie D. Lipschutz, *Global Civil Society and Global Environmental Governance* (Albany: State University of New York Press, 1996), and Paul Wapner, *Environmental Activism and World Civic Politics* (Albany: State University of New York Press, 1996).

33. For a survey, see Malcolm Rutherford, *Institutions in Economics: The Old and the New Institutionalism* (Cambridge: Cambridge University Press, 1994).

34. For a survey, see W. Richard Scott, *Institutions and Organizations* (Thousand Oaks, Calif.: Sage, 1995).

The view of regimes as mechanisms intended to solve collective-action problems rests on utilitarian premises in that it treats the actors in international society as coherent units possessing well-defined utility functions and seeking to advance their own interests through a process of weighing the benefits and costs associated with alternatives in situations featuring interactive decision making. Regimes, on this account, are regulatory mechanisms created to solve or manage social dilemmas.[35] Behavioral prescriptions—rules, norms, principles—are the essential elements of regimes, and efforts to implement them and elicit compliance with their requirements are critical to their success. The central link in this analytic chain is clear: the operation of regimes alters incentives in such a way as to prevent individualistic behavior that can lead to collective-action problems in situations involving strategic interaction. Recently, an interesting debate has arisen among those who think in these regulatory terms about the extent to which compliance is better understood as a matter of management rather than enforcement.[36] The issue here centers on the relative importance of sanctions in contrast to various forms of debate, exhortation, and capacity building as factors affecting behavior in international society.[37] Nonetheless, the focus of arrangements designed to solve collective-action problems is on forces determining the extent to which the actual behavior of subjects conforms to the requirements of regulatory standards.

The social-practice perspective, by contrast, approaches regimes as arrangements that affect behavior through nonutilitarian mechanisms, such as inducing actors to treat prescriptions as normatively compelling, enmeshing actors in communities that share a common discourse, or stimulating processes of social learning. Such practices may even affect the identities of actors by influencing the way in which they conceptualize their roles in social interactions and define their interests.[38] This way of thinking treats institutions as "structures and activities that provide stability and meaning to social behavior."[39] It directs attention to processes through which actors become participants in complex social practices that influ-

35. Robyn M. Dawes, "Social Dilemmas," *Annual Review of Psychology* 31 (1980), 169–93, and Keohane, *After Hegemony*.

36. Abram Chayes and Antonia Handler Chayes, *The New Sovereignty: Compliance with International Regulatory Agreements* (Cambridge: Harvard University Press, 1995), and George W. Downs, David M. Rocke, and Peter N. Barsoom, "Is the Good News about Compliance Good News about Cooperation?" *International Organization* 50 (Summer 1996), 379–406.

37. Ronald B. Mitchell, "Adversarial and Facilitative Approaches to On Site Inspection in Arms Control and Environmental Regimes," paper presented at the annual meeting of the International Studies Association, Minneapolis, March 1998.

38. Alexander Wendt, "The Agent-Structure Problem in International Relations," *International Organization* 41 (Summer 1987), 335–70.

39. Scott, *Institutions and Organizations*, 33.

ence their behavior more through de facto engagement and through their impact on the discourses in terms of which these practices are conducted than through conscious decisions about compliance with prescriptive rules.[40] The LRTAP regime offers a clear example: Even with the addition of substantive protocols concerning sulfur dioxide, nitrogen oxides, volatile organic compounds, and persistent organic pollutants, this regime is relatively short on regulatory content. Yet it has played a role of considerable importance in raising awareness of transboundary air pollution as a significant item on the international political agenda, changing how the issue is addressed and drawing its members into an increasingly complex social practice that has altered responses to long-range air pollution over a period of several decades.

What are the implications of this contrast between collective-action and social-practice perspectives on the nature of international regimes and the roles they play in international society? The key point is that these perspectives direct attention to different research agendas. The research puzzles that arise in connection with the collective-action perspective center on utilitarian accounts of the behavior of regime members with regard to such matters as compliance with institutional commitments, the relative merits of different policy instruments available for use in implementing the provisions of specific regimes, and the prospects for avoiding or resolving differences regarding the application of rules to specific situations.[41] Issues that loom large on the horizons of those who think in terms of the social-practice perspective, by contrast, involve the sources of behavioral change in general in contrast to compliance more specifically, the prospects for socializing actors to conform to rules without making conscious calculations regarding the benefits and costs of doing so, and the processes through which regimes integrate individual actors into communities engaged in practices that are not governed by utilitarian calculations.[42]

Is one of these research agendas right, while the other is wrong? Certainly not! Each points to a set of questions that arise from a distinct perspective on the mechanisms through which regimes affect the behavior of participants. Is this bifurcation a good or a bad thing in terms of its implications for the enhancement of our understanding of international institutions? I believe that it will constitute a healthy development for regime

40. Litfin, *Ozone Discourses*.

41. Weiss and Jacobson, *Engaging Countries*, and Victor, Raustiala, and Skolnikoff, *International Environmental Commitments*.

42. Lee Botts and Paul Muldoon, *The Great Lakes Water Quality Agreement: Its Past Successes and Uncertain Future* (Hanover, N.H.: Institute on International Environmental Governance, 1996), and William C. Clark, J. van Eijndoven, and Jill Jaeger, eds., *Learning to Manage Global Environmental Risks: A Comparative History of Social Responses to Climate Change, Ozone Depletion, and Acid Rain* (Cambridge: MIT Press, forthcoming).

theory, so long as we treat the collective-action perspective and the social-practice perspective as complementary points of departure that can serve to enrich our thinking rather than as competing analytic platforms to be defended by committed adherents. Although the development of a unified theory of institutions should remain as a long-term goal for students of international regimes, further explorations of the perspectives under consideration here can play an important role in clearing up some of the persistent sources of confusion that have plagued efforts to identify regimes clearly and to think systematically about their place in international society.

MEETING THE CONSTRUCTIVIST CHALLENGE

From the start, regime theory has featured a distinctly pluralistic orientation on matters of methodology and epistemology, which has been a source of both strengths and weaknesses. Pluralism has allowed a diverse community of scholars to join forces around a common set of substantive concerns relating to the roles institutions play in international society. At the same time, it has undoubtedly contributed to the persistence of ambiguities about the conceptual and empirical boundaries of the category of international regimes. On the whole, it seems fair to conclude that these concerns have not crippled the efforts of those seeking to define and energize a coherent research program dealing with international institutions. During the 1990s, however, deeper concerns—I group them for convenience under the rubric of the "constructivist challenge"—have come into focus. Roughly speaking, we can address this challenge at three levels: conceptual issues, causal concerns, and matters of ontology and epistemology. As I endeavor to show here, the nature of the challenge implicit in these concerns becomes increasingly fundamental as we move from one level to the next.

Constructivist thinkers have introduced several concepts that bring into focus a range of questions ignored or downplayed in mainstream research on regimes. By and large, I believe, these conceptual contributions have served to broaden and deepen our understanding of institutionalized cooperation at the international level. The first and, in many ways, the most interesting of these constructivist concepts concerns what has become known as the "agent-structure problem."[43] Mainstream regime theory has proceeded by assuming the prior existence of actors that possess well-

43. Wendt, "Agent-Structure Problem," and Alexander Wendt, "Collective Identity Formation and the International State," *American Political Science Review* 88 (June 1994), 384–96.

defined utility functions or preference structures. When a problem arises, those actors whose interests are affected seek to solve it by entering into negotiations aimed at formulating the provisions of a mutually agreeable regime. In essence, the actions of participating actors play a constitutive role with regard to the character of the regime. As the constructivists have pointed out, however, institutions can play a constitutive role in shaping the identities of their members and, to be more specific, influencing the way in which these actors define their interests. In effect, regime formation may produce collections of actors who identify themselves—at least in part—as members of the relevant institutional arrangements and view participation in these arrangements as an essential component of their roles in international society.[44] It follows that regimes may exert a significant influence on the course of world affairs, whether or not they prove effective in solving the particular problems that lead to their creation.

Similarly, the constructivists have drawn attention to the fact that the problems regimes are created to solve are themselves socially constructed. The movement of sulfur dioxide across jurisdictional boundaries, the annual thinning of the stratospheric ozone layer, and increases in levels of carbon dioxide in the Earth's atmosphere are all facts of life that can be measured and monitored with considerable accuracy. But the framing of air pollution as a problem to be dealt with at the international level is a human artifact arising from processes often treated under the rubric of agenda formation. Is long-range air pollution best thought of as an emissions problem or as a transboundary flux problem? What are the pros and cons of focusing on production rather than consumption of ozone-depleting substances in thinking about the thinning of the stratospheric ozone layer? Is there a case to be made for joining together such issues as long-range air pollution, stratospheric ozone depletion, and climate change in the interest of developing a comprehensive law of the atmosphere? There are no correct answers to these questions. It is easy enough to see why individual actors would prefer some answers over others, and there is considerable room for regime theorists to debate the probable consequences of framing the problem in one way or another in thinking about the effectiveness of the institutions eventually created. But any effort to rank problems according to the ease or difficulty of finding solutions must come to terms with the prospect that key participants may frame the problems under consideration quite differently and that the ways in which problems are conceptualized may undergo change dur-

44. See Nicholas Greenwood Onuf, *World of Our Making: Rules and Rule in Social Theory and International Relations* (Columbia: University of South Carolina Press, 1989).

ing processes of regime formation or, for that matter, later on in the life of specific regimes.[45]

The constructivists have also pointed out that there is an intersubjective element to the rules or, as they frequently say, "norms" that constitute key elements of most regimes.[46] Partly, this phenomenon results from the fact that rules in use can and often do differ significantly from rules as stated in formal agreements. No doubt, considerable variance exists among cases in the size of the resultant gap. While the rules of most parlor games are relatively unambiguous, for instance, there is a great deal of room for disagreement about the operational meaning of many rules pertaining to, for example, the production and consumption of ozone-depleting substances or emissions of greenhouse gases. Small wonder, then, that the problem of devising procedures for generating authoritative interpretations is a central feature of all complex social institutions. But beyond this, the constructivist argument about the nature of rules suggests that these prescriptive standards have no real existence outside the minds of those who are subject to them.[47] Although this observation clearly underlies some of the difficulties associated with answering questions about the existence of regimes and the occurrence of watersheds in their operations, it need not become a fatal flaw in efforts to understand the dynamics of international regimes. Just as lawyers and judges recognize the gap between formal legal texts and actual legal practices and accept the prospect that legal processes—constitutional interpretation is the classic case—will alter the operational meaning of laws over time, students of international regimes will need to go beyond the provisions of formal agreements to determine when regimes come into existence and how to characterize their defining elements.

More broadly, the constructivists have performed a useful service in drawing attention to the importance of discourses in connection with international regimes.[48] *Discourses* are systems of thought that not only provide a way of framing and addressing problems and the behavioral complexes within which they are embedded but also contain normative perspectives on the importance of the problems and appropriate ways to

---

45. For a prominent example, see Steinar Andresen, "Science and Politics in the International Management of Whales," *Marine Policy* 13 (1989), 99–117.

46. For a review of recent work on international norms, see Gregory A. Raymond, "Problems and Prospects in the Study of International Norms," *Mershon International Studies Review* 41 (November 1997), 205–45.

47. Friedrich Kratochwil and John Gerard Ruggie, "International Organization: A State of the Art on an Art of the State," in Kratochwil and Edward D. Mansfield, eds., *International Organization: A Reader* (New York: Harper Collins, 1994), 4–19.

48. Litfin, *Ozone Discourses.*

resolve them. The key idea here is that the emergence and diffusion of a suitable discourse constitutes a critical determinant both of success in efforts to form regimes in the first place and of the effectiveness of regimes once they become operational. On this account, much of the success of the regime created to protect stratospheric ozone is attributable to the emergence of a consensual discourse regarding the role of ozone-depleting substances such as chlorofluorocarbons and halons and the importance of controlling ozone depletion in the interests of protecting human health and the functioning of vital ecosystems. A fundamental problem facing the climate regime, by contrast, is that the discourse of climate change remains seriously contested, despite the vigorous efforts of the Intergovernmental Panel on Climate Change to formulate a consensus view of the sources of climate change and its probable trajectory over a period of decades to centuries.[49] Fundamentally, this argument is not about the role of epistemic communities in creating or operating international regimes. This is not to deny that epistemic communities sometimes emerge as significant forces in connection with the development of international regimes.[50] But as cases like the development of public health regimes at the end of the nineteenth century and the beginning of the twentieth century make clear, it is the development of a consensual discourse rather than the emergence of a particular group of disseminators that really energizes the process of regime formation.[51]

Bearing in mind these observations about conceptual issues, I turn now to the level of causal concerns. The constructivist challenge provides backing for the social-practice perspective on regimes. On this account, it would be a mistake to treat regimes as external arrangements whose requirements members choose to conform to or ignore on the basis of some calculation of the costs and benefits of compliance. To the extent that regimes play a role in structuring the interests and even the identities of members and that regime norms are absorbed into the behavioral repertoire of these actors, it makes sense to think of regime members as participants in social practices that give rise to behavior which is controlled by internalized standards rather than guided by ongoing streams of efforts to

49. See J. J. Houghton, L. G. Meiro Filho, B. A. Callander, N. Harris, A. Katenberg, and K. Maskell, *Climate Change, 1995 — the Science of Climate Change* (Cambridge: Cambridge University Press, 1996).

50. Haas, *Knowledge*, and Ernst B. Haas, *When Knowledge Is Power: Three Models of Change in International Organizations* (Berkeley: University of California Press, 1990).

51. See Richard N. Cooper, "International Cooperation in Public Health as a Prologue to Macroeconomic Cooperation," in Barry J. Eichengreen, Robert D. Putnam, Richard N. Cooper, C. Randall Henning, and Gerald Holtham, *Can Nations Agree? Issues in International Economic Cooperation* (Washington, D.C.: Brookings Institution, 1989), 178–254.

weigh the costs and benefits of different courses of action. The introduction of the idea of discourses reinforces this line of analysis. Discourses typically become second nature, so that those who absorb them seldom stop to question the validity of the premises and propositions that underlie their behavior. When such matters do surface at the conscious level, it is apt to involve efforts to defend a dominant discourse against criticisms launched by outsiders rather than to question the role of the discourse as the canon of the regime in question.[52] In effect, regimes become integral components of behavioral complexes rather than exogenous arrangements created and maintained by actors seeking to avoid or ameliorate collective-action problems associated with various behavioral complexes.

What is the significance of these causal concerns for the future of regime theory? In essence, they highlight the need to engage in more systematic analyses of the mechanisms or pathways through which regimes guide the behavior of their members and by so doing affect the content of collective outcomes in world affairs.[53] What has emerged here is the prospect of a healthy debate between exponents of two distinct perspectives on the causal significance of institutions: those who adhere to the rational-choice model characteristic of the fields of economics and public choice, and those who are drawn to the constructivist model characteristic of the fields of anthropology, sociology, and some segments of political science. Is this intellectual confrontation a good thing, and how is it likely to influence regime theory? Because regimes are not actors in their own right, they must affect the course of world affairs by influencing the behavior of members and others subject to their provisions. In this regard, the emergence of a focused debate dealing with the behavioral mechanisms through which regimes operate can only be regarded as a healthy development. Will one perspective or the other emerge triumphant from this debate during the foreseeable future? There is little likelihood of this occurring. In my judgment, both the rational-choice and the constructivist models of actor behavior are capable of capturing important elements of the roles that institutions play in international society; neither offers a way of thinking that can account for all the variance in these terms. Thus I believe that we should encourage a sustained and productive debate about the uses of each model in illuminating key issues relating to international institutions. So long as the debate does not degenerate into sterile exchanges about the superiority of one dogma or another, all those inter-

52. For a sustained account of environmental discourses, see John S. Dryzek, *The Politics of the Earth: Environmental Discourses* (Oxford: Oxford University Press, 1997).
53. Young, *Effectiveness of International Environmental Regimes*.

ested in understanding the role of institutions at the international level stand to benefit from this intellectual dialogue.

This brings me to the third level of the constructivist challenge. This set of issues arises from a line of reasoning—espoused by some but by no means all those who think of themselves as constructivists—concerning the ontological status of regimes. As Friedrich Kratochwil and John Gerard Ruggie state in a well-known formulation, "Regimes are conceptual creations not concrete entities." It follows, they say, that "we *know* regimes by their principled and shared understandings of desirable and acceptable forms of behavior. Hence, the ontology of regimes rests upon a strong element of intersubjectivity." Among other things, this means that "the concept of regimes will reflect commonsense understandings, actor preferences, and the particular purposes for which regimes are undertaken. Ultimately, therefore, the concept of regimes, like the concept of 'power,' or 'state,' or 'revolution,' will remain a 'contestable concept.'" From this ontological vantage point, Kratochwil and Ruggie seek to derive epistemological consequences. Referring to the mainstream of regime theory, they point to "the most debilitating problem of all: epistemology fundamentally contradicts ontology."[54] In other words, mainstream regime theorists have been busily applying empiricist procedures for formulating and testing knowledge claims to a subject that by its very nature does not lend itself to this approach to knowledge. The solution, on this constructivist account, is to supplant the "epistemological ideal of positivism, which insists on a separation of 'object' and 'subject'" with "a more interpretative approach that would open up regime analysis to the communicative rather than the merely referential functions of norms in social interactions."[55]

What should we make of this ontological and epistemological component of the constructivist challenge? It is important to acknowledge the seriousness and sophistication of the critique; certainly, no basis exists for dismissing the interpretavist line of reasoning out of hand. That said, however, there is a compelling need to put this line of reasoning into a broader perspective. In essence, this view of international regimes is a specific manifestation of a debate that recurs throughout the social sciences and that divides most social science disciplines into distinct—though not necessarily hostile—camps. As experience in many fields makes clear, the constructivist position is not about to triumph over positivist perspectives, whatever its merits in framing a research program that is appealing to its

54. Kratochwil and Ruggie, "International Organization," 9.
55. Ibid., 15.

own adherents. Consider the following examples: Markets and the rules regarding property, contracts, liability, and so forth that are essential to their operation are socially constructed. But this has not prevented economists from carrying out sophisticated empirical work on the performance of a wide variety of market mechanisms. Similarly, the roles that actors play in various human communities are socially constructed. But this has not vitiated the efforts of sociologists and political scientists to conduct empirical studies of the behavior associated with distinct roles. Much the same can be said of systems of laws or legal prescriptions and the work of legal scholars who carry out empirical research on the performance of specific legal arrangements as well as comparative studies of the performance of different legal systems. I do not suggest that social science based on the tenets of positivism can provide persuasive answers to all the interesting questions that arise in the realm of human affairs. But to ignore the accomplishments of positivistic research in the social sciences would be just as unsatisfactory as a posture that ignores the ontological and epistemological arguments set forth by the constructivists.

How, then, should we proceed? One response is to say that the ontological differences between constructivists and mainstream regime analysts are so fundamental that we should conclude they are looking at separate realities and leave it at that. To borrow a perspective associated with dialectical reasoning, however, it may make more sense to think of the constructivist perspective as focusing on the internal relations of regimes, whereas the positivist perspective deals with the external relations of these arrangements.[56] Employing an interpretative mode of analysis, constructivists can be expected to use methods like process tracing, thick description, and linguistic analysis to probe the normative content of regime rules and to understand how the evolution of shared meanings gives rise to social practices that are intelligible to participants, whether or not outsiders are able to comprehend the intersubjective content that turns a collection of otherwise empty prescriptions into a vital social institution. They will be more interested in analyzing the role that discourses play in allowing regime members to arrive at common understandings about the nature of environmental problems and how to address them than in assessing levels of compliance with regulatory rules or the various processes involved in implementing interstate agreements in such a way as to influence the behavior of a wide range of nonstate actors. Deploying an empiricist mode of analysis, by contrast, positivists tend to focus on the external facets of re-

56. See Bertell Ollman, *Alienation: Marx's Conception of Man in Capitalist Society* (Cambridge: Cambridge University Press, 1976).

gimes and, more often than not, on matters that can be examined through a study of various forms of behavior. This leads, for instance, to an interest in institutional bargaining as a process of regime formation, in conformance with specific commitments as a measure of regime performance, and in processes of change in regulatory rules or decision-making procedures as a way of thinking about regime dynamics.

Whereas the constructivists use interpretative techniques to examine the inside of regimes, then, the positivists deploy empirical methods to assess the outside of regimes. Is there an opportunity to integrate the two modes of analysis in such a way that the whole of regime theory is greater than the sum of its parts? Thoughtful commentators on both sides of this divide have sought to avoid the onset of a sterile debate over matters of ontology. Kratochwil and Ruggie, for example, say that they "are not advocating a coup whereby the reign of positivist explanation is replaced by explanatory anarchy."[57] Conversely, no thoughtful observer would deny the force of the constructivist challenge, though some see it as an effort to "revitalize and expand . . . conceptual lenses" rather than as a call for major changes at the level of epistemology.[58] What remains puzzling, however, is the matter of integration. The two modes of analysis do not and cannot produce streams of propositions that can be compared with one another in some straightforward manner, evaluated through the application of a common methodology, and eventually joined together to produce a cumulative body of knowledge relating to regimes.

Perhaps the best hope for mutually beneficial interaction lies in a conscious effort to frame questions in such a way that they can be addressed systematically from both perspectives. Consider, for example, this question: Why are some regimes (such as the Antarctic Treaty System or the ozone regime) more effective than others (the whaling regime or the LRTAP regime)? Of course, the first issue to arise in tackling such a question concerns the meaning of effectiveness and whether the two modes of analysis can find common ground regarding this conceptual matter. Assuming that this issue does not doom the exercise from the outset, however, it would be instructive to examine the answers offered by the two approaches to questions about the determinants of effectiveness. Where the constructivists and the positivists reach similar conclusions about the effectiveness of a particular regime, our confidence in the result should be

57. Kratochwil and Ruggie, "International Organization," 11.

58. Jeffrey T. Checkel, "The Constructivist Turn in International Relations Theory," *World Politics* 50 (January 1998), 324–48; quotation on page 347. Consider also Checkel's observation that "constructivists do not reject science or causal explanation; their quarrel with mainstream theories is ontological, not epistemological" (327).

high. Where the two modes of analysis produce divergent conclusions, by contrast, we should be alerted to the occurrence of an anomaly and the need for a more sustained effort to arrive at compelling answers to our questions. There is nothing in this procedure that is likely to lead to a genuine integration of constructivist and positivist thinking about international regimes; it seeks to capitalize on the differences themselves as a means of building confidence in consensual results and of pinpointing areas where there is a need for additional analysis. Yet such a procedure does offer a way forward that may allow the two groups to work together rather than engaging in sterile arguments about the relative merits of their respective modes of analysis.

ACHIEVING POLICY RELEVANCE

Regime theory is a scientific exercise in the sense that it seeks to develop a body of valid propositions about such matters as the formation, effectiveness, and evolution of international institutions. The broader the scope of the resultant propositions and the more parsimonious the logic required to derive them, the better. Nonetheless, there are compelling reasons for regime theorists to take a lively interest in the policy relevance of the conclusions they reach. Once initial barriers are overcome, a dialogue between scholars and practitioners can produce substantial benefits for members of both groups. The allocation of resources to the study of regimes depends in large measure on the promise that this line of research can produce results that will improve the capacity to solve or at least to ameliorate real-world problems. Regime theorists themselves are typically motivated, at least in part, by a desire to make a constructive contribution to efforts to solve one or another real-world problem. The importance of the quest for policy relevance is therefore not in doubt. Yet it turns out that achieving success in this realm is easier said than done.

One appealing way to respond to this challenge is to develop what Elinor Ostrom and her colleagues, in their work on institutions governing the use of common pool resources (CPRs), call *design principles*.[59] As she explains it, a design principle is "an essential element or condition that helps to account for the success of these institutions in sustaining the CPRs and gaining the compliance of generation after generation of appropriators to the rules in use." Examples of the design principles that Ostrom has de-

---

59. Elinor Ostrom, *Governing the Commons: The Evolution of Institutions for Collective Action* (Cambridge: Cambridge University Press, 1990), chap. 3.

rived from examining a large collection of CPR institutions include "most individuals affected by the operational rules can participate in modifying the operational rules," and "monitors, who actively audit CPR conditions and appropriator behavior, are accountable to the appropriators or are the appropriators."[60] What makes such principles attractive in policy terms is that they can be applied directly to the activities of those engaged in efforts to create new institutions or to modify existing arrangements. In evaluating the attractions of any proposed regime, for instance, we can ask whether its provisions include suitable arrangements regarding collective-choice processes or monitoring procedures and suggest the need for revised provisions in situations where the requirements of such principles are not met.

Since these design principles have emerged from an extended study of small-scale, local arrangements, it is natural to ask whether we can scale them up for application to international regimes.[61] Ostrom and her colleagues have adopted an affirmative stance on this issue.[62] Yet several factors make this procedure anything but straightforward. Partly, this is a consequence of heterogeneity in the set of problems that lead actors to create regimes in international society. Although accountable monitors are important in dealing with collaboration problems, for example, the issue of monitoring is not a central concern in regimes that deal with coordination problems at the international level.[63] More generally, problems that can be interpreted sensibly as common pool resource issues constitute only a subset of the range of concerns that prompt actors to create regimes at the international level. In part, the difficulties of adapting Ostrom's design principles for use at the international level are consequences of the transition from one scale to another. Efforts to solve international environmental problems, for example, typically involve two-step processes in which the governments of member states are responsible for implementing the provisions of regimes within their own jurisdictions, and there is no simple way to think about the accountability of monitoring systems to those (for example, municipal power plant managers, tanker operators, or individual car owners) whose behavior is ultimately at stake with regard to various

60. Ibid., 90.
61. For an extended discussion of the problem of scale in this context, see Oran R. Young, "The Problem of Scale in Human/Environment Relationships," *Journal of Theoretical Politics* 6 (October 1994), 429–47.
62. Michael McGinnis and Elinor Ostrom, "Design Principles for Local and Global Commons," in Oran R. Young, ed., *The International Political Economy and International Institutions* (Cheltenham: Edward Elgar, 1996), 2:464–93.
63. Stein, "Coordination and Collaboration."

problems.[64] In effect, the actors at the international level (states) are complex entities whose behavior is difficult to capture using only the models of individual behavior on which the analysis of CPR arrangements is based.

Where does this leave us in thinking about the policy relevance of regime theory at the international level? I think it is unlikely that we will be able to formulate a set of simple generalizations that spell out necessary conditions for success in efforts to create international regimes or to operate them effectively to solve problems once they are in place. This is a significant limitation with regard to policy relevance. Even so, it strikes me that regime theory has much to offer those in the policy community responsible for forming regimes in the first place or administering them once they become operational.

With regard to regime formation, the theory offers valuable insights about the character of the problems to be solved and about the nature of the processes involved in regime formation. Because the range of problems that stimulate efforts to form regimes is great, there is much to be said for making a sustained effort to think through the institutional implications of specific problem structures. It makes no sense, for example, to focus on devising compliance mechanisms for inclusion in regimes dealing with coordination problems. It is essential to design institutional arrangements so that they fit the biophysical features of the problems to be solved. The elements needed for programmatic regimes are not identical to those required for regulatory regimes. Systems for implementation review are particularly important in cases where the behavior in question is that of actors—including large numbers of individuals or far-flung transnational corporations—that the governments of regime members find difficult to control. With regard to processes, by contrast, those engaged in creating regimes can profit from a clear understanding of the differences among the stages of the formation process and of the distinctive features of institutional bargaining as opposed to the legislative bargaining that is more familiar to most policymakers.[65] These contributions do not add up to simple recipes for success in efforts to form international regimes to solve specific problems. In fact, they suggest the need to analyze problems on a case-by-case basis and to devise institutional arrangements that are tailored to the distinctive features of each case. While this process is obviously more complex than simply applying a well-defined set of design principles, it is no less important for that.

Similar observations are in order when it comes to addressing policy

64. Victor, Raustiala, and Skolnikoff, *International Environmental Commitments*.
65. Young, *International Governance*, chap. 4.

issues that relate to the operation of international regimes. We cannot assume that creating a regime will produce a solution to the problem at hand. One of the most significant things we have learned about the effectiveness of international regimes is that implementation processes are both complex and critical to success. Not only is there an important distinction between implementation at the international level (such as activating relevant decision-making bodies) and at the domestic level (such as translating international commitments into effective regulations directed toward a variety of private actors), but the success of implementation procedures may differ sharply from one regime member to another.[66] With regard to most regimes, moreover, there is a need for flexibility to accommodate changes in our understanding of both the problems to be solved and the efficacy of the problem-solving procedures built into regimes. Yet the pursuit of flexibility must not become an excuse for watering down arrangements to the point where they are mere arenas in which those able to wield the greatest bargaining power call the shots in dealing with one issue after another. We are just beginning to produce conclusions about the determinants of variation in the success of international regimes. These conclusions are not likely to take the form of simple generalizations that those responsible for managing regimes can use as recipes for success. Even so, the study of effectiveness promises to yield insights that will contribute substantially to the ability of managers to identify and avoid a variety of governance failures that can undermine the performance of regimes as mechanisms for solving international problems.

This discussion points to a more complex link between theory and practice than the link implicit in the idea of design principles. Responsible parties can go through a checklist of design principles, asking whether each principle has been met and taking steps to deal with any principle that remains unmet. In effect, the checklist amounts to a recipe. It tells actors what they must do to achieve success and offers them some confidence that their efforts will be crowned with success if they follow the recipe faithfully. Policy relevance with regard to international regimes, by contrast, is apt to involve an ongoing consultative process in which analysts and practitioners work together to identify the major features of the problem to be solved, understand the dynamics of institutional bargaining in the relevant behavioral complex, and devise strategies to maximize the success of the resultant regime treated as an evolving arrangement. It is

66. For an account that differentiates among the members of the European acid rain regime in these terms, see Don Munton, Marvin Soross, Elena Nikitina, and Marc A. Levy, "Acid Rain in Europe and North America," in Young, *Effectiveness of International Environmental Regimes*, 155–247.

this interactive relationship that has led me to conclude that the achievement of policy relevance requires the analytic skills of a good diagnostician rather than the expository skills of someone who prepares a collection of recipes expected to work under a wide range of circumstances.

THE NEW INSTITUTIONALISM in international relations has roots in a variety of theoretical and epistemological traditions ranging from economics to sociology and from positivism to constructivism. Undoubtedly, this heterogeneity can become a source of problems. Efforts to identify regimes can bog down into disagreements about matters of ontology which raise questions about the extent to which students of international institutions are addressing one phenomenon or several. Debates about the effectiveness of regimes sometimes run afoul of theoretical differences about the nature of the actors in international society and the sources of their behavior. Nonetheless, I believe that there is no reason for this analytic pluralism to sink regime theory as a going concern. The most profound challenge appears to derive from the ontological concerns. If we cannot agree on a procedure for identifying international regimes that produces a single universe of cases, it may prove necessary to divide the field into two enterprises that may flourish on their own merits but have little to contribute to each other's efforts. Short of this, it strikes me that the pluralism of regime theory can be treated as a source of strength. The use of distinct procedures designed to probe the role of regimes as determinants of collective outcomes can reinforce the conclusions we reach or, alternatively, pose new questions that require careful consideration.[67] Even more to the point, in my judgment, are questions about the behavioral impacts of institutional arrangements arising from the collective-action perspective and the social-practice perspective on international regimes. The challenge is not to determine which perspective is right; institutional arrangements can affect the behavior of actors through a number of causal mechanisms. Rather, thinking in terms of these theoretical perspectives and drawing on the larger streams of institutional analysis from which they flow should allow us to broaden and deepen our understanding of the nature of governance in world affairs.

67. On the uses of two such procedures, variation-finding analysis and tendency-finding analysis, see Young, *Effectiveness of International Environmental Regimes*, chap. 5.

Index

actor behavior
  constructivist model, 208
  Oslo/Seattle approach to problem structure, 58–63
  rational-choice model, 208
  Tübingen approach to problem structure, 52–58
actors
  in constructivists' agent-structure problem, 204–5
  in contractarian and constitutive perspectives, 4
  noncompliant, 95
  obeying or complying with regulatory rules, 98
  organizations as, 110n4
  in regime theory, 204–5
  role in problem solving, 66–69
actors, nonstate
  in global civil society, 9–10
  as players in international environmental regimes, 128
  role in international regimes, 9–10, 19, 22
  role in problem solution, 68–69
  See also nongovernmental organizations
Ad Hoc Group on the Berlin Mandate (AGBM), 104
air pollution. See Long-Range Transboundary Air Pollution
Alliance of Small Island States, 20
Antarctic Treaty System (ATS), 7
  administration of, 7–8
  effectiveness of, 115
  harmonizing components of, 171

nesting structure of, 182
Protocol on Environmental Protection, 175, 183
  as regulatory regime, 182
Arctic Council
  nesting under, 177
  opposition to, 174–75, 178
  range of coverage, 169
  regime formation process for, 35
Arctic Environmental Protection Strategy (AEPS), 34, 174, 177–78
  as programmatic regime, 182
arms control regimes, 11
ATS. See Antarctic Treaty System
authoritativeness, as mechanism of procedural regimes, 46

Barents Euro-Arctic Region (BEAR), 174
bargaining
  effect of asymmetries on, 70–71
  integrative and distributive, 74–75
  in programmatic regimes, 38–39
  in regulatory regimes, 36–37
bargaining, institutional
  ambiguity of rules as product of, 103
  impediments to, 74–75
  reaching consensus, 67
  regime formation as process of, 74–75, 193–94
behavior
  regime prescriptions related to, 202
  related to regime's effectiveness, 110–12
  rule-following, 97–99
  See also actor behavior

217